I0881423

The Ancient Red Sea Port of Adulis, Eritrea

Results of the Eritro-British Expedition, 2004–5

The Ancient Red Sea Port of Adulis, Eritrea

Results of the Eritro-British Expedition, 2004–5

Edited by
David Peacock and Lucy Blue

Assisted by
Darren Glazier

Illustrations by
Julian Whitewright, Jillian Phillips
and Penny Copeland

With the collaboration of
Yohannes Gebreyesus, Daniel Habtemichael
and Rezene Russom

Oxbow Books

First published in the United Kingdom in 2007. Reprinted in 2016 by
OXBOW BOOKS
10 Hythe Bridge Street, Oxford OX1 2EW

and in the United States by
OXBOW BOOKS
1950 Lawrence Road, Havertown, PA 19083

Paperback Edition: ISBN 978-1-84217-308-4
Digital Edition: ISBN 978-1-78570-405-5 (ePub)

A CIP record for this book is available from the British Library

For a complete list of Oxbow titles, please contact:

UNITED KINGDOM
Oxbow Books
Telephone (01865) 241249, Fax (01865) 794449
Email: oxbow@oxbowbooks.com
www.oxbowbooks.com

UNITED STATES OF AMERICA
Oxbow Books
Telephone (800) 791-9354, Fax (610) 853-9146
Email: queries@casemateacademic.com
www.casemateacademic.com/oxbow

Oxbow Books is part of the Casemate Group

Cover design is by Julian Whitewright and Penny Copeland

Contents

List of illustrations

Tables

Preface

David Peacock and Lucy Blue

In 2002 the editors, in the company of Dr David Williams, visited Eritrea for the first time. We travelled the length of the country from Massawa to Assab examining volcanic rocks which may have been the source of basalt ships' ballast found on Egyptian sites such as Quseir al-Qadim and Berenike (Peacock, Williams and James 2007). On this trip we made our first acquaintance with the site of Adulis which has posed so many problems, not least because it was described as a port in the ancient literature and yet lay 20 stades (or 3.3km) from the sea. It was at once apparent that there had been major coastal change in the area and we surmised that if we could understand this change we would better understand the development and siting of this important town. On this trip we were fortunate to meet Yohannes Gebreyesus of the Northern Red Sea Regional Museum in Massawa, who shared our enthusiasm for a new study of Adulis. In 2003 we were encouraged to present a proposal to the Research Committee of the University of Asmara by its then chairman, Dr Ghebrebrhan Ogubazghi. It was endorsed and Daniel Habtemichael, then of the University, and Rezene Russom of the National Museum joined the leadership of the team.

In 2004, with the encouragement of the new chairman of the Research Committee, Dr Zemenfes Tisghe, and Dr Yousief Libsekal, Director of the National Museum, we were able to start work which we continued in 2005. These two field seasons were highly productive and enabled us to answer the most pressing questions on our agenda. We had hoped for a third season in 2006 to investigate the harbour on Dese in more detail and to erect information boards in an effort to make Adulis more comprehensible to the layperson with limited archaeological knowledge. These plans were thwarted by new regulations prohibiting foreigners from working on antiquities and by draconian new travel restrictions that made it hard for foreigners to leave Asmara.

The project was a truly collaborative venture between two Universities and two museums and while this report is, of necessity, put together by three of us, all those whose names appear on the title page contributed equally to the success of the field work and to developing the field strategy. However, the success of our project was in large measure due to the willing and skilled staff recruited from the University, the National Museum, the Northern Red Sea Regional Museum and the University of Southampton. In addition to the above, we thank particularly Daniel Dagnew, Graeme Earl, Asmaret Kiros, Tesfalidet Leake, Elias

Mehari, Jillian Phillips, Dawit Tesfay and Julian Whitewright. It is seldom possible to recruit such a harmonious group and there is no doubt that our ability to work together contributed markedly to the speed and success of the project.

We gratefully acknowledge the help of the custodian of the site, Sahla Hallo of Foro, whose cheerful disposition and detailed knowledge of the topography of the site and region were indispensable. A true polyglot, he was able to talk to everyone in their own language.

We also received much practical help and advice from Tedros Kebbede of Travel House International in Asmara, without which it is doubtful the project would have started at all.

We warmly thank Professor Jeroen Poblome, Dr Philip Kenrick and Dr Roberta Tomber for helping us with the fine-wares, Dr Sonia Zakrzewski and Sarah Inskip for examining photographs of the bones from the surface of Samidi, Ismini Nina for reporting on the petrology of certain hand-made sherds, Kerlijne Romanus for contents analysis, and Beta Analytic Inc. for radiocarbon dates. We are also indebted to Dr Keith Matthews and the British Museum for permission to publish his manuscript report on the isotopic analysis of five marble fragments from Adulis now in the British Museum.

We are particularly grateful to Professor John Murray and Dr Charlie Thompson of the National Oceanographic Centre, University of Southampton for all their help with the sediment samples analysis, and facilitating the ostracod analysis kindly undertaken by John Whittaker of the Natural History Museum.

We are indebted to David Buckton of the Department of Medieval and Later Antiquities for making the objects available which were sampled in Keith Matthews' report and to Geoffrey House for supplying the historical information about these pieces. Professor Norman Herz of the University of Georgia, U.S.A. kindly made his database of marble quarry analyses available to Dr Matthews.

Finally, we gratefully thank our funders, The Arts and Humanities Research Council and the British Institute in East Africa, for providing the finance which made the work possible. We are also grateful to our referees for helpful comments which have enabled us to make improvements to this report.

David Peacock
Lucy Blue
Southampton

Chapter I
Introduction

David Peacock and Lucy Blue

Since Eritrea gained its independence in 1993, very little archaeological work has been possible as the country was rebuilding itself after 30 years of war with Ethiopia. The scars of this war remain and present a considerable hazard to field work, in the form of minefields and unexploded ordnance, as we were to discover. After a preliminary visit in 2002 and more extensive discussions in Asmara in 2003, we were able to launch the Adulis project in 2004, although by 2006 tightening government regulations made continuation impracticable. The project was conceived as a non destructive survey without recourse to excavation. The latter seemed premature in the current state of Eritrean archaeology, where even a basic topographic map of the site and its surroundings was lacking.

The Environment

Adulis is situated on the Bay of Zula on the western shore of the southern Red Sea (Fig. 1.1). It comprises a series of low mounds covering an area of nearly 40 hectares, now partly covered with low scrub (Fig. 1.2). The bedrock here is a fine yellowish alluvium, but volcanic rocks are found near Foro and in the Galala Hills. To the north is the metamorphic Ghedem massif, which dominates the site and in the rainy season often capped with cloud. This is almost certainly the Montuosa Chersonesus of Claudius Ptolemy (*Geog*.Book 4, chapter7; Stevenson 1932).

From June to September it becomes very hot (40–50° C). In the period December to February (rainy season) the temperature varies from 20 to 35° with an average annual temperature of 30° C and an annual precipitation of about 200 mm. Around Adulis are fields, which are farmed by the inhabitants of the neighbouring villages of Zula and Afta, although many of these are barren perhaps because of climate change. The main economy seems to be based on the herding of sheep, goats and camels, with relatively little exploitation of marine resources. The coastal strip is also home to local Rashaida nomads, whose tents are usually in evidence. The local fauna is rich and varied with significant numbers of gazelle and ostriches.

At the entrance to the Bay of Zula is the hilly island of Dese, which contrasts with the flat Dhalak islands further to the north-east (Fig. 1.3). The waters in this area are easily

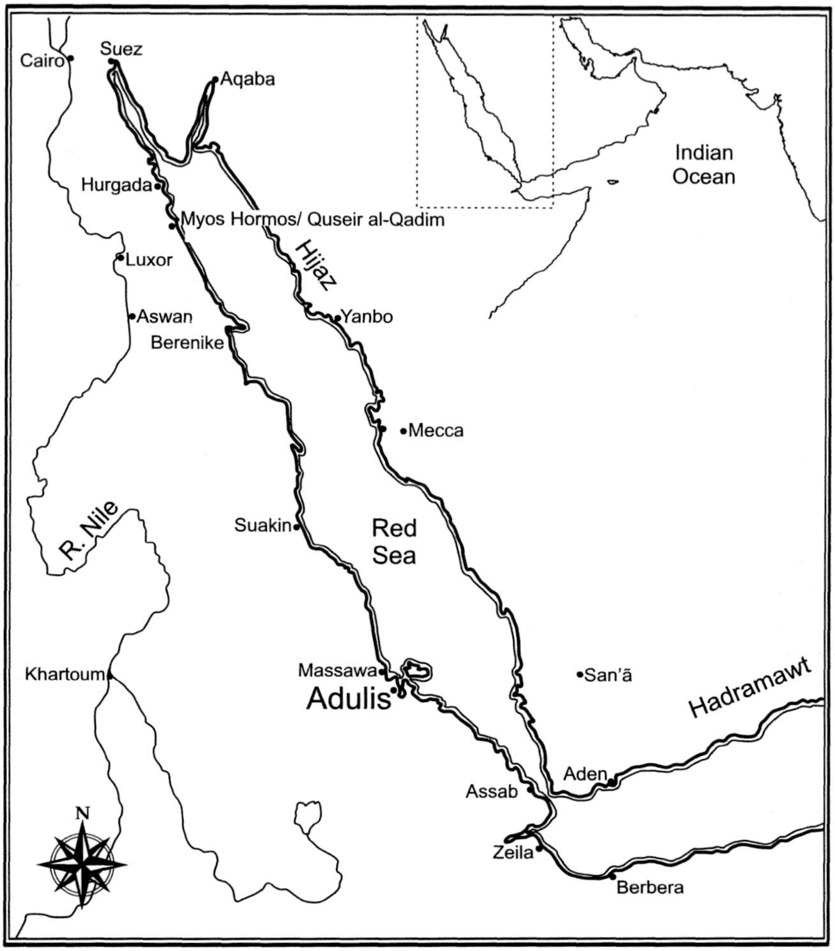

Figure 1.1 Map of the Red Sea showing the location of Adulis

navigable and generally much more sheltered than the northern Red Sea which is dominated by northerly winds for much of the year. Massawa, 50 km to the north of Adulis, is the main port of Eritrea and capable of accommodating sizable vessels. The sea abounds in fish, no doubt attracted by the coral reef.

Adulis in Antiquity

The port of Adulis was one of greatest significance in Antiquity. It is best known for its role in Aksumite trade during the 4th–7th centuries AD. It is connected to Aksum in Ethiopia by a tortuous mountain route to Qohaito, thence across the plateau to the city itself. However, it is also a major port of the *Periplus of the Erythraean Sea*, a sailors' hand-book of the mid 1st century AD, concerned with the journey between Egypt and India (Casson 1989). We learn that, not only did Adulis offer a good harbour on the route to India, but it was also a

Figure 1.2 A view of Adulis showing the typical topography with scrub covered mounds

source for luxuries such as ivory, tortoise-shell and rhinoceros horn. Whilst the equation of the site with the historically attested town of Adulis is broadly acceptable, from the outset it appeared that there were a number of chronological and topographical issues which could be economically addressed by field survey. Firstly, the surface pottery appeared to be late in date, according with the Aksumitic importance of the town. There must however, have been earlier activity on the site, because of its mention in the *Periplus* and because pre-Aksumitic pottery from this region has been found at Quseir (Myos Hormos), in Egypt, in 1st century contexts (Tomber 2005b). Paribeni (1907) conducted excavations at the beginning of the 20th century which revealed two phases of occupation: a later Aksumite and an archaic phase, which it seemed dated many centuries earlier. It was felt that careful, gridded study of the surface pottery might well reveal that parts of the site were occupied at the earlier and perhaps Roman date.

In addition, there were significant topographic problems. Adulis is referred to as a port, yet it now stands some 7 km from the sea. At the time of the *Periplus* it was 20 stades (3.3 km) from the coast. It is therefore clear that there has been major coastal change in the area, which at present remains relatively poorly understood. The site does appear to have been connected to the sea by a silted river channel, and if this was active in the Roman and Aksumite periods then Adulis may have been a fluvial rather than a maritime port. The *Periplus* itself refers to ships mooring near an island approached by a causeway, for which there is no evidence at Adulis. Theories have thus evolved that suggest that the site was

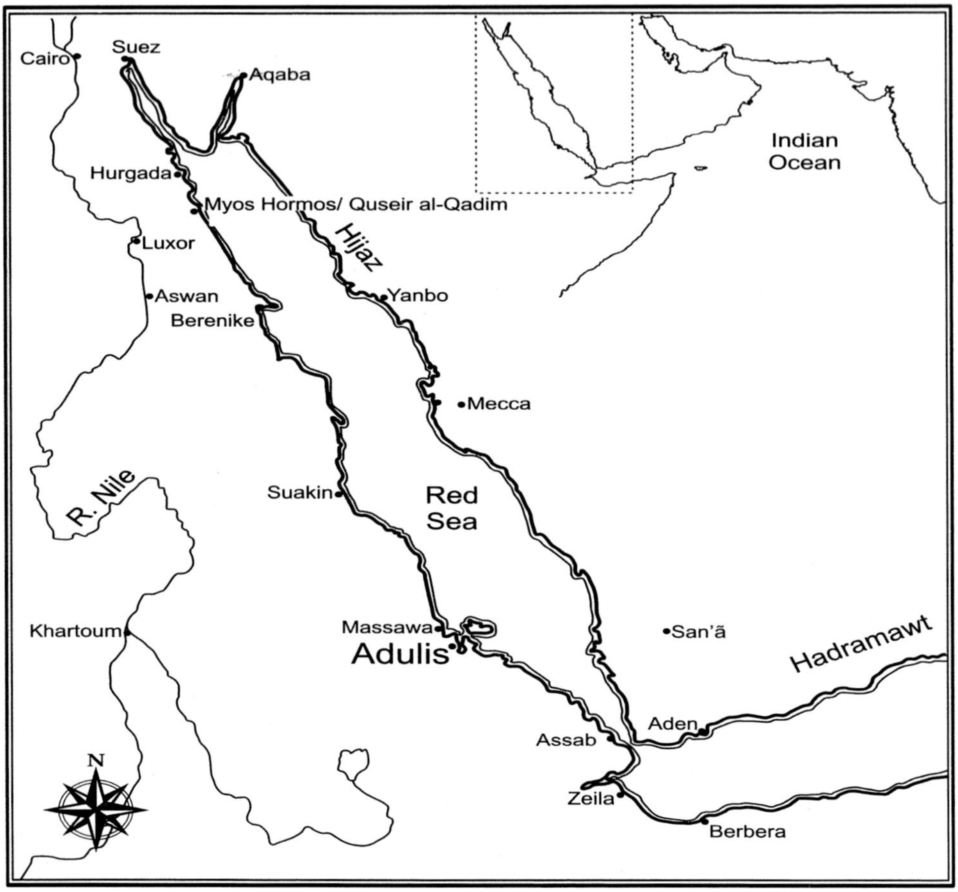

Figure 1.3 The maritime approaches to Adulis

originally at Massawa, 60 km to the north, which today comprises islands connected by causeways (Casson 1981), though it is equally plausible that an island and causeway, now obscured by coastal change once existed much closer to the site of Adulis. These questions could only be answered through a detailed analysis of the maritime environment on the plain of Zula.

The work of Cosmas Indicopleustes, *'Christian Topography'*, written in the 6th century AD provides us with an introduction to the town in the Aksumite period. It contains a sketch map showing Adulis a little way from the coast, clearly connected with Aksum (Wolska-Conus 1968; here Fig. 2.1). It seems to have been an important place with a throne and inscription which Cosmas recorded. On the shore are two other places Gabaza and Samidi, which have never been identified. However, 3.5 km to the south-east are some low hills in a region now known as Galala, at the foot of which large quantities of 6th century pottery have been noted. It was suggested by Sundström (1907) that this could be the site of

Aksumite Gabaza, the port of Adulis in this period. If this were indeed the case then it may also have been the location of the port in the earlier, Roman period.

The present project

It was felt that the problems outlined above were crucial to understanding this important site, and they could be answered simply and cost effectively by field survey. The work was therefore designed to comprise the following elements:

- topographic survey with a total station, recording the mounds and structures within them,
- geophysical survey using a fluxgate gradiometer (as the ground is too dry for effective resistivity) to investigate sub-surface structures,
- study of the surface pottery through systematic collection,
- study of decorative stones in the same manner,
- regional survey and geomorphological evaluation of the sedimentary strip between the site and the sea, involving coring the sediments,
- a coastal study of the area from Massawa to the Bay of Zula, including the island of Dese and the western coast of the Bure peninsula.

The following academic outcomes were anticipated:

- an assessment of the status and wealth of the town of Adulis,
- an insight into the urban layout of Adulis,
- an explanation of the whereabouts of Adulis of the *Periplus*,
- an enhanced knowledge of Aksumitic trade from surface evidence on its most important port,
- an understanding of the development of the harbour or rather harbours of Adulis.

As this report demonstrates all these objectives were achieved to some extent. This is, in itself, quite remarkable for it is seldom to match research design and outcomes in such an unambiguous way.

Chapter II
Historical background and previous investigations

Darren Glazier and David Peacock

Despite the prominence of Adulis in the antique world, surprisingly little is known of its origins. It is suggested by Huntingford (1980, 168–170) that the city may be equated with Strabo's Saba and its elephant hunts, though this appears to be based upon little more than the absence of any mention of Adulis in Strabo's account. The city does feature in Pliny's *Natural History*, written *c.* AD 70, where it is described as a large trading centre for both the coastal and highland populations of the region (*NH* VI, 34) though it is unclear whether 'large' refers to the size of the settlement or the volume of trade. It is in the *Periplus of the Erythraean Sea*, however, that we find the first detailed description of the ancient settlement: the anonymous author of the *Periplus*, a remarkable sailor's log of the mid 1st century AD, describes Adulis as 'a fair sized village' some twenty stades (3.3 km) from the sea (Casson 1989, 53). The author suggests that ships with cargo bound for Adulis had previously moored at 'Diodorus Island', connected to the mainland by a causeway, but that attacks on the port installation from local *barbaroi* had forced ships to seek an alternative anchorage offshore at the island of 'Oreinê' (meaning 'hilly').

The *Periplus* refers to Adulis as 'a legally limited port', though there has been considerable debate about what this means (*e.g.* Casson 1989, Appendix 1). Only three of the ports mentioned in the *Periplus* appear to be designated in this way, so trade could clearly take place elsewhere. It is suggested by Casson that the term indicates a market where trade was limited and controlled by a ruler, rather than a 'free' bazaar. In contrast, Huntingford (1980, 81) argues that the *Periplus* divides ports into four distinct types: appointed, or customary marts, established marts, legal marts and local marts. For Huntingford, Adulis belongs to the second category, meaning simply that it was recognised as the official market for the region. The *Periplus* is enigmatic, but our work in the region does suggest another alternative *viz.* that the phrase 'legally limited port' refers to a situation in which the port and market is separated from the town itself. This will be discussed in more detail in Chapter X. Whichever theory is accepted, however, it is clear that, by the middle of the 1st century, Adulis had become a thriving centre of international trade.

Adulis is described in the *Periplus* as 'a fair sized village', though most of the trade does seem to have taken place elsewhere, around the harbour itself. The *Icthyaphagoi* of the Dhalak Archipelago appear to have conducted a fairly substantial trade in tortoise shell through the market, whilst large quantities of cloth, fabric, brass, glass, copper and coinage and smaller quantities of wine, olive oil and jewellery were imported (Munro-Hay 1982). It is generally accepted that Adulis exported tortoise-shell, ivory, horn and obsidian (Munro-Hay 1982,109), whilst human trafficking in the form of slaves was substantial enough to be highlighted by Pliny (see Connah 1987, 72, 89 on slave trading in ancient East Africa). Wild animals for the Roman arena may also have attracted merchants to the region, as both elephants and rhinoceroses were found close to Adulis itself. It is interesting to note that no manufactured goods seem to have been exported from the region, whilst the imports consist mostly of luxury items for which there is unlikely to have been a mass market in the interior (Munro-Hay 1996, 405, 407). It is questionable therefore whether trade in these goods alone could sustain the sheer quantity of trade suggested by the *Periplus*, or indeed, a trading station as significant as Adulis. However, if we accept the hypothesis that the Eritrean hinterland was exploited as a source of gold in antiquity (D. Habtemichael *pers.comm.*), then the scale of the trade appears more plausible. Significantly, the *Periplus* describes the ruler of the region, King Zoscales, as 'well versed in Hellenic sciences'. This would naturally require fluency in Greek, the *lingua-franca* of the ancient economy. Clearly this was no isolated outpost.

Adulis certainly seems to have been well known during the Roman period, featuring in the works of both Pliny and Claudius Ptolemy (Stevenson 1932). What is not clear from the sources, however, is the relationship between Adulis and Aksum in this early period. It is suggested by Munro-Hay (1996a, 405) that Adulis began trading with southern Arabia during the Kingdom of D'MT (the late first millennium BC), significantly earlier than the first recorded mention of Aksum. Others have argued for an even earlier date, equating the Eritrean coast with the Land of Punt made famous by the expeditions of Hatshepsut (*e.g.* Doresse 1967; Kitchen 1971, 1993, 1999; *c.f.* Gardiner 1961), though this is far from certain. Equally uncertain is whether Eratosthenes of Alexandria (276–194 BC) knew of Adulis, as is suggested by the *Dictionary of Classical Geography*. Though he clearly influenced Greek geographers and cartographers, *Geographica* survives only in fragments found in the work of later scholars such as Strabo, who fails to mention Adulis in his *Geography* (though see above). Pliny does, however, describe a trading centre used by 'the cave-dwellers and also the Ethiopians' (*NH* VI, 172), which may suggest the existence of two distinct groups in the region in the 1st century AD, whilst Claudius Ptolemy's *Geography* (IV, 7, 8) of the 2nd century distinguishes between the local Aduliate and the inhabitants of Barbaria, the East African interior (Stevenson 1932). It is nevertheless possible that the term Adulitae was used simply to identify individuals resident at the port itself, rather than any political entity – Procopius too refers to 'harbour of the Adulitae' (*History of the Wars* I xix) in the 6th century (though see p.11 below).

We know from both the *Periplus* and from material evidence that Aksum had begun to assert a growing influence upon the region by the middle of the 1st century (Phillipson 2000; Munro-Hay 1991) – the *Periplus* describes 'the city of the Axômite', through which the majority of the ivory traded at Adulis was transported, the first known mention of the city (Schoff 1912, 61). It is suggested by Munro-Hay (1989a, 43) that Zoscales himself was an early king of Aksum, which would imply that the port had already been incorporated into the Aksumite Kingdom by the time of the *Periplus* (see also Huntingford 1980, 148 on Zoscales the 'Sea-King'), though this is unproven. The development of Aksum also appears to have been heavily influenced by contact with other cultures, most notably those in southern Arabia (Munro-Hay 1996, 403–4). Inscriptions suggest that the Kingdom was powerful enough to exert an influence on Arabian politics by the 3rd century, recording a number of Aksumite naval expeditions to the region which could only have been launched from Adulis (Munro-Hay 1996a, 408).

It is clear that Aksum could not have achieved or maintained its hegemony without Adulis. With the port, the Kingdom controlled not only the raw materials of the region, but also its trade routes (Munro-Hay 1996a, 405). Adulis was doubtless as vital to Aksum as Aksum was to Adulis: a dialectical relationship existed between the two metropolitan centres, with both drawing their power from the other. It is tempting therefore to speculate that the port was gradually incorporated into the Aksumite Empire from the 1st century onwards, whilst retaining the degree of autonomy expected of any city a considerable distance from the administrative centre. It is of course possible that the Adulis of the 1st and 2nd centuries AD was the centre of an independent state, home to the Adulitae, which facilitated trade between Aksum and the rest of the classical world.

Whenever Adulis became absorbed into the Aksumite Empire, the city had by the 4th and 5th centuries become the pre-eminent port of north-east Africa, its harbour filled with ships from Egypt, India, Ceylon and the Arabian peninsula (Kirwan 1972, 168). It is suggested by Kirwan (1972) that the predominance of Adulis resulted in the demise of the Nilotic Kingdom of Meroe, but this would seem unlikely. Although the vast majority of trade was conducted through Adulis, the inland Nile Valley routes still retained an importance for Aksum (Munro-Hay 1996a). By acting as Aksum's point of contact with the outside world, the city nevertheless appears to have played a significant role in the politics of antiquity: it was at Adulis, for example, that the otherwise excellent relationship between Aksum and the Roman Empire was tested, following the capture of the ship carrying Frumentius of Tyre, (later Bishop Frumentius); a breach in relations occurred following the death of an Aksumite King and the failure of his successor to ratify a peace treaty between the two empires, culminating in the execution of the majority of the ship's crew. Such breaches are common in absolute monarchies when each treaty needs to be ratified by successive monarchs (Munro-Hay 1996a, 410). Any delay can thus have potentially fatal consequences. It is possible, though unproven, that a similar breach led to the transfer of the 1st century port of Adulis from Diodorus Island, to Orienê.

Archaeological evidence demonstrates the extent of Adulis' involvement in the trading networks of antiquity. Material exported through Adulis has been recovered from archaeological contexts from Egypt to India (see for example Munro-Hay 1996; Tomber 2005; Peacock, Williams and James 2007), whilst amphorae from the Mediterranean and the Arabian peninsula are found on the site itself. Whether its influence ever reached further east is, however, open to question: it has been suggested that the Kingdom of Huang-Chi in the Chinese chronicles of the 1st century AD may be Aksum (Sergew Hable Sellassie 1972; see also Munro-Hay 1996), and if this is the case then the contact can only have occurred through Adulis. However, Leslie and Gardiner (1996, 326) refer to Huang-Chi as 'an

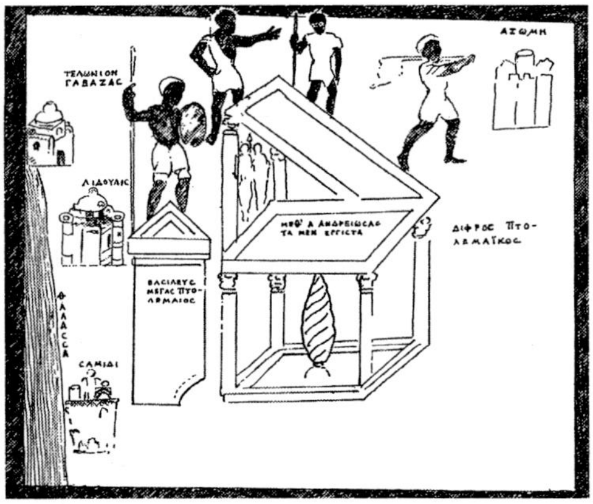

Figure 2.1 Sixth century map by Cosmas Indicopleustes (from Wolska-Conus 1968). Note the town of Adulis with its inscriptions, the 'customs house of Gabaza', Samidi and the route to Aksum.

unidentified country in South-East Asia or India' and significantly it does not figure in either the *Hou Han shu* (AD 25–220) or the *Weilue* (AD 239–265), which deal with Chinese exploration of the west (Hill 2003, 2004). It is true that the exports of Huang-Chi described by the chroniclers match those of the *Periplus*, including a live rhinoceros gifted by the Kingdom to the ruler Wang-Mang in 6 AD. There is, however, little other evidence to suggest formalised contact with the Far East.

The city does feature in Stephanus of Byzantium's 6th century manuscript *Ethnica* and more prominently in *Christian Topography*, written anonymously in the 6th century by a Nestorian Christian from Alexandria (Wolska-Conus 1968). He was later given the pseudonym Cosmas Indicopleustes, or Indian Voyager, in the 11th century (Kirwan 1972, 169), though this is somewhat misleading: there is little evidence to suggest the author ever journeyed to India (Kirwan 1972, 169), though he clearly travelled as far as Adulis and the East African interior. Cosmas was a religious zealot with good reason to prefer anonymity. *Christian Topography* was designed to convince readers that the earth was not round, as the pagan geographers and cosmographers claimed, but flat – something of a controversial position for an Alexandrian in a city that prided itself on being the seat of Greek geographical learning. Hidden amongst the religious rhetoric, however, are ethnographic and geographical accounts of various journeys made along the coast of the Red Sea, including a map of Adulis (Fig. 2.1) upon which two sites appear for the first time: the customs house of Gabaza, situated to the south of Adulis, and the site of Samidi, located to the north. That the city of Adulis featured so prominently in what is essentially a religious tract is testimony to the prestige of the port in the late antique world.

It is likely that the customs house of Gabaza was located in the harbour of Adulis, which must have been considerable. Indeed, the 6th century Geez document *The Martyrdom of Saint Arethas* relates that King Kaleb of Aksum amassed a fleet of some sixty ships there, ten of which were made locally:

> It followed that Elesbaas [= Kaleb], servant of God, amassed in a short time an army of 120,000 soldiers, drawn from all over his kingdom and from other nations. And by the providence of the Saviour, there came 70 ships of Roman, Persian and Ethiopian merchants and from the island of Farsan; that is to say from the city of Ayla 15 ships, from Klysma 20, from Iotabe 7, from Berenike 2, from Farsan 7, from India 9. Elesbaas gathered the same ships in a certain port called Gabaza, which is situated in *the district* of Adulis, and he ordered them to work for the country. And in the same winter he ordered the making of 10 ships, bringing the total to 70 (Pereira 1899, verse 29; translation from the Portuguese by DPS Peacock).

Ayla was of course Aqaba, Klysma can be equated with Suez, Iotabe is perhaps the island of Tyran at the entrance to the Gulf of Aqaba, the site of Berenike can be found in southern Egypt, whist Farsan is clearly the Farasan islands on the southern edge of Saudi Arabia. Gabaza was thus simultaneously customs house, naval base and shipyard. That it was a place of great maritime importance is confirmed by Procopius' (*History of the Wars*, I, xix, 17–22) assertion that the 'harbour of the Adulitae', 20 stades from Adulis and a journey of 12 days from Aksum, was the major port of arrival for journeys across the Red Sea. He also mentions sewn boats, used by both the Indians and the Aethiopians.

Of particular interest is Cosmas' description of the famous *Monumentum Adulitanum* of Adulis, in reality two inscriptions detailing the territorial claims of separate monarchs: Ptolemy III Euergetes of Egypt and an unknown Adulitic /Aksumitic king. Given that Ptolemy III Euergetes ruled Egypt from 246–221 BC, the first inscription offers a tantalising glimpse into the *potential* antiquity of Adulis. It is of course possible that the basanite stone (see below p. 109), already inscribed, was brought to Adulis at a later date, with Ptolemais of the Hunts (possibly modern Aqiq, Sudan) suggested by Kirwan as a likely source (1972, 172). The stone, featured upon Cosmas' map, would appear to be portable, and there is as yet no material evidence that would lend credence to such an early date for the foundation of Adulis. Indeed, until large-scale, systematic excavations are conducted at the site, then the existence of a Ptolemaic port at Adulis must remain speculative at best.

The second inscription was found upon a marble throne and appears to outline the military achievements of an anonymous King of Aksum. It may be presumed that this inscription was deemed to be of the most importance in the 6th century, as Cosmas was asked to provide copies of the inscriptions to King Kaleb in Aksum, prior to the onset of the military expedition to the Arabian peninsula described by the *Martyrdom of Saint Arethas*. The inscription would therefore have provided the expedition with an air of historical legitimacy. The force seems to have been gathered at Adulis at the request of the Emperor Justin in Constantinople, a punitive expedition retaliating against the massacre of Christians at Najran in southern Arabia (Kirwan 1972, 171). Cosmas himself provides us with a clear indication of the symbolic importance of the throne and its inscription within the city, with public executions regularly taking place before it (Kirwan 1972, 176). Unfortunately, no trace of the throne or these inscriptions has been recovered and the description of Cosmas remains the only surviving record of the *Monumentum Adulitanum*.

The city begins to fade from view in the 7th century, though the underlying reasons for its demise are difficult to determine. The complete destruction of the site at some point is undeniable: unlike so many cities of antiquity, no extant architecture remains at Adulis, merely mounds of debris marking the location of once substantial buildings. It has been postulated that the city was razed by the Arab naval expedition of 640, led by Umar ibn al-Khattab (*e.g.* Budge 1928, 274; Hourani 1995, 54; see Munro-Hay 1982). Yet the expedition was described by the Caliph as a failure (unlikely if the chief port of Aksum had been destroyed) whilst coinage recovered from the site seems to suggest continued occupation until *c.* 700AD (Munro-Hay 1982, 117). It is likely therefore that the expedition destroyed little more than a minor base of piracy in the Red Sea (Munro-Hay 1989a). An episode of fierce burning is nevertheless clearly visible in the archaeological record: Paribeni (1907, 536) describes a church he excavated as collapsing in flames, whilst Sundström (1907, 174,

179) documents finding copper objects fused together at *certain* parts of the site. There is, however, little evidence to suggest that these fires can be attributed to a single event, much less that they were set deliberately. Paradoxically, it is suggested by Salt (1814, 452) that legend attributes the demise of Adulis to a great torrent of water, presumably a substantial wadi flush. Again, there is no evidence to support this.

It is perhaps likely that political shifts in the southern Red Sea contributed most to the decline of Adulis. Though Adulis /Aksum had excellent diplomatic relations with the nascent Islamic empire of the 7th century, the continued rise of Islam, combined with the corresponding unification of Byzantine lands and the decline in traditional trade networks may have forced Aksum to look inwards to guarantee its longevity – civilisations based in the Ethiopian highlands maintained a strong presence in the East African interior for many centuries following the collapse of the Red Sea trade routes (Munro-Hay 1982, 121; 1996). Of equal significance were the Persian conquests of Arabia and Egypt in the late sixth, early 7th centuries, resulting in a loss of the tribute paid by the Arabian provinces to Aksum and an increase in hostile ships in once friendly seas (Munro-Hay 1996, 413). The fierce fires that clearly ravaged the site may have signalled the death knell for one of antiquity's most important ports: certainly Adulis appears to have lost authority in the region by 702 AD, when the Arab 'Abd al-Malik occupied the Dhalak Islands to counter the threat of piracy (Munro-Hay 1982, 121).

Previous investigations

The ruins of Adulis were first identified by Henry Salt in the early 19th century. Salt's plan of Annesley Bay (the Gulf of Zula; Fig. 1.2) clearly shows the ruins of 'Adule', close to the village of Zulla [*sic*]. His plan marks the 'village of Zulla near which are the ruins of the ancient city of Adule' though they are placed too far south near the head of the bay. Also marked is the island of Dese, which we identify as Orienê, the 'hilly island' of the *Periplus*. Salt's (1814, 451) name is Valentia Island. Though Salt's representatives were prevented from visiting Adulis, he does include a drawing of a stone pot recovered from the site in the account of his travels (1814, plate 31), although it is not of a type recognised by the present writers. Salt (1814, 451) also records the presence of an 'Egyptian style column' at a landing place opposite Massawa, brought to the area from Annesley Bay. Yet despite the considerable amount of evidence presented by Salt, his attribution has not been without controversy: a dearth of 1st century material led Casson (1989) to speculate that Massawa was in fact the site of the port of the *Periplus*, the city moving to Annesley Bay only at a later date. There is, however, no real evidence to support Casson's claim, and the results of our survey indicate this to be an extravagant explanation for what is essentially a gap in our knowledge occasioned by a lack of fieldwork. It is worth noting that Salt's identification accords extremely well with the *Periplus*, lying in a deep bay of the right proportions, opposite the hilly island of Dese. There can be little doubt that the ruins on the plain of Zula are those of Adulis.

The first survey at the site was conducted by Vignaud and Petit in 1840, part of a French scientific mission to Abyssinia led by Theophile Lefebvre (1845). The survey clearly defines the large mounds that distinguish Adulis (Fig. 2.2), detailing the presence of three temples

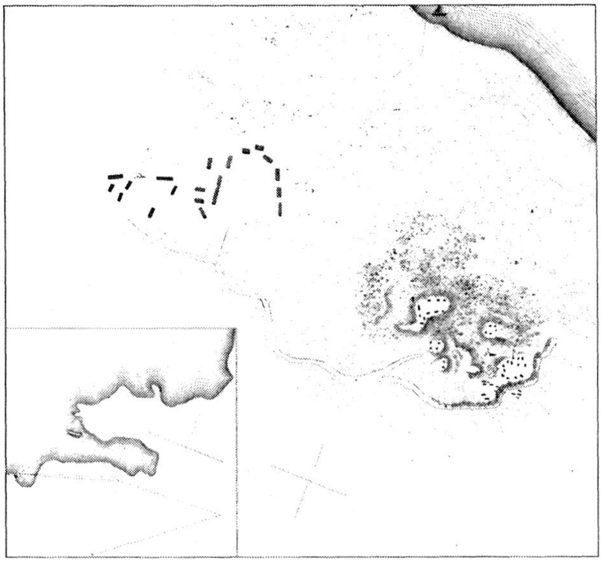

Figure 2.2 Lefebvre's plan of Adulis. The hatched rectangles may represent modern houses

(a 'triangle of temples') identified by the mission as Byzantine (Lefebvre 1845 vol III, 437–39). The existence of a modern cemetery covering a substantial part of the south-eastern corner of the site is highlighted, with many seemingly ancient architectural blocks reused as tomb stones; clearly the site retained relevance for the local population over many generations. Of particular interest is the description of the extant architectural remains at Adulis – Vignaud and Petit provide sketches of three different pillar types, discussing in some detail the features and dimensions of their triangle of temples. Their survey would thus seem to suggest that there was significantly more standing architecture at Adulis in the 1840s than today, or indeed the latter part of the 19th century: later explorers all appear struck by the *lack* of visible archaeology to be found at the site (*e.g.* Bent 1896; Sundström 1907). Given the inaccessibility of Adulis and the sheer size of the architectural blocks recorded by subsequent investigations, it is difficult to determine what happened to these remains. It is possible that they were removed by a 'Commandant Russell', part of a French expedition that conducted brief explorations at Adulis in 1859 (see Munro-Hay 1989a, 44), although this does seem somewhat implausible: Munro-Hay's is the only mention of the expedition, and it is likely that such a large-scale operation would be better documented. It is equally possible that 'Russell' refers simply to a French frigate active in the southern Red Sea in 1859. The presence of three churches is highlighted by the French geographer Vivien de Saint-Martin (1863; after Kirwan 1972). It is however likely that his account draws heavily upon the published description of the site in Lefebvre.

The triangle of temples certainly does not feature in the report of the ancient city's first excavators: the British Army, under the auspices of the British Museum. Accompanying the 1868 force charged with the rescue of two British diplomats held hostage by Emperor Tewodros II in Magdala was Richard Holmes, a representative of the British Museum, intent on acquiring ethnographic and archaeological artefacts for the museum's collection. Whilst Holmes himself accompanied the main march to Magdala, William West Goodfellow, a Captain with the Royal Engineers, was instructed to explore the ruins of Adulis, just 5 km from the military camp at Malcatto, with the assistance of the Madras and Bombay Sappers and Miners. Goodfellow excavated a Byzantine church at the south-east corner of the site, one of the earliest archaeological excavations in sub-Saharan Africa (Munro-Hay 1989a, 44), but no further excavations were conducted. The site was later visited by another Briton,

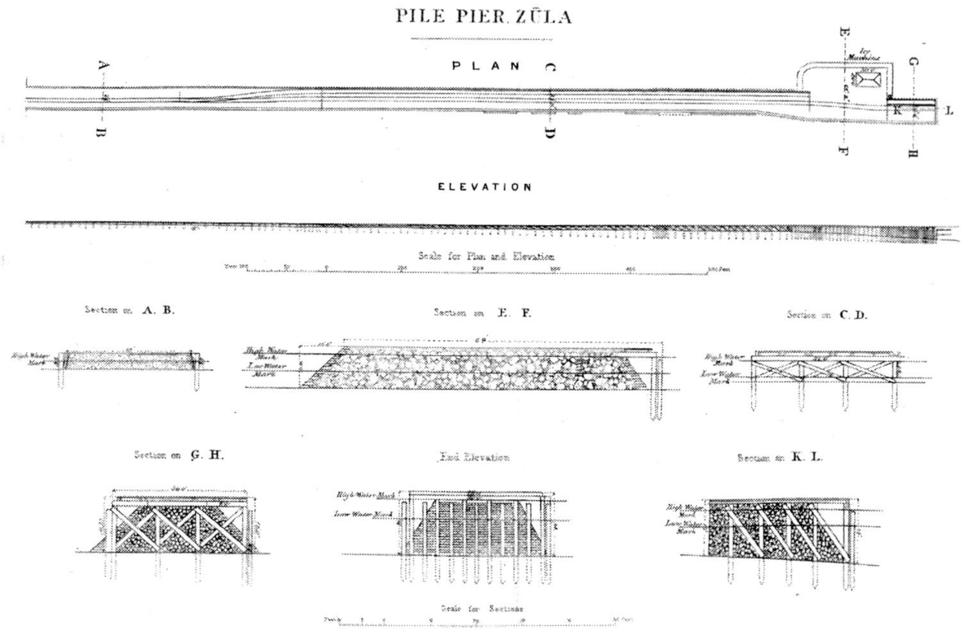

Figure 2.3 The construction of Napier's disembarkation pier (from Holland and Hozier 1870)

Theodore Bent, who noted similarities between the few architectural features that remained at Adulis and those at Aksum and Koloe. Though Bent produced sketches of the capitals and columns excavated by the British Museum, he does not appear to have conducted any exploratory excavations himself (see Bent 1896, 228–30).

The 'Napier campaign' of the British Army did, however, leave its own archaeological signature in the region. Malcatto, a small landing point on the edge of the plain of Zula, was chosen ahead of Massawa because of the presence of fresh well water just 2 km inland, whilst Annesley Bay itself afforded a large, sheltered anchorage capable of harbouring a number of substantial vessels in 7 fathoms of water, deepening to 12–15 fathoms towards the middle of the bay (Holland & Hozier 1870; Myatt 1970). The army that arrived in the bay in September 1867 nevertheless faced a considerable obstacle: though the bay is indeed capable of sheltering large ships, it shallows to a depth of just 1.2 m 180 m from the shore. The construction of a stone jetty was thus considered a necessity, with fishermen from Zula hired to bring suitable stone from the opposite shore of the bay (Myatt 1970, 71). The line of the jetty was marked by fascines fastened to the sea-bed, with stone walls built outside them and the cavity filled with loose stone (Fig. 2.3). The completed jetty stretched some 270 m into the bay to a depth of 1.5 m, sufficient to allow most of the vessels to unload and the expedition to begin in earnest (Myatt 1970, 71–2). An artificial island was subsequently

Left: Figure 2.4 Remains of the railway and pier at Malcatto in 2005

Above: Figure 2.5 A photograph showing the construction of the railway and the British camp (from Myatt 1970)

added at the end of the pier to support a condenser plant; later still a second jetty was built and tramway laid to the beach (Myatt 1970).

The plain itself would have been a hive of activity in 1867. Hundreds of prefabricated huts were brought ashore and erected at Malcatto (Myatt 1970, 79), whilst the surrounding area took on the appearance of a tented city. Conditions were far from sanitary and, for a while at least, chaos reigned:

> The desert for miles round the base was littered with swollen carcasses [of pack animals]. By day they attracted hundreds of vultures, by night the hyenas and jackals came out to feast on the unexpected bounty, not always waiting till their victims were dead. Corruption followed as a matter of course and in a few days the whole area was buzzing with flies and foul with the smell of rotting flesh (Myatt 1970, 75).

The harshness of the landscape makes the existence of the archaeological site of Adulis, not to mention the persistence of the colonial armies of the 19th century, all the more remarkable.

What is perhaps most remarkable, however, is the *lack* of evidence for the British landing at Zula. The army retained a presence there throughout the Magdala campaign, yet very little survives to the present. At Malcatto today can be found the buildings of a modern fishery, alongside concrete structures most probably constructed by the Italians. Indeed, the presence of the Italians is very much in evidence at Malcatto with heaps of broken beer and wine bottles lying around the concrete installations, many of which are inscribed with the legend 'birra esportazione' and appear to date from the 1930s onwards. In contrast, the vast majority of the equipment used during the Magdala campaign was returned to India, whilst the railway and several buildings were handed to the Egyptians at Massawa (Myatt 1970, 176). All that remains of this enormous encampment are the footings of the jetties at Malcatto and a trace of the tramway which evidently had iron sleepers to judge from the

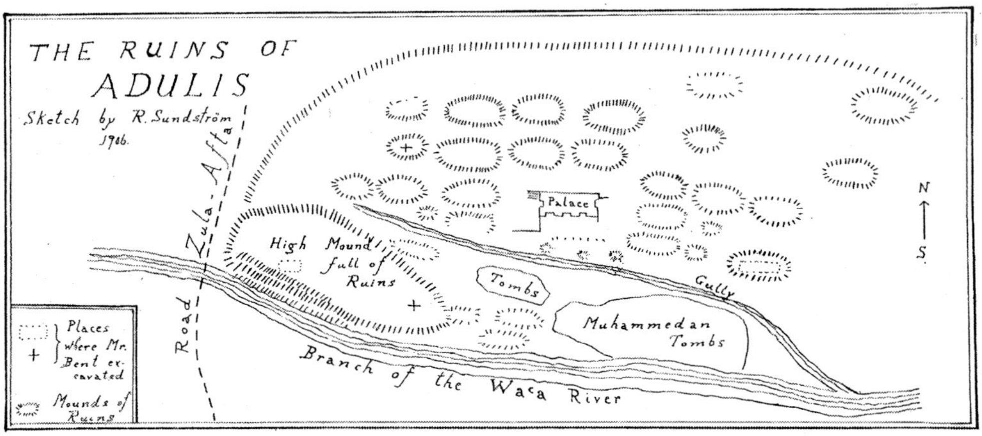

Figure 2.6 Plan of Adulis by Sundström (1907)

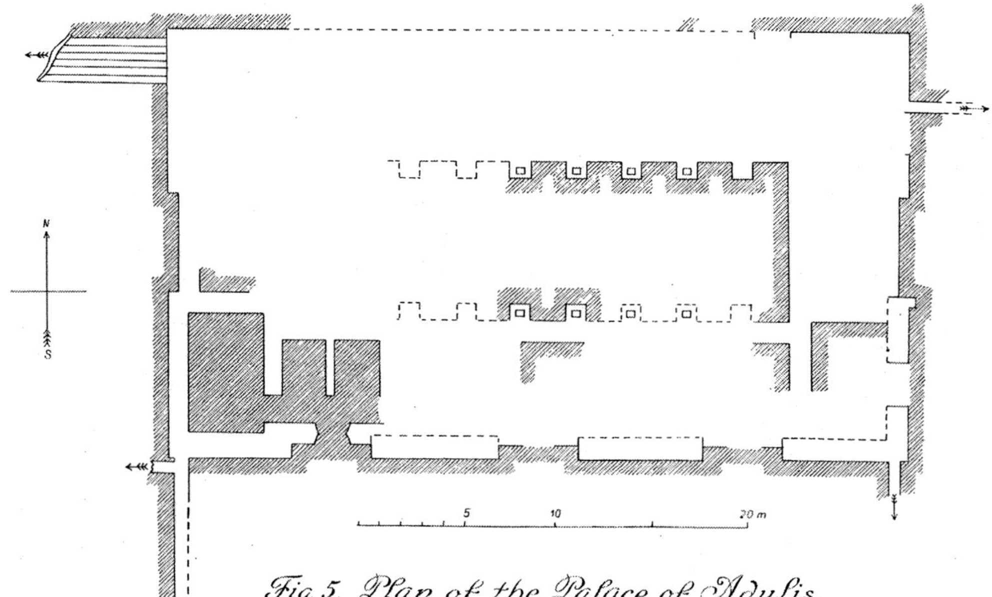

Fig. 5. Plan of the Palace of Adulis.

Made by R. Sundström.

Figure 2.7 Sundström's plan of the so-called palace he excavated (1907)

extant rust marks (Fig. 2.4 and 2.5). These were photographed by the present authors and their locations recorded, though no further archaeological investigation were undertaken.

The first decade of the 20th century did, though, see two further archaeological investigations at Adulis. In 1906 Richard Sundström, part of Enno Littman's Princeton expedition to Abyssinia, excavated a substantial structure to the north-west of the British Museum excavations. Sundström's report includes a sketch map of the 'Ruins of Adulis', clearly showing modern tombs, the 'palace' and 'a high mound full of ruins' (Fig. 2.6). He also marks 'places where Mr Bent excavated', despite Bent's failure to mention any excavations himself (see above). One of these localities correlates well with the church excavated by the British Museum and would therefore appear to be the same excavation, the other, in the 'high mound full of ruins', remains something of a mystery. Sundström (1907, 176) himself excavated the palace, so named because of the grandeur of the architecture and quality of many of the artefacts recovered, though there is little evidence that it was indeed a royal household (see also p.23 below); his plan is shown in Fig. 2.7. The high mound on Sundström's plan was investigated by an Italian expedition later that year. Led by Roberto Paribeni and sponsored by the Italian government, the team conducted substantial excavations at the south-west corner of Adulis, as well as at the site of two Byzantine churches (Paribeni 1907). The last excavations were conducted by François Anfray in the early 1960s; though he uncovered a substantial structure in the centre of the site his findings were published only briefly in a more general, comparative article (Anfray 1974).

Chapter III
Topographic and geophysical survey

Darren Glazier, Julian Whitewright and Graeme Earl

Although Adulis has received considerable attention from scholars of the Red Sea, of East African archaeology, and of trade and exchange in the late Roman Empire, there has, as yet, been no systematic survey of the ancient site. Researchers have had to rely on classical sources or on the investigations of Holmes, Sundström, Paribeni or Anfray for their evidence, at best 40 years out of date, at worst over a century. A modern archaeological assessment of the site, comprising topographical, geophysical and architectural surveys, was thus considered a priority. This survey will prove indispensable to future investigations at Adulis, whilst answering the pleas of existing scholars (*e.g.* Munro-Hay 1996; Pedersen 2003) and providing much needed assistance to heritage specialists and conservationists as they develop management strategies for the site.

Topography

Methodology

A comprehensive topographic survey was conducted at Adulis, plotting both the topography of the ancient site and the disposition of extant architectural features, using a Leica TC 600 Total Station and three staff mounted prisms. An arbitrary orthogonal survey grid was established around the site, with Station 1 as its focal point (Fig. 3.1). This station was assigned the grid co-ordinates 2000 m East, 5000 m North, with a vertical reading of 25 (2000, 5000, 25). An orientation point was established due east of Station 1 at grid co-ordinates 2232, 5000, 20.998; this became Station 2. Station 3 was subsequently established at grid co-ordinates 2079.711, 5190.722, 24.078. The use of stable reference points in the form of grid pegs secured in the ground allowed us to re-establish the grid over two successive field seasons and ensured that data maintained consistency. Though the local grid was arbitrary, it has been possible to incorporate it into real-world co-ordinates using GPS data acquired on site. UTM readings were taken daily at all survey stations in an effort to assess positional errors.

For the majority of the survey the height of the prism was set at 1.300 m; given the topography and the presence of a considerable amount of scrub, it was occasionally necessary to increase the prism height to 2.00 m. The site was traversed east-west following a course plotted with hand held compasses, with readings taken at least every 5 m, or more when the topography demanded it. Data was then 'roughly' processed in the field using Leica Liscad software and ArcView, allowing us to assess the quality of the data and ensure total site coverage. The final survey was processed in the Archaeological Computing Research Group laboratory in the University of Southampton using both ArcGIS and AutoCAD.

The importance of the town is emphasized by the sheer scale of the ancient site which, as defined by the survey, covers some 38 hectares (see Fig. 3.1), significantly more than the 400 m x 600 m (or 24 hectares) estimated by Kirwan (1972, 169). The western and eastern extent of Adulis was deemed to be the point at which the topography levelled to match the rest of the plain of Zula, the southern and south-eastern edge defined by wadi walls that have cut into the site over time, the northern edge by modern field boundaries.

To produce a useful map of the site it was also necessary to locate, as far as possible, and undertake the survey of previous excavations (Fig. 3.2). Of these, the 19th century excavation and some of those of Paribeni are exposed, but in a poor state of preservation; the trench of Anfray is better preserved, but obviously decaying; the 19th century British Museum church excavation at the eastern end of the site is visible but much ruined, while the site identified as the 'palace' by Sundström is represented by a large and partly back-filled hole in the ground (see Holland & Hozier 1870; Paribeni 1907; Sundström 1907; Anfray 1974; Munro-Hay 1989a). Given the nature of the extant remains, re-survey was only viable at the trenches of Paribeni and Anfray: the edges of the 'palace' and the British Museum church were also surveyed, but little architecture remains within, at least in its original location. Two further churches excavated by Paribeni at the beginning of the 20th century appear to have been back-filled, but their approximate sites are indicated by a pottery dump and by spoil heaps. Interpretation of geophysical data has allowed us to pinpoint the position of at least one of these churches with more accuracy (see below).

Results

Figs 3.1 and 3.2 show the distribution of mounds, most of which probably represent the sites of important buildings. There are, however, four mounds that are extremely prominent: one to the south of the site, one to the west of Anfray's trench, one to the north and one far to the east (only just on the plan). These are almost certainly excavation dumps and while they are useful as vantage points they are of no archaeological significance.

Fig. 3.2 indicates the presumed position of the two churches excavated by Paribeni and the position of earlier excavations:

A. The trench excavated by Captain William West Goodfellow in 1868, under the auspices of the British Museum. Figs. 3.3 and 3.4 show a view during excavation and a more detailed plan taken from the original report. Note the column fragments and the threshold at the west end.

Holmes' report to the trustees of the museum identifies the building as a Byzantine church, the east end of which was apsidal (see Munro-Hay 1989a, 46). Goodfellow notes that the foundations of the building were 4 m deep, though it is unclear whether the church was built upon the remains of an earlier structure. The total area excavated was some 24.4 m and included the discovery of a number of square stone columns, though no capitals were found at the site. Small quantities

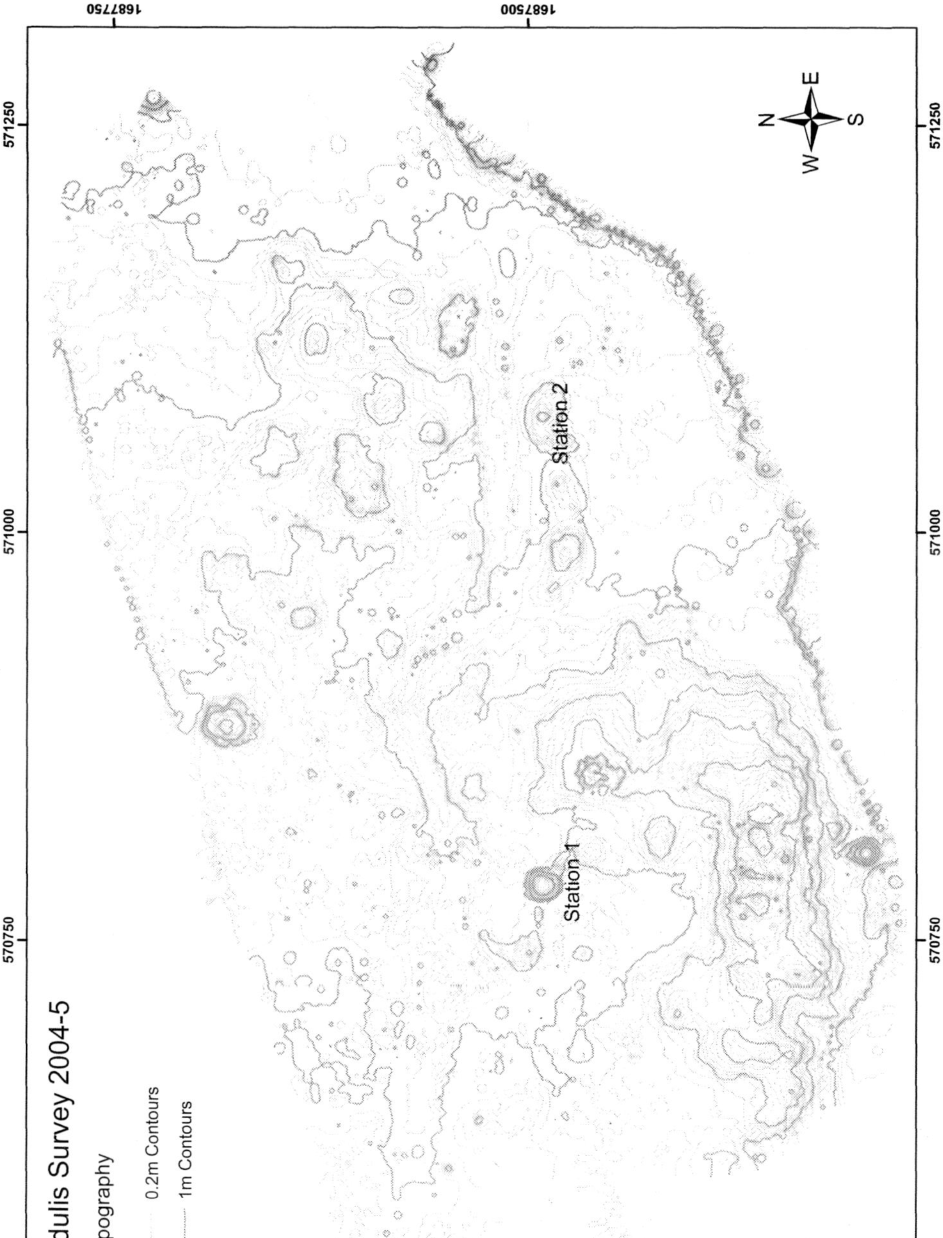

Figure 3.1 The topography of the site of Adulis

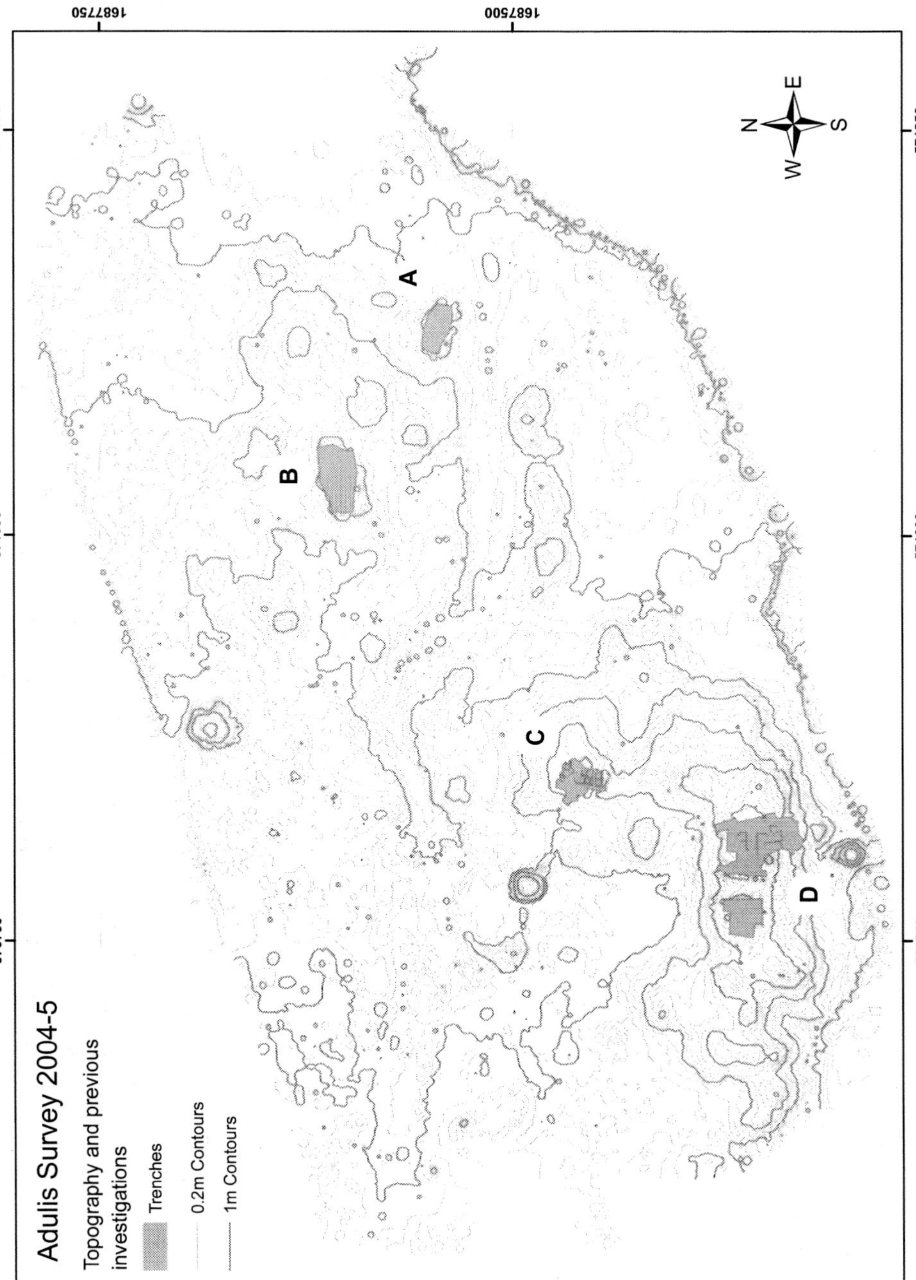

Figure 3.2 The topography of the site of Adulis showing sites of previous excavations. Letters correspond to discussion in the text.

Figure 3.3 A view of the church during the exacavtion by the British Museum.

of architectural fragments were, however, recovered during excavation, including the remains of a marble cross (Holland & Hozier 1870; Munro-Hay 1989a). Several items of church furniture, including columns and screen-posts of Proconnesian marble, appear to have their origin in Asia Minor, and were transported prefabricated for assembly at their destination. Such trade was fairly common in the 6th century, though this appears to be the southernmost find of its kind, indicative of the close contact between Adulis/Aksum and the court of Justin and Justinian at Constantinople (Munro-Hay 1982; 1989a, 50).

The location of this church is interesting and suggests that it served a different suburb of the city from those excavated by Paribeni at the northern and eastern edges of the site (Munro-Hay 1989a, 48) – the finds from this location and Paribeni's northern church would certainly seem to indicate that they were contemporaneous (Munro-Hay 1989a).

B. The site of the two-storey structure excavated by Sundström (1907). This is now an overgrown hollow and was clearly partially backfilled. Fig. 2.8 shows a plan in Sundström's report.

The trench was originally dug to a depth of 4 m (the same depth as Goodfellow's) and revealed the stepped walls or 'graduated masonry' characteristic of both the site and the region. (see Sundström 1907, 176 and below). The excavated structure measured 22.5 m x 38 m and contained sixteen rooms, a central 'pillar-hall' and a 'splendid flight of stairs' (1907, 178). Finds from the building include coins, painted glass, human bones and marble slabs replete with vine and grape reliefs.

It is suggested by Sundström that the building was an 'important house or palace' (1907, 178) and in his subsequent plan it is labelled the 'Palace of Adulis' (see Fig 2.7). This attribution is based solely upon the presence of a 'screw pillar' or spiral column (see Fig 9.7) and the relative size of pillars compared to those found on the surface at other areas of the site. There is little evidence, however, to confirm that this was indeed the site of a Royal household, nor, given the relative lack of excavation across the site, can we make adequate comparisons with other structures.

Sundström's report states that the 'palace' was destroyed by a fierce fire, perhaps set deliberately: it is suggested that all the combustible material within the building was piled in front of the doors to the lower storey (1907, 179). This would concur with the oft-expressed theory that the town was razed to the ground in the mid 7th century, though Sundström does not record evidence that might allow us to extrapolate a chronology for these events. It is equally plausible that the building (and the town) was ravaged by a fire that began accidentally.

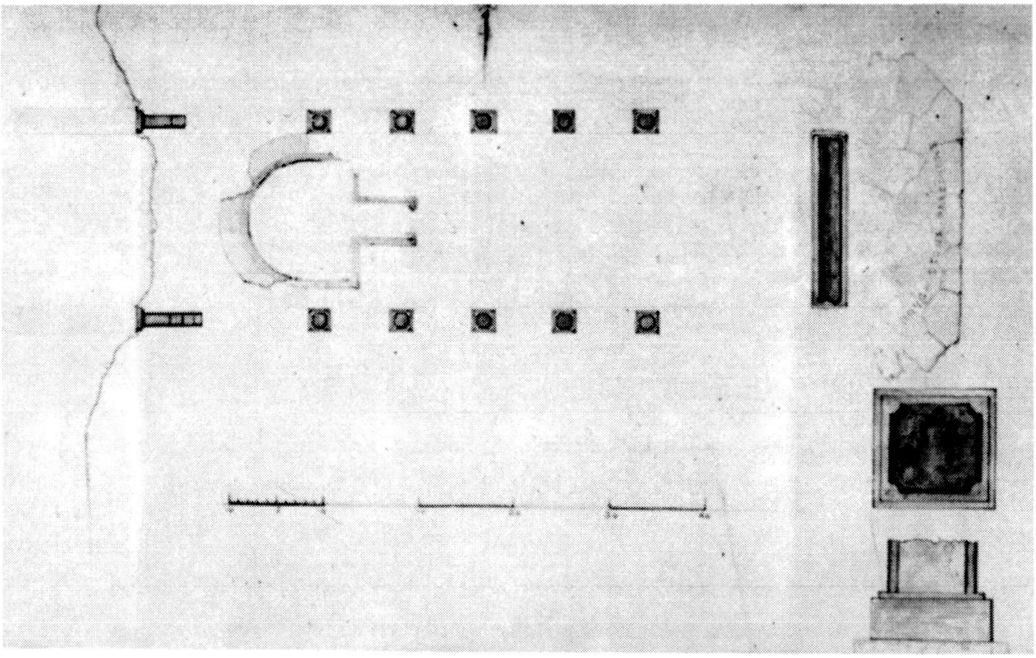

Figure 3.4. Plan of the church excavated by the British Museum

C. The site of Anfray's unpublished excavation in the 1960s, sponsored by the Ethiopian Institute of Archaeology. Fig. 3.5 shows a plan and Figs 9.1–3 a well exposed wall. The architecture of the trench is discussed below (pp.109–111).

D. A complex of trenches excavated by Paribeni in 1907. It is in a poor state of preservation, but some of the main wall courses are shown in Fig. 3.6. Interestingly, Sundström's plan of 1906 (Fig. 2.6), produced prior to the excavations of Paribeni, indicates the presence of an open trench on this mound, attributed by Sundström to Theodore Bent. This would appear to be unlikely; Bent (1896, 228–30) does not mention conducting any excavations at the site, and his stay of just a couple of days would be insufficient to do anything significant. It is possible that either the French mission of Vignaud and Petit or the British Museum expedition conducted exploratory excavations in this area, though neither team records doing so.

Geophysics

Integral to the survey at Adulis was the use of non-invasive survey techniques to explore the layout and extent of the ancient city, facilitating the direct interpretation of material beneath the subsoil without recourse to destructive, not to say logistically problematic, large-scale excavation. Though the aridity of the Zula plain made a resisitivity survey unfeasible, it was decided that a survey conducted using a magnetometer might render useful results. The depth of architectural deposits excavated in previous investigations did, however, mean that the success of the survey was by no means assured.

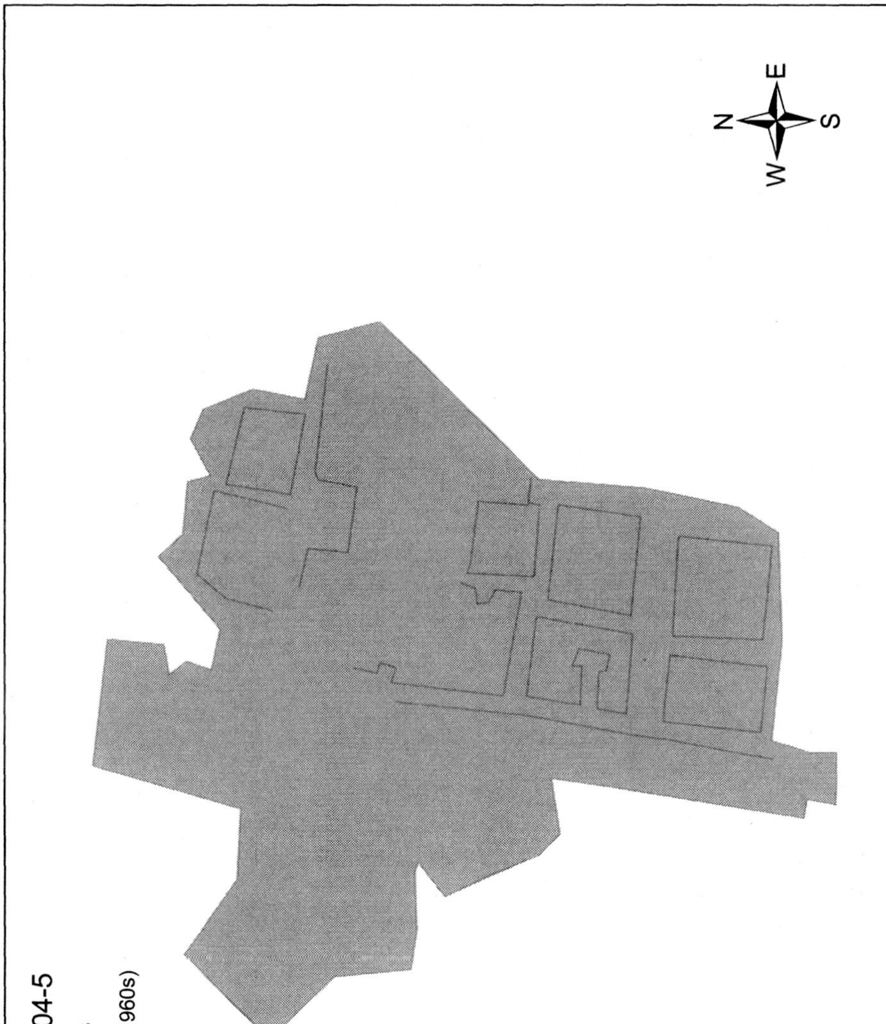

Figure 3.5 A plan of structures in Anfray's trench

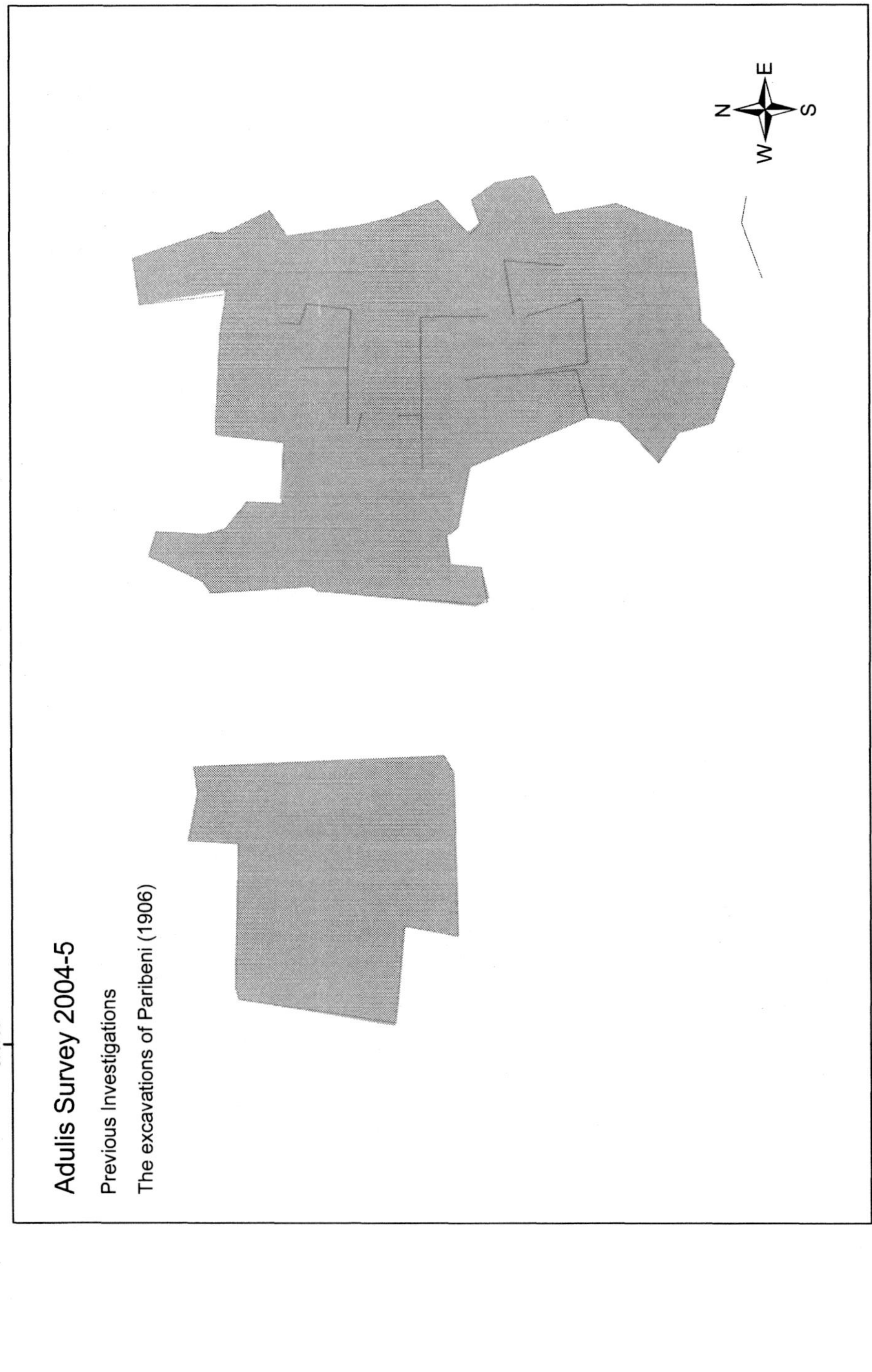

Figure 3.6 A schematic plan of Paribeni's excavations in the south-west corner of Adulis

Magnetometry

The survey was conducted using a GeoScan Research Fluxgate Gradiometer FM36. In comparison to other geophysical instruments, the magnetometer is a mobile instrument, allowing for the rapid assessment of large areas of the site. Magnetometry is widely used in archaeology, and is based upon the detection of variation in magnetic gradients: human processes affect the magnetic profile of the soil permitting human interventions to be inferred. Different natural materials have different magnetic signatures. Igneous rocks such as basalt have a high magnetic signature and thus produce peaks in the survey data, whilst limestone, sand and other materials will be less magnetic and therefore produce a lower reading. As basalt appears to have been the primary building material used by the inhabitants of Adulis, it would be expected that the structures beneath the soil would present a very visible signature. The magnetism of any soil matrix is, however, intrinsically variable, with topsoil usually having a higher magnetism than lower levels – natural processes on the surface increase the magnetism of iron compounds, thus producing a stronger magnetic signature. These natural processes are coupled with the human introduction of fired and organic materials that can also considerably increase local magnetism.

This differential magnetism between topsoil and lower levels is fundamental to the identification of archaeological anomalies. A pit cut through topsoil, for example, and later filled with material of a lower signature will be identified in the geophysical survey as a region of lower magnetism. Conversely, a pit cut into the natural and later filled with topsoil will have a correspondingly higher magnetic signature. Similarly, a bank formed from topsoil deposits may be more magnetic than the surrounding soil matrix. Wall features can give very clear anomalies where a foundation trench containing either a positive or negative building material is packed with material of the opposite charge: for example, a limestone wall surrounded by a topsoil fill. Such anomalies show up as 'shadow' bands of alternating positive and negative values. The firing of materials also leads to very great increases in magnetic signature, with areas of human activity such as hearths or dumps of fired pottery producing a very visible signal.

The survey area

The survey grids were positioned with the Leica Total Station used for the topographic survey. Each grid was 20 m square, providing coverage of 400 m per grid. A total of 71 grids were surveyed throughout the course of the project, amounting to a total coverage of some 28,400 square metres. The grids were walked in twenty west-east traverses (the x axis), with a sample taken every 0.5 m; each grid is thus composed of 800 individual readings. The instrument is, however, capable of taking samples at a maximum of 0.25 m intervals, allowing for a greater accumulation of information. Given this degree of sampling in the x axis, a corresponding increase of density in the y axis to either 0.5 m or 0.25 m would be required to avoid over-sampling anomalies running perpendicular, relative to those running parallel. It is also widely recognised that the sample interval for any geophysical survey should be a maximum of half the size of the smallest anomaly considered to be of interest. At Adulis, we can therefore confidently and consistently identify anomalies that have a total

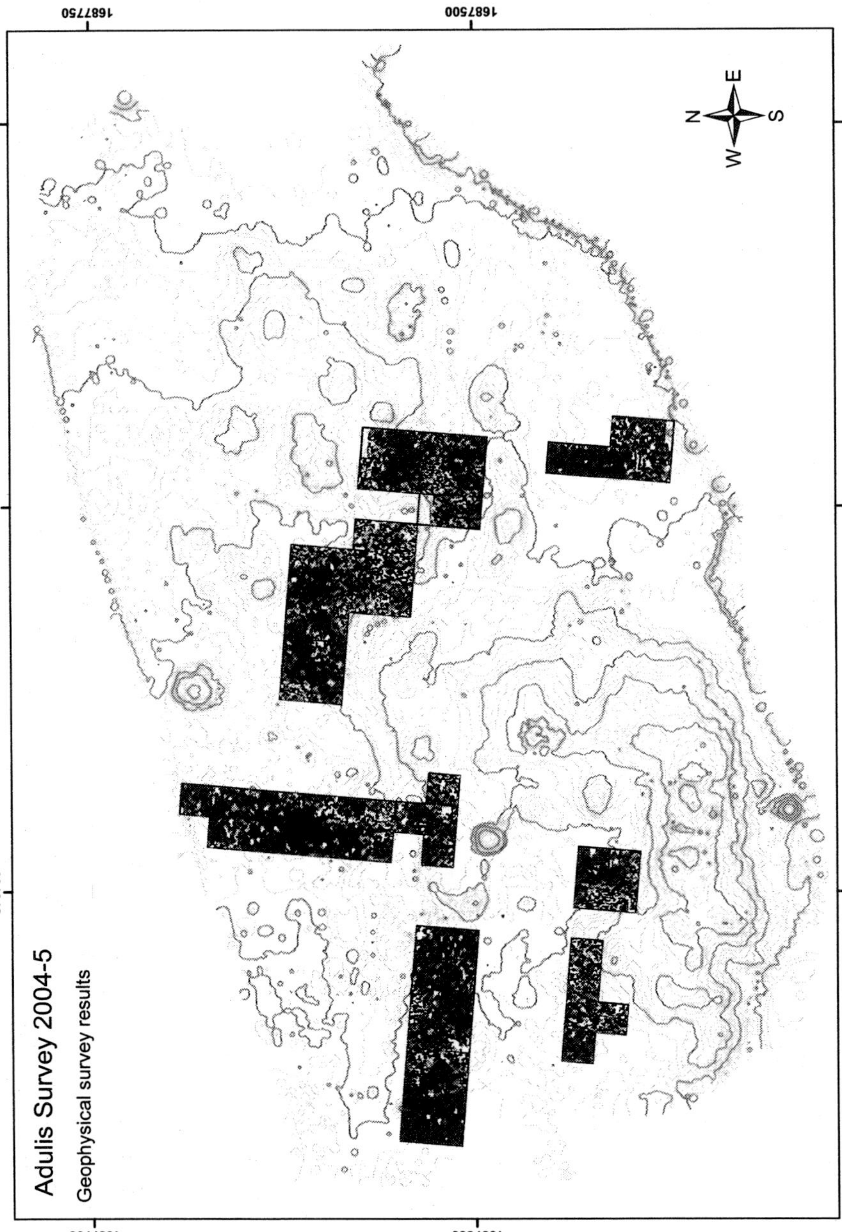

Figure 3.7 Results of the geophysical survey

area of 1 m or more, sufficient to demonstrate the potential of geophysical survey at the site and to provide some interesting, promising results.

Effectively the 0.5 m by 1 m sample size results in a grid of rectangular sample data. At the processing stage this grid is converted into a 0.5 m by 0.5 m grid – a square sample size. Only where features run due east will there be any chance of missed information. The GeoScan Research GeoPlot software was used to download the instrument readings each day and to process the results. The resulting data were exported as ASCII text and imported for further processing into the project Geographic Information System (ArcGIS) as an ArcInfo GRID.

Somewhat paradoxically, the survey at Adulis was hindered by one of its perceived strengths: the predominance of basalt. Whilst this produces a very strong magnetic signature underground, its presence in large quantities on the surface, particularly around the trenches and spoil heaps of previous investigations, made geophysical survey unfeasible in some areas; surface peaks would render anomalies beneath the soil all but invisible. Extensive survey was nevertheless carried out in transects that reach the northern, the southern, the eastern and the western extent of the ancient site.

Results

The results of the geophysical survey are presented in Fig. 3.7, and as interpretation in Fig. 3.8. We have been able to clearly define a large number of major anomalies beneath the subsoil, demonstrating the sheer scale of ancient Adulis. Indeed, the success of the geophysical survey has allowed us to address two questions fundamental to our understanding of Adulis: *viz.* was the town protected by a defensive wall, and how was it laid out?

Examination of the results show that most structures appear to be aligned upon a rough north-west – south-east axis, with the exception of those buildings already identified as churches by previous excavations. There is also the suggestion of a structure running along an east-west axis in the centre of the survey area, which is likely to be the church identified and excavated by Paribeni and subsequently back-filled; pottery scatters and the presence of a large spoil heap nearby would seem to confirm this. The structures surveyed within the trench of Paribeni, and to a certain extent those of Anfray, do not, however, appear to conform to this grid. It is feasible to suggest that these structures relate to a different building phase not visible in the geophysics. Paribeni (1907) and now our radiocarbon dates (see p.93 below) suggest that this may indeed be the site of the earliest extant evidence of Adulis, albeit perhaps with some Aksumite overlay. Thus it is not necessary for every structure within the civic boundary to have been aligned upon the same, rigid axis. Similarly, the depth of the excavated features suggests that the geophysical survey reveals structures of a later date, perhaps dug through by both Paribeni and Anfray. Paribeni himself argued that the church he excavated was built upon the foundations of an earlier building (1907, 477 and figure 15), lending credence to the notion that the geophysics represents the Adulis of the late antique. Older parts of the town may have been built to a different plan, as they were at many of the Roman sites of the period, or indeed have grown up organically: we know that the town grew from the 'fair sized village' of the *Periplus* to the cosmopolitan centre of commerce described by Cosmas in the 6th century, and this is unlikely to have

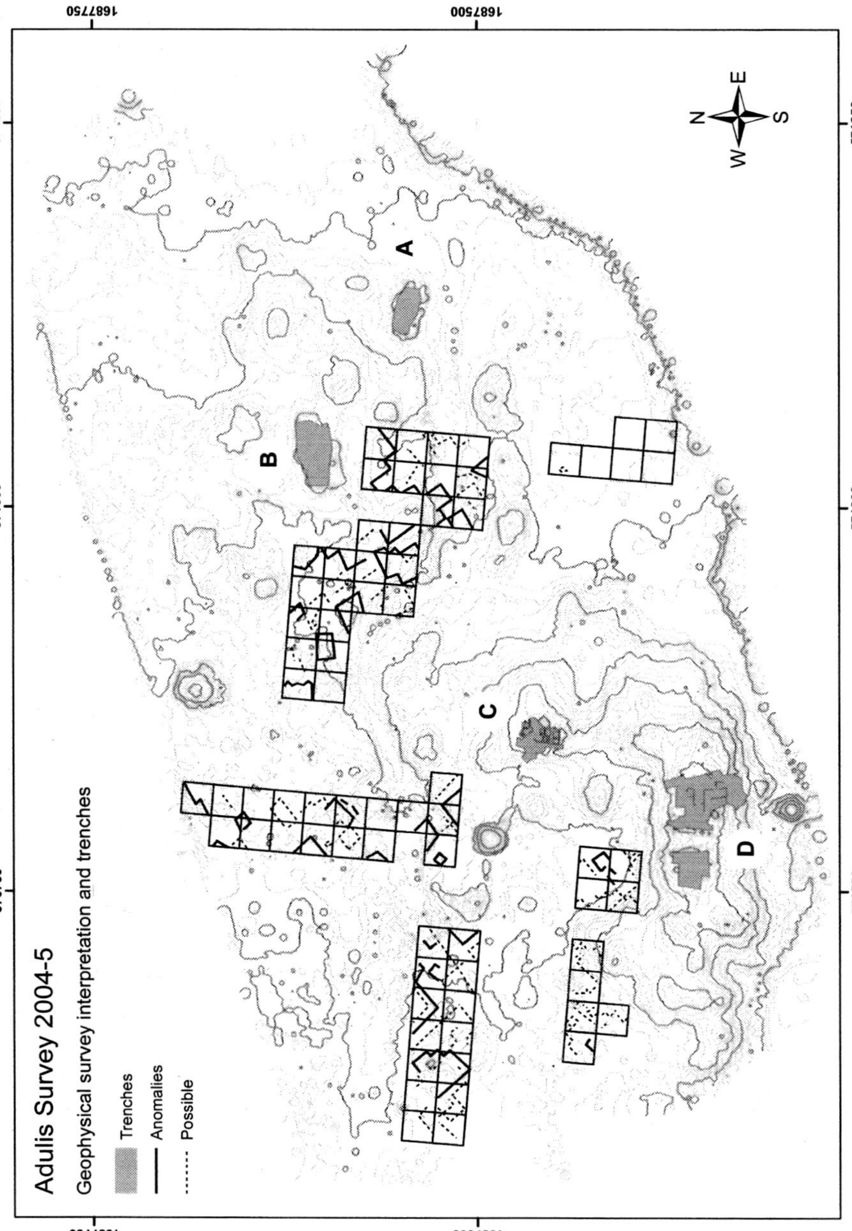

Figure 3.8 Interpretation of the geophysical survey

occurred instantly. Pottery surveys conducted at the site seem to suggest that this area of occupation is indeed older than other parts of the site, with the highest proportion of pre-Aksumite pottery and obsidian flakes found at the south-west corner of Adulis (see below). It would appear therefore that *parts* of Adulis were built according to a regulated grid plan, in contrast to the more scattered growth of Adulis' earliest phases. It is unclear whether this growth was continuous, as would seem likely, or whether a period of desertion separated the 1st century settlement from the 4th. This will only be settled by excavation.

It is possible that the significant number of features identified around Sundström's 'palace' form part of a complex, perhaps incorporating a wall; more survey is required to verify this. However, given the contentious labelling of the building as a 'palace', it would be somewhat premature to talk of Royal, or Palatial precincts. Unfortunately this area has too much basalt scatter on the surface for more geophysical survey to be viable – perhaps the remains of the debris of the upper storey suggested by Sundström (1907, 178), based upon his excavation of 'a splendid flight of stairs on the west side' of the structure. Similar problems are associated with the survey at the south-western edge of the site, close to the trenches of Paribeni. Due to the large amount of surface basalt, the results are difficult to interpret. There does, however, appear to be a significant number of substantial structures in the area, of similar size to those visible in the trenches and aligned upon the same north-west, south-east axis. It is tempting to suggest that the strong signature and somewhat chaotic readings result from tumble, *i.e.* the collapse of walls into the structures, during the same destructive phase recorded by Sundström, Paribeni and Anfray at other areas of the site. Until these results are ground-truthed through excavation this will remain only a hypothesis, albeit a tempting one.

The results would also seem to support Paribeni's claim that Adulis was unwalled (1907; see Munro-Hay 1982, 107) and there is certainly no clear evidence of a defensive wall in the survey data. It is true that there are still a number of anomalies appearing in the grids at the northern and western extent of the survey area, which might suggest that the town extended into the area now covered by modern field systems. Within the survey grids, however, which the topographic survey would suggest covered at least the southern and eastern extent of the site, there is clearly no defensive wall. Given the size of the grids, their location and the apparent success of the survey in identifying substantial anomalies, we can be fairly confident that we would have traced the remains of such a wall had it ever existed in this area. The lack of a defensive wall is a common feature of other Aksumite settlements of a similar period, and must be indicative of a central authority capable of ensuring and maintaining security in the region – although a number of revolts or uprisings amongst 'subordinate tribes' are mentioned in Aksumite inscriptions, none of these appear to have occurred at Adulis or its environs (Munro-Hay 1982, 107; 1991). It is certainly testimony to the power and reach of Adulis / Aksum that the town, in such an isolated, indefensible position on the plain of Zula, appears to have lacked any permanent, substantial fortifications.

This would nevertheless appear to contradict the claim made in the *Periplus* that an alternative anchorage was necessary at Orienê following attacks on Diodorus Island. It makes little sense to emphasise the power and authority of Adulis /Aksum, whilst simultaneously recognizing that security issues in the middle of the 1st century AD forced ships to harbour offshore. This is less problematic if we accept that the geophysics represents later period growth, following the consolidation of the region more fully into the Aksumite Empire. It cannot be assumed that the Adulis of the *Periplus* was undefended.

It is nevertheless suggested by Kirwan (1972, 171) that the famous *Monumentum Adulitanum* of Cosmas Indicopleustes was located 'outside the western gate of the city, on the side of the road'. Kirwan's claim is based upon Wolska-Conus'(1968) translation of *Christian Topography*, which actually reads '*á l'entrée de la ville, du cote ouest*'. Similarly, the MacCrindle (1897) translation of Cosmas reads simply: 'here is to be seen a marble chair, just as you enter the city on the western side by the road which leads to Axômis'; there is no explicit mention of a gate. The Greek text itself is equally ambiguous, reading 'άρχη τηζ πόλεωζ', 'at the edge, or the boundary of the city. Given the lack of any structures significant enough to be a wall around the ancient city, it would seem most likely that Kirwan simply substituted gate for entrance. One does not have to pass through a gate, or indeed a wall, to enter a city.

Chapter IV
The Galala Hills

David Peacock and Lucy Blue

To the south of Adulis, two ranges of low hills of the order of 50 m or so high, can be seen on the horizon. They dominate the plain of Zula as they are the only significant prominences which break this flat area. According to the custodian of Adulis, Sahla Hallo, who has unsurpassed local knowledge, the low flat western hill is known as Gamez. It lies 4.96 km south of Adulis on a bearing of 178 degrees. A visit to this hill produced no antiquities and no local knowledge of any. The easternmost hill comprises two parts: a larger hill to the west and a series of smaller ones to the east with a valley or gully between them. They are collectively known as the Galala Hills and lie 5.61 km south-east of Adulis on a bearing of 143 degrees (Fig. 4.1–2).

These hills offer protection from the prevailing winds and form an excellent defensive look-out point, with views out to sea and across the plain far to the north and south. It is likely that they would have been used as such in antiquity and it is thus no surprise that they were occupied by Ethiopians in the recent conflict. Their trenches are clearly visible around the westernmost hill and the steep sides are known to have been extensively mined: four people and numerous sheep have lost their lives on these hills in recent years. In view of this, our inspection of the hills was circumspect and we were only able to climb part of the way up the eastern hill under the guidance of a local shepherd. The minefield was reported to the United Nations Mission to Ethiopia and Eritrea (UNMEE) de-mining section, but there were more pressing needs elsewhere and it was not felt appropriate to devote resources to clearing this relatively minor field. The hills must therefore wait for more detailed archaeological exploration sometime in the future.

We were able to ascend the eastern hill about two thirds of the way to the top and on the way we saw several recent Ethiopian stone-built rifle emplacements. However, we also encountered two much older, overgrown, stone structures, apparently circular and approximately 5 m in diameter. Their elevated position would have made them ideally suited to defensive rather than domestic duties and they may have been the footings of towers. Small quantities of pottery were found in or around them including ribbed sherds of Aqaba amphorae, suggesting that they were contemporary with Aksumite Adulis. Further pottery, both imported and local, was found at the foot of the slope and this may have washed down from the structures above. Significant sherds are described below (pp.84–5).

Figure 4.1 View of the Galala hills from the north

It seems likely that these structures relate to the harbour of Gabaza (Fig. 2.1) mentioned in the works of Cosmas Indicopleustes and Procopius (see above, pp.10–11); although the harbour itself is likely to lie buried by more recent sedimentation. This conclusion concurs with that of Sundström (1907, 181) who wrongly names the hills Gamez, a name which he claims recalls the form of Gabaza. The correct name is Galala, which might equally hark back to the ancient name.

Today the gully between the hills is dry, although the smooth, fresh, rocks suggest the flow of water. It appears to have been widened by modern quarrying, perhaps by the Italians when they occupied the plain of Zula around Malcatto. It appears that the British Expeditionary Force quarried rock for making piers from the opposite shore on the Bure Peninsula (Holland and Hozier 1870, 291). Sundström (1907, 182) does not mention quarrying, which may not have existed in his day, but states:

> 'Between the northernmost [*sic*] hill and the others runs a gully of fresh water. When I visited the place, situated 1½ hours from Adulis, I found near the water pits dug by the natives in order to water their cattle, large heaps of potsherds of different kinds like those found at Adulis, pieces of glass, broken tiles, beads, ashes and charcoal. The natives told me that they found such objects in the earth every year. This indicates that a town was situated here. On account of the name and of the fact that fresh water and ancient fragments are to be found here, I presume that Gabaza, the harbour of Adulis was situated on this spot.'

Figure 4.2 View of the westernmost hill from the eastern hill of the Galala hills

Figure 4.3 View of Diodorus Island off the eastern end of the hills

Figure 4.4 View of Diodorus island from the foot of the Galala hills

Figure 4.5 Pot still in situ

Diodorus Island

Off the eastern end of the Galala Hills, at a distance of 112 m, is a fossil skerry (Figs. 4.3–5). It comprises a lozenge shaped mass of lava (including pillow lava) 173 m long, 35 m wide and 15 m high. On the flat surface were sherds of Roman amphorae, Eastern Sigillata A and local wares (see p.82 below). The surface is very eroded and no structures could be discerned, but at one point a pot appeared to have been set in the ground, suggesting that they may once have existed (Fig. 4.6). The sedimentological analysis suggests that in antiquity this fossil skerry could have been surrounded by sea (see below p.47). It is therefore almost certain that this is Diodorus Island of the *Periplus* and the hills that currently stand proud of the surrounding flat salt marsh, would once have provided the only shelter along this coastline from the prevailing northerly winds to vessels anchored in their lee.

The area between the island and the main Galala Hills is occupied by modern silt with a wadi channel cutting through it, which has exposed some very ephemeral structures, 20 m from the western tip of the island on a bearing of 203°. In the wadi bed is one course of a mud brick wall 15 m long and 1.2 m wide on a bearing of 95°. It is made of bricks which appear to be about 30 cm square and a few body-sherds of Roman pottery suggest it to be contemporary with the material on the rock. 10 m south of the first wall, is an even more ephemeral wall running parallel, but the scant traces are very difficult to discern. These structures might represent buildings or be associated with the causeway that connected Diodorus Island to the mainland, attested to by the *Periplus*.

Chapter V
The ancient shoreline and maritime landscape

Lucy Blue and David Peacock

A comprehensive appreciation of Adulis in the context of its maritime landscape is critical to an understanding of the history of the site. The site is located on the plain of Zula some 7 km from the coast, linked to the sea by the now dry wadi bed of the River Haddas. The relationship of the site to the sea in antiquity is, however, somewhat ambiguous: accounts of the *Periplus* and the writings of Procopius and Cosmas Indicopleustes all suggest that the site was originally 20 stades (or 3.3 km) distant from the shore. The current location of the site some 7 km from the present shore-line, would indicate that there has been considerable coastal change since the site was occupied. Prior to the research presented here, the exact location of the harbours of Adulis was also unknown. To address this lacuna in our appreciation of the changing coastal geomorphology and the location of the harbour, a careful study was made of the coastal strip of the plain of Zula, from some 8 km to the north of Adulis and 3.5 km to the south of the site to the Galala Hills, with the objective of trying to locate the ancient shoreline and enable the identification of the harbours of Adulis.

Our studies of the region were greatly aided by a QuickBird satellite image taken on 24th October 2003 (Fig. 5.1). With 60 cm resolution and a total absence of cloud and haze, detail is visible with incredible clarity. The image covers the area from Adulis to the sea. The two are separated by an area of fields and irrigation channels, apparently laid out at the time of Haile Selassie, but now, due to climate change, largely unused. To the east of them is a band of salt marsh about 1 km wide. The fields occupy slightly higher ground than the salt marsh and it was therefore thought probable that the ancient beach might be located somewhere on the interface between the two zones. The area to the east would represent sedimentation that occurred subsequent to the occupation of Adulis. This interface is located approximately 4 km (or 24 stades) to the east of the town, which accords broadly with the ancient sources. Careful study of this area revealed six localities (Fig. 5.2), with rolled basalt pebbles, pieces of worn and eroded pottery, a few flakes of obsidian and shells, which seem to be beach deposits. One of these was undated, one produced a mixture of wheel and hand-made pottery, possibly suggesting a Roman date, while the remaining four produced hand-made pottery associated with Aksumite pottery of the type found on Adulis itself. The area to the north of these beach deposits, north of the Haddas River, was covered with more extensive dune topography in which were found a further four sites with hand-made pottery and obsidian flakes, probably of prehistoric date (Fig. 5.2 Sanda, North of Afta 1–3).

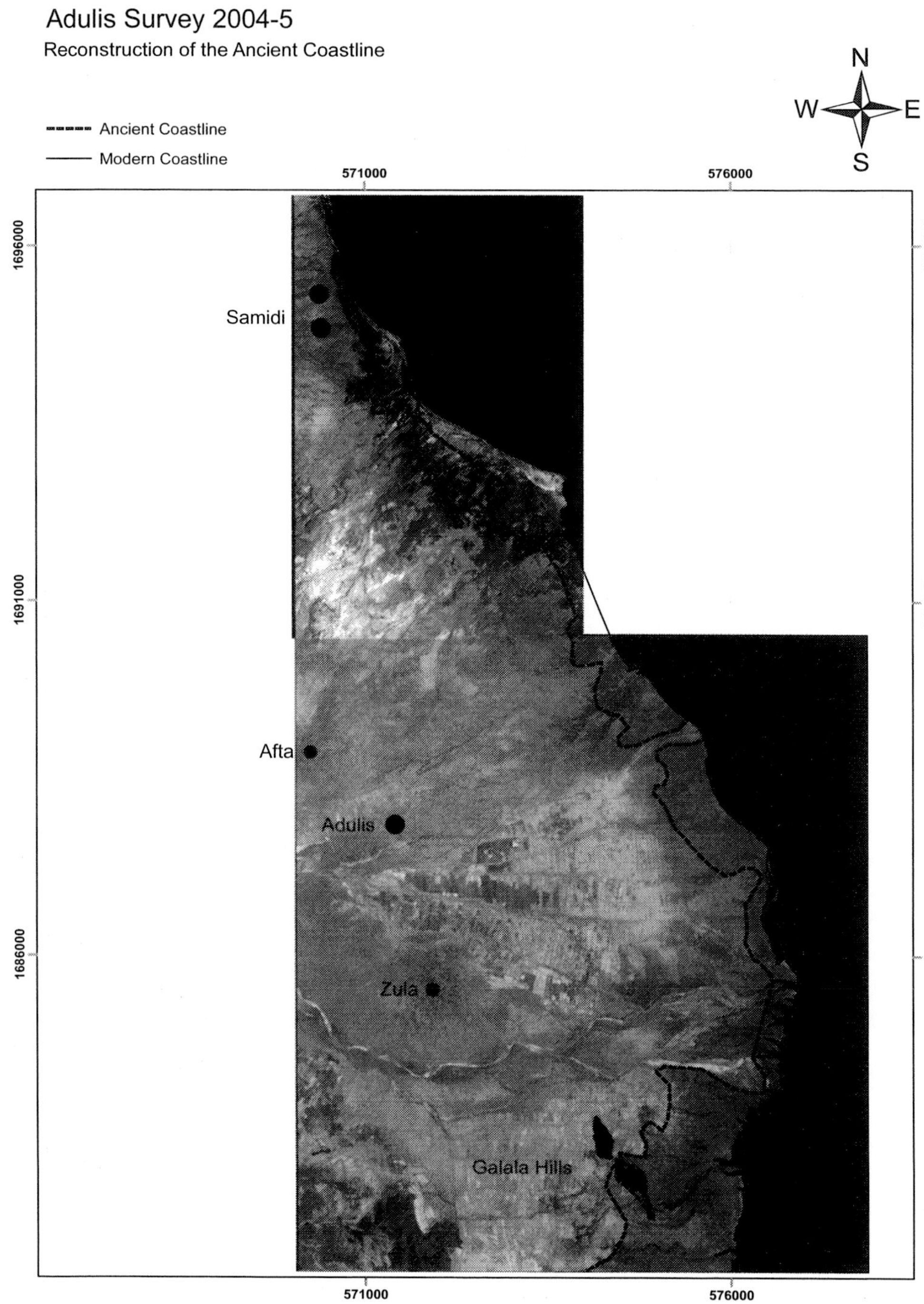

Figure 5.1 Satellite image showing coast and suggested configuration of the ancient shoreline.

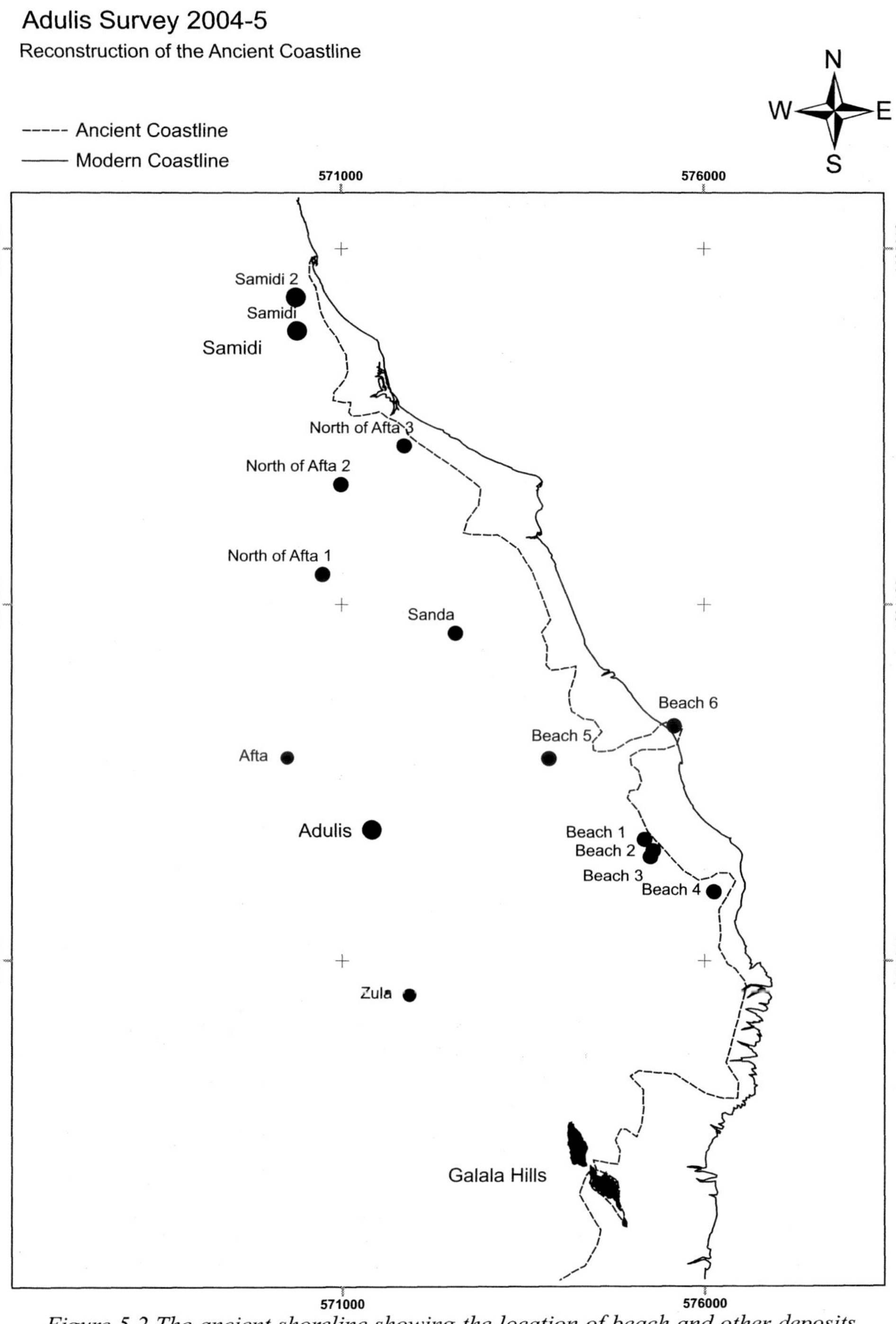

Figure 5.2 The ancient shoreline showing the location of beach and other deposits

Results of the regional survey

The following relate to Fig. 5.2.

Beach deposits

Beach 1 comprises a small collection of badly worn body-sherds, much degraded by salt. Some are hand-made while others are wheel turned and the predominant fabric is reddish buff with medium sand and a little mica (see below p.85). A few flakes of obsidian are present.

Beach 2 comprises a scatter of eroded sherds, nearly all wheel made. The presence of rilled Aqaba pottery suggests an Aksumite date. See below p.86 for illustrated sherds.

Beach 3 is a collection of worn sherds including three rilled Aqaba pots. Most are wheel turned with some hand-made. See below p.86 for illustrated sherds.

Beach 4 is a small collection of body-sherds nearly all hand-made. They are in a black fabric with coarse sand fragments and some mica. One was tempered with vegetable matter. A single flake of obsidian was found.

Beach 5 could be of prehistoric date for it comprises a few red brown hand-made body-sherds associated with obsidian flakes.

Beach 6 comprises five red brown hand-made body-sherds with a prehistoric aspect.

The nature of this material and their location in the landscape helps support the idea of delta progradation and indicates the possible location of the ancient shoreline. The other sites identified further to the north are inland and comprise hand-made sherds associated with much obsidian. They are probably the remains of prehistoric camps and cannot be used to gauge the position of the ancient shoreline with the same certainty.

To the north of Adulis

The coastal strip was examined as far north as the naval station of Ghedem some 29.5 from Adulis. In this stretch the coastal sediments disappear and the shoreline is more rocky. No antiquities were seen and there was no evidence for significant coastal change. The US hydrographic map published by Casson (1981) marks 'tombs' about halfway between Afta and the Ghedem headland. These were located and believed to be of relatively recent date perhaps associated with the local nomadic tribes.

Arkiko

The village of Arkiko (or inland from it) was regarded by Casson (1981) as a potential site of the Adulis of the *Periplus*. The area around it was carefully examined for antiquities but without success. Nothing pre-Islamic was found and the existing ruins all seem to date from the Turkish occupation.

Massawa

Casson (1981) regarded Massawa as a likely place for 1st century AD Adulis as it is the only place where islands connected to the mainland by causeways can be found. It is indeed an excellent port and the most important in modern Eritrea. However, the causeways are modern and there is no evidence that they existed in antiquity. It is also worth noting that there is no water on the islands and today it has to be brought from springs at Dongola, some 15 km inland. Despite considerable building work in and around Massawa in the last few

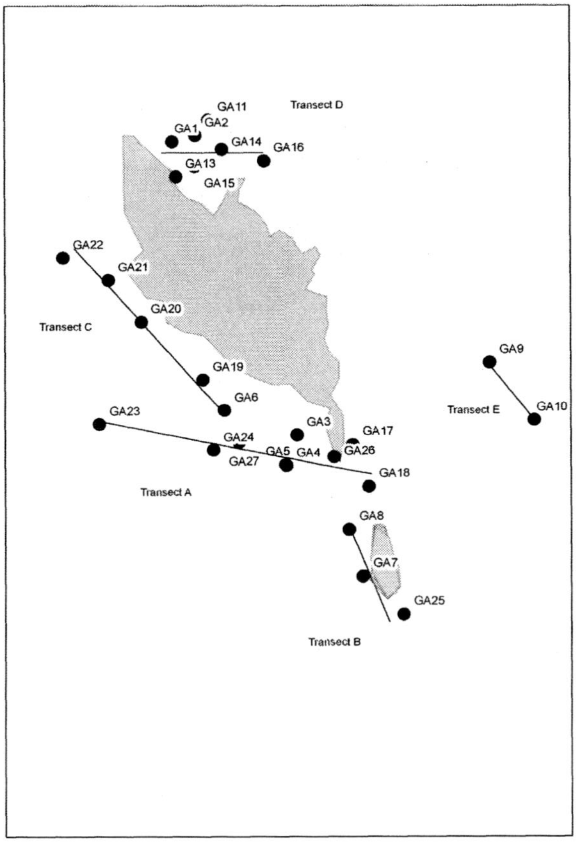

Figure 5.3 Location of sedimentological transects around the Galala Hills

years, no pre-Islamic antiquities have come to light.

Thus, the beach deposits described above are indicated in Fig. 5.2. If, as seems probable, they represent the ancient coastline, it is reasonable to use them as a guide to indicate the position of the ancient sea level. If this evidence is combined with the contrasting sedimentary regime and topography revealed by the satellite image, it can be used as a guide to map the ancient coastline with some degree of certainty.

Sedimentological survey of the Galala Hills

The theory relating to the location of the ancient coastline was tested in the region around the hills of Galala. Here the interface between the apparent area of easterly prograded coastline and the higher ground identified on the satellite image, falls around the easterly base of the Galala Hills. Furthermore, if this is an accurate interpretation, then it would appear that a small prominence to the south, identified as the site of Diodorus Island (see p.37, above), and the area surrounding and to the east of the most south-easterly of the two small hills near Galala, would previously have been surrounded by water, whereas the adjacent hill to the north-west would have been on dry land. As mentioned above, Sundström (1907) reported finding large quantities of 6th century pottery at the foot of the hills and suggested that this could be the site of Aksumite Gabaza, the customs house and port of Adulis in this period. This suggests that the coastline was indeed closer to the Galala.

Five transects (Fig. 5.3) were established around the low hills of Galala to test the theory that the area was on the coast in antiquity. In total some twenty seven cores were extracted using a gouge auger that extracted 50 cm sections at a time to a maximum depth of *c.* 5 m (Fig. 5.4). The location of each core was recorded using a handheld GPS which allowed us to plot their relative distribution to a reasonable degree of accuracy, but did not determine to any degree of reliability, their relative heights. Within these cores some 185 samples were taken. Selected samples have subsequently been subject to grain-size analysis and some tested

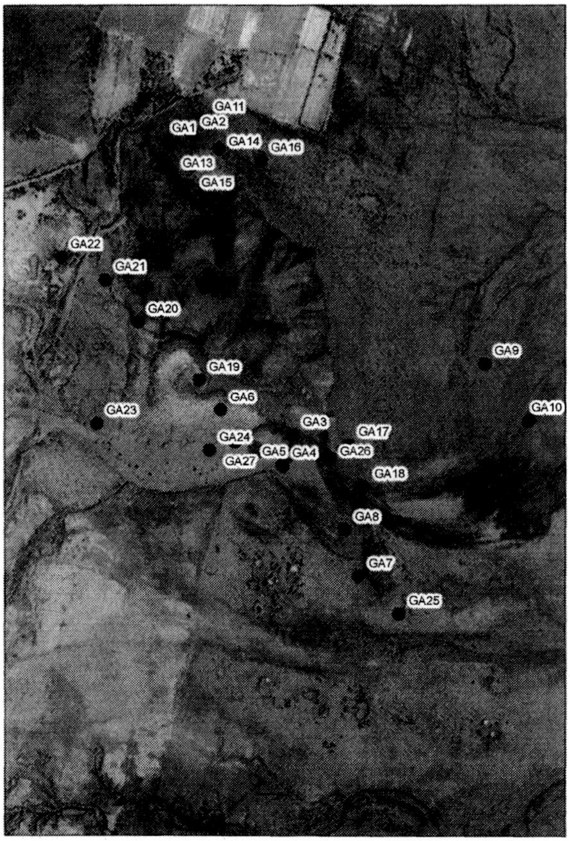

Figure 5.4 Location of auger holes around the Galala Hills. ©Digital Global Inc. All rights reserved.

to see if any foraminifera or other micro-organisms were present in the samples that are indicative of environment.

Criteria for selection of transects and individual core localities, was to primarily ascertain the location of the proposed marine environment in antiquity. The satellite image and current topography acted as a guide to the predicted location of the sea. The hypothesis was that water once divided the small fossil skerry that is located at the extreme south-eastern end of the chain of hills, from the rest of the hills that extended inland to the west, and that to the north and east of these hills was a narrow shoreline adjacent to the sea. To the south of the Galala Hills, was an area of water that would have formed an ideal anchorage sheltered in the lee of the hills from the prevailing northerly winds of the region. The most south-easterly island would have been separated from the other inland hills of Galala by a stretch of shallow water and thus may have been accessible by a shallow causeway, as fitting the *Periplus* description of Diodorus Island.

Data pertaining to relative Holocene sea-level stands, recent tectonic activity and sediment progradation is not available for the region. A detailed relative sea-level curve has yet to be determined for the Holocene period (Siddall *et al.* 2003) and recent tectonic activity is negligible and the tidal range in the region minimal *c.* 0.6 m (Said 1990).Whilst sediment progradation particularly in the region of the delta of Zula, appears to have been substantial, there is no detailed data. The Galala Hills are located some 1.2–1.3 km to the west of the current shoreline and yet due to poor relative height data no measure of relative sea-level can be ascertained. Much work needs to be done in this area to determine the nature of the current landscape and how it has formed, to interpret past landscape change. However, an attempt is made here to provide a broad understanding through the sedimentology and archaeology, of the changing nature of the region around the Galala Hills over the last two thousand years.

Sediment sampling (Fig. 5.5a–g)

Transect A (cores 23, 24, 27, 4/5, 3, 26, 17, 18; Fig. 5.5a–b) was selected as it effectively ran the length of the wadi bed from west to east eventually emerging on the east side of the Galala Hills.

Transect B (cores 8, 7, 25; Fig. 5.5c) was selected as it was hoped this would provide information about the environment in lee of the most south-easterly skerry.

Transect C (cores 22, 21, 20, 19, 6; Fig. 5.5d) provided information about the environment in the lee of the south-easterly large hill of Galala.

Transect D (cores 1, 2, 11/12, 13, 14, 15, 16; Fig. 5.5e–f) denotes an area to the north of the south-easterly large hill of Galala, and was selected to determine the nature of this embayment.

Transect E (cores 9, 10; Fig. 5.5g) was selected as a 'control' area as these two cores are 'seaward' of the Galala Hills and if the sea did reach this area in the past then these two cores would have been submerged.

Sediment analysis – Initial observations based upon grain size and sediment colour/ context of the cores within transects

The easterly extension of Transect A appears to comprise finer sediments which are coloured blue-grey at depth, indicative of a water-logged environment. Likewise sediments in lee of the skerry (Transect B) have similar characteristics. There are less blue-grey sediments in the embayment to the north of the south-easterly hill (Transect D) and organic matter was also extracted from these cores, indicating that it was unlikely that this area was inundated. In contrast, both cores 9 and 10 (Transect E) located to the east *i.e.* to seaward of the Galala Hills, had predominately fine sediments and were almost blue-grey in colour throughout, indicating a marine environment

Of the twenty-seven cores taken, five were selected for grain-size analysis (Cores 2, 10, 16, 18, 26). These were selected as they were comprehensive samples, with a good sequence and they were located in areas that either could potentially provide control information or specific environmental information. Core 10 for example, was the most easterly of the cores taken and would therefore indicate whether or not this region was a marine environment at some point in the past. Cores 18 and 26 were located between the seastack and the south-eastern hill, an area that we believed to have been water-logged in antiquity. The results of the grain-size analysis are shown in the tables below.

The sediment samples that were subject to grain-size analysis were also analysed for foraminifera and other micro-organisms. The upper levels of all the cores contained large quantities of mica, presumably washed down from the surrounding mountains. Unfortunately, no foraminifera were found but samples in cores 10, 18 and 26 contained shell fragments. The shell tended to be concentrated towards the base of the cores, with abundant quantities of coral fragments at the bottom of core 18 (sample 9). Cores 10 and 18 contained gypsum, a diagenetic mineral often associated with sabkha environments (Fig. 5.6 top). Core 10, sample 7 contained a *serpulid* (Fig. 5.6 bottom) which usually lives in a marine environment, commonly attached to sea-grass close to the shore. However, none of these samples were dated and none can be guaranteed to have been deposited in context *i.e.* they may have been transported prior to deposition. Cores 10, 18 and 26 also contained samples with ostracods. A specimen from core 26, sample 6 (Fig. 5.6 middle), was an undamaged bi-valued ostracod

Sample Summary: Core 2

Sample #	*% fines*	*% sand*	$D_{50(\mu m)}$	*Size Classification Wentworth*
S1	90.68	9.32	11.82	Fine silt
S2	7.63	92.37	255.06	Medium sand
S3	69.12	30.88	43.14	Coarse silt
S4	15.96	84.04	250.41	Medium sand
S5	86.87	13.13	15.45	Fine silt
S6	60.67	39.33	30.09	Medium silt
S7	19.52	80.48	104.64	Very fine sand
S8	51.39	51.39	64.19	Very fine sand
S9	18.29	81.71	132.26	Fine sand
S10	61.39	38.61	23.61	Medium sand
S11	41.91	58.09	76.13	Very fine sand
S12	79.81	20.19	14.42	Fine silt
S13	88.44	11.56	9.05	Fine silt
S14	51.51	48.49	45.87	Coarse silt
S15	86.13	13.87	16.41	Medium silt
S16	32.13	67.87	112.31	Very fine sand
S17	62.39	37.61	25.74	Medium silt
S18	26.71	73.29	98.35	Very fine sand
S19	59.19	40.81	25.73	Medium silt
S20	31.56	68.44	95.99	Very fine silt
S21	90.71	9.29	11.37	Fine silt
S22	48.03	51.97	66.98	Very fine sand
S23	66.04	33.96	20.59	Medium silt
S24	16.61	83.39	143.13	Fine sand
S25	53.09	46.91	33.94	Coarse silt
S26	16.74	83.26	145.78	Fine sand
S27	90.75	9.25	13.49	Fine silt
S28	20.12	79.88	157.19	Fine sand
S29	33.07	66.93	117.30	Fine sand

Table 5.1a. Sediment samples

which would indicate that it had been deposited *in situ*. This has been kindly analysed by John Whittaker, Department of Palaeontology, The Natural History Museum and he has determined that it is of the genus *Cyprideis*. 'Whether it is *Cyprideis torosa* is another matter. That species is ubiquitous in Europe, the Middle East and North Africa and lives in estuaries, lagoons, tidal rivers, saline lakes and the like, in salinities from near-freshwater to hypersaline. In very low salinities the shell develops nodes (on up to 7 sides), hence its name. In salinities above about 5 ppt it is usually "smooth", like yours [Core 26, sample 6]'. This means that a freshwater environment for the sample can be discounted because the shells are smooth so the salinity was at least 5 ppt (brackish).

The sedimentological results from the area around the Galala Hills have helped provide further insight into the nature of the past environment. The results are not conclusive evidence of marine environment, but a number of pointers suggest that the sea would have surrounded the seastack and reached the easterly slopes of the south-easterly Galala Hills, perhaps with water encroaching to the south of this hill and thus providing shelter to vessels in its lee. The abundant quantities of shell and some coral fragments in cores analysed and of course the ostracod which does on preliminary analysis, appear to have been deposited in a marine environment, do however, provide interesting results. They would therefore seem to confirm the hypothesis that the ancient shoreline bisected the Galala Hills, supporting the identification of the seastack as Diodorus Island, one of the harbours of the *Periplus*.

Sample Summary: Core 18

Sample #	*% fines*	*% sand*	$D_{50(\mu m)}$	*Size Classification Wentworth*
S1	12.88	87.12	117.3	Very fine sand
S3	7.56	92.44	185.4	Fine sand
S4	15.95	84.05	234.6	Fine sand
S5	70.31	29.69	20.66	Medium silt
S6	12.27	87.73	218.35	Fine sand
S7	74.21	25.79	17.43	Medium silt
S8	75.66	24.34	17.12	Medium silt
S9	28.24	71.76	1225	Very coarse sand

Sample Summary: Core 26

Sample #	*% fines*	*% sand*	$D_{50(\mu m)}$	*Size Classification Wentworth*
S1	6.07	93.93	228.05	Fine sand
S2	11.25	88.75	217.80	Fine sand
S3	74.95	25.05	10.34	Fine silt
S4	80.17	19.83	13.16	Fine silt
S5	87.51	12.49	15.93	Medium silt
S6	79.06	20.94	18.83	Medium silt

Table 5.1b. Sediment samples

Sample Summary: Core 10

Sample #	*% fines*	*% sand*	*$D_{50(\mu m)}$*	*Size Classification Wentworth*
S1	63.68	63.32	29.83	Medium silt
S2	13.18	86.82	271.38	Medium silt
S3	51.29	48.71	58.71	Coarse silt
S4	14.57	85.43	114.55	Very fine sand
S5	74.61	25.39	24.12	Medium silt
S6	39.05	60.95	61.95	Coarse silt
S7	43.16	56.84	68.44	Very fine sand
S8	22.33	77.67	115.08	Very fine sand
S9	28.49	71.51	103.78	Very fine sand

Sample Summary: Core 16

Sample #	*% fines*	*% sand*	*$D_{50(\mu m)}$*	*Size Classification Wentworth*
S1	63.14	36.86	25.24	Medium silt
S2	83.64	16.36	12.82	Fine silt
S3	16.44	8356	152.30	Fine sand
S4	38.57	61.43	66.72	Very fine sand
S5	73.85	26.15	17.86	Medium silt
S6	40.63	59.37	64.89	Very fine sand
S7	21.52	78.48	98.68	Very fine sand
S7.5	70.19	29.81	19.14	Medium silt
S8	58.54	41.46	25.43	Medium silt
S9	37.32	62.68	68.14	Very Fine sand
S10	90.61	9.39	12.62	Fine silt

Table 5.1c. Sediment samples

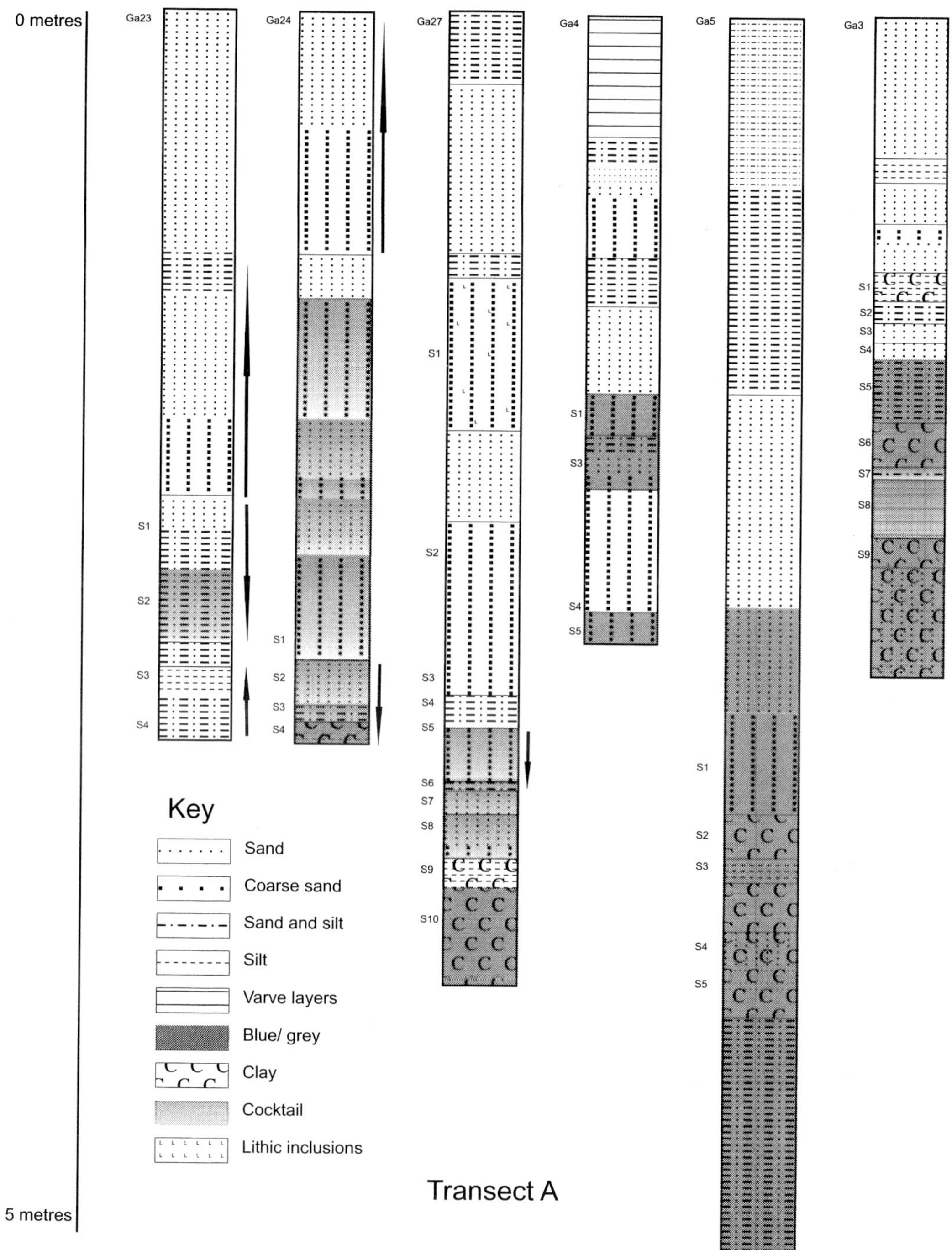

Figure 5.5a Sedimentological stratigraphy of auger cores around Galala Hills

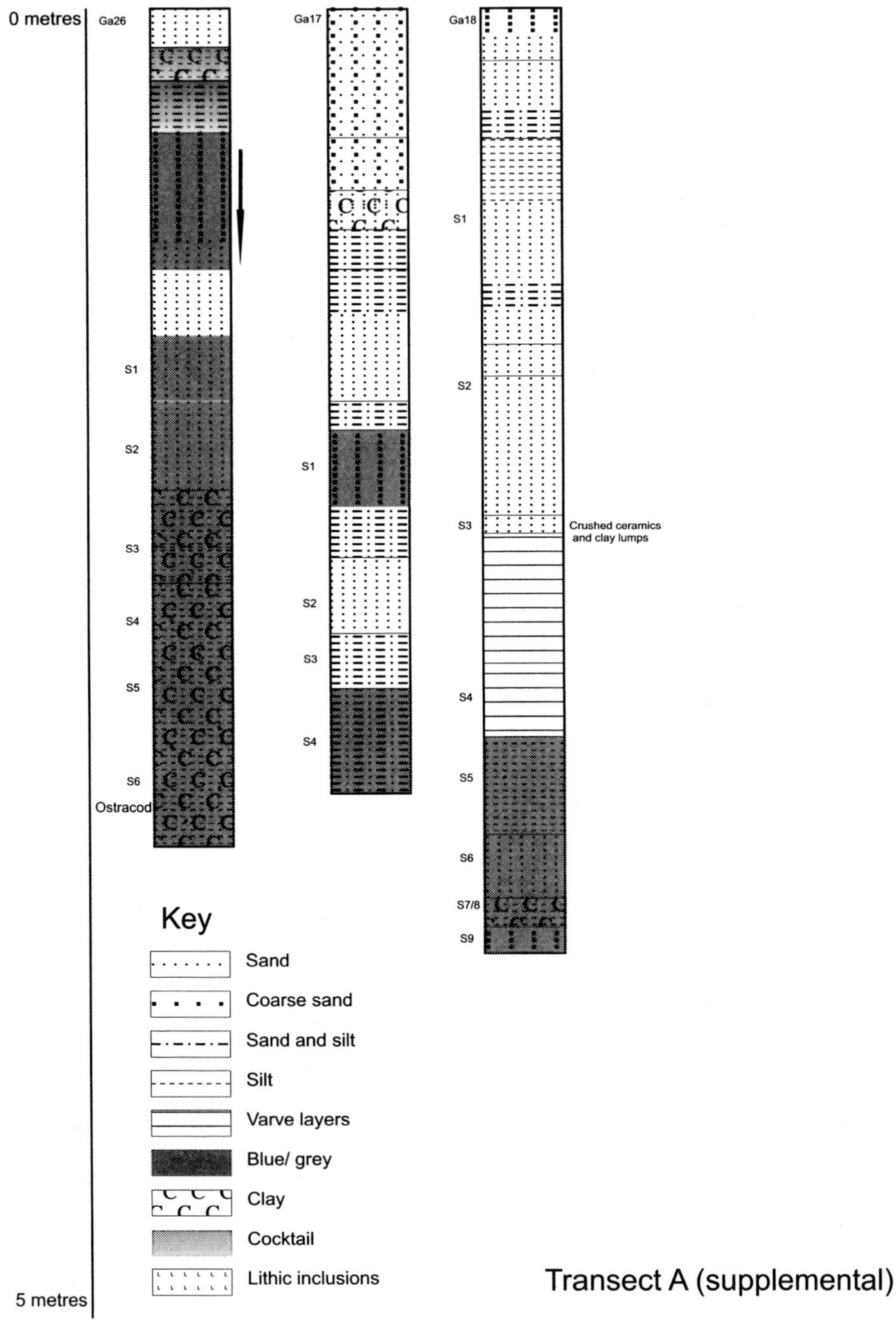

Figure 5.5b Sedimentological stratigraphy of auger cores around Galala Hills

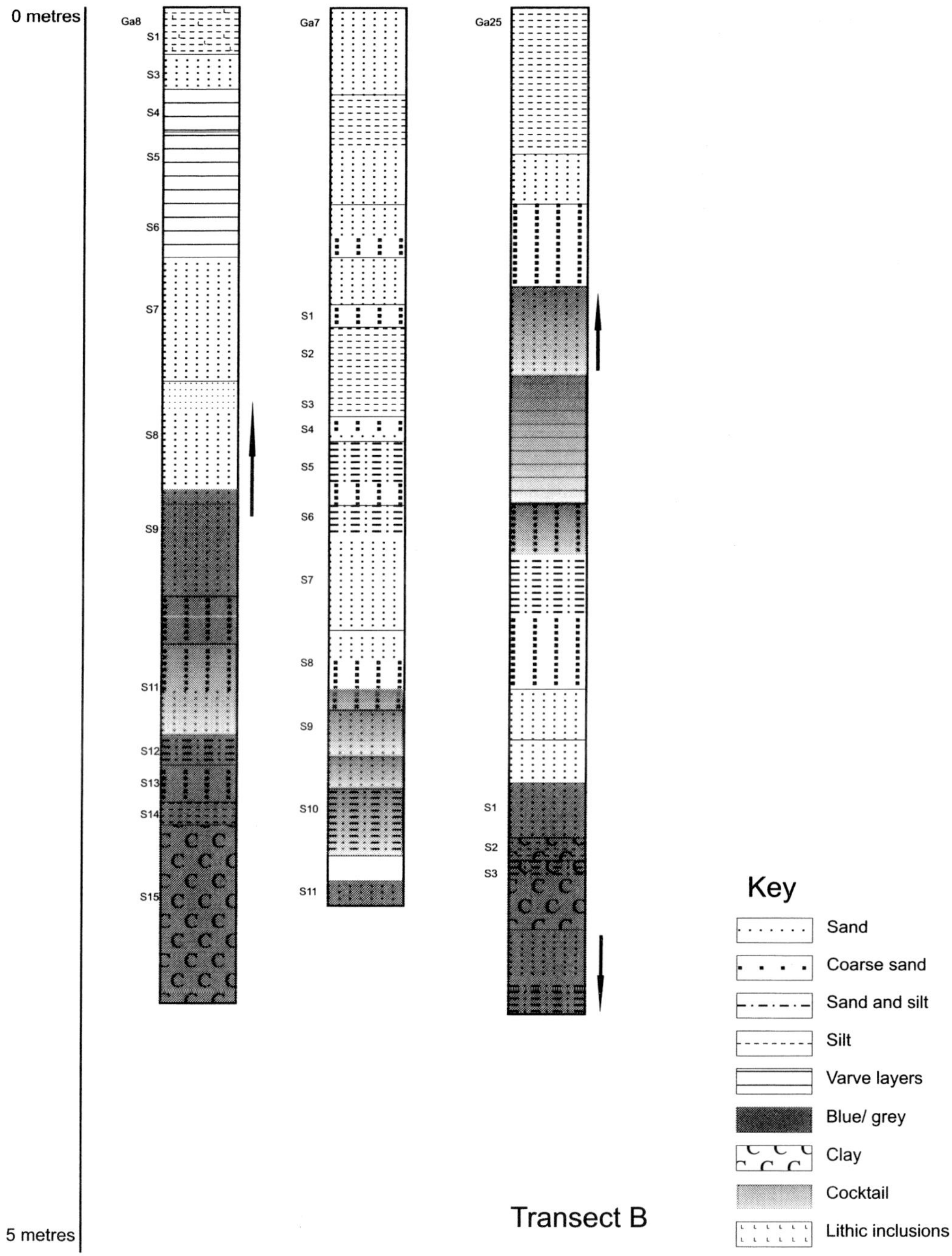

Figure 5.5c Sedimentological stratigraphy of auger cores around Galala Hills

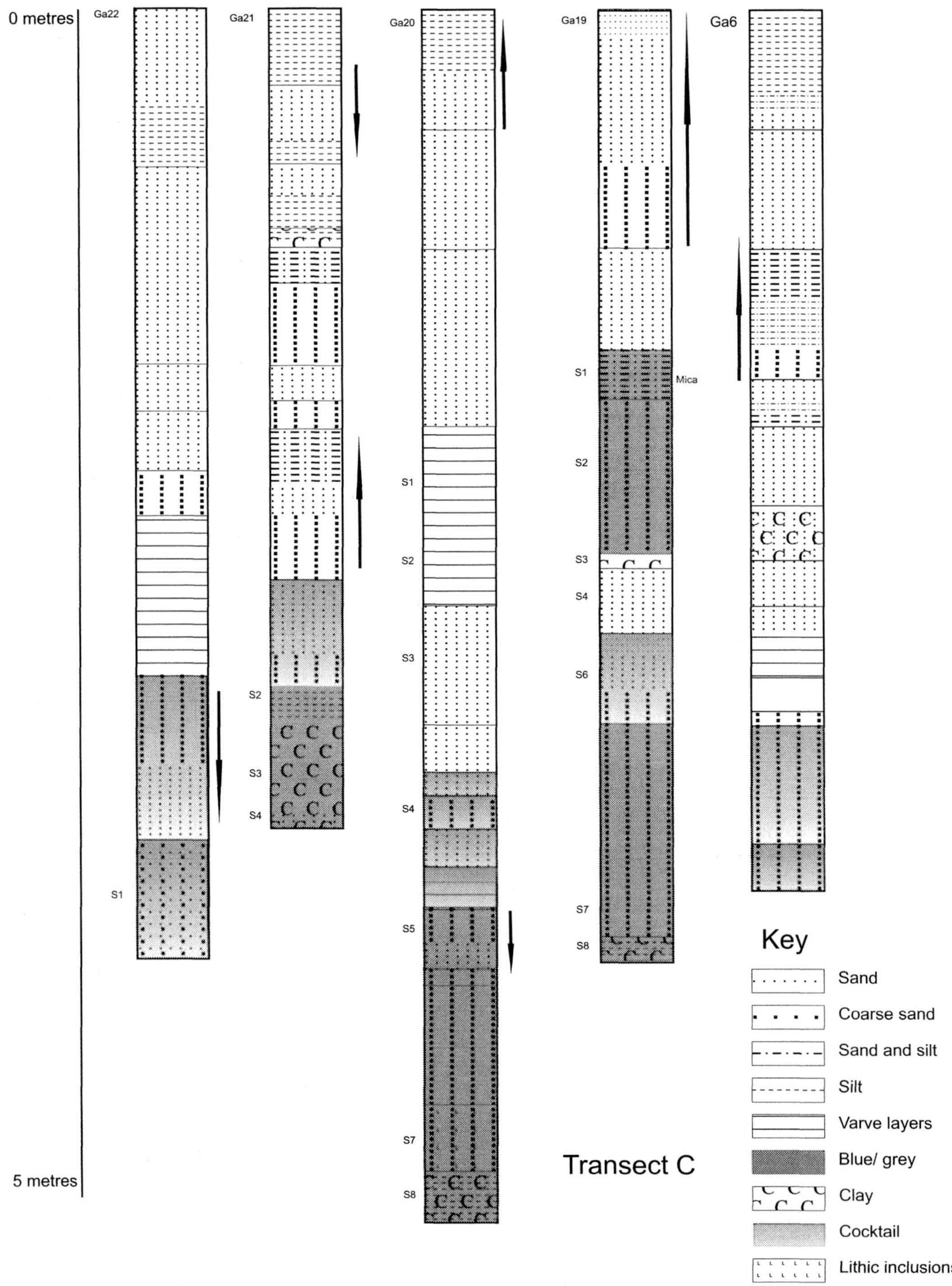

Figure 5.5d Sedimentological stratigraphy of auger cores around Galala Hills

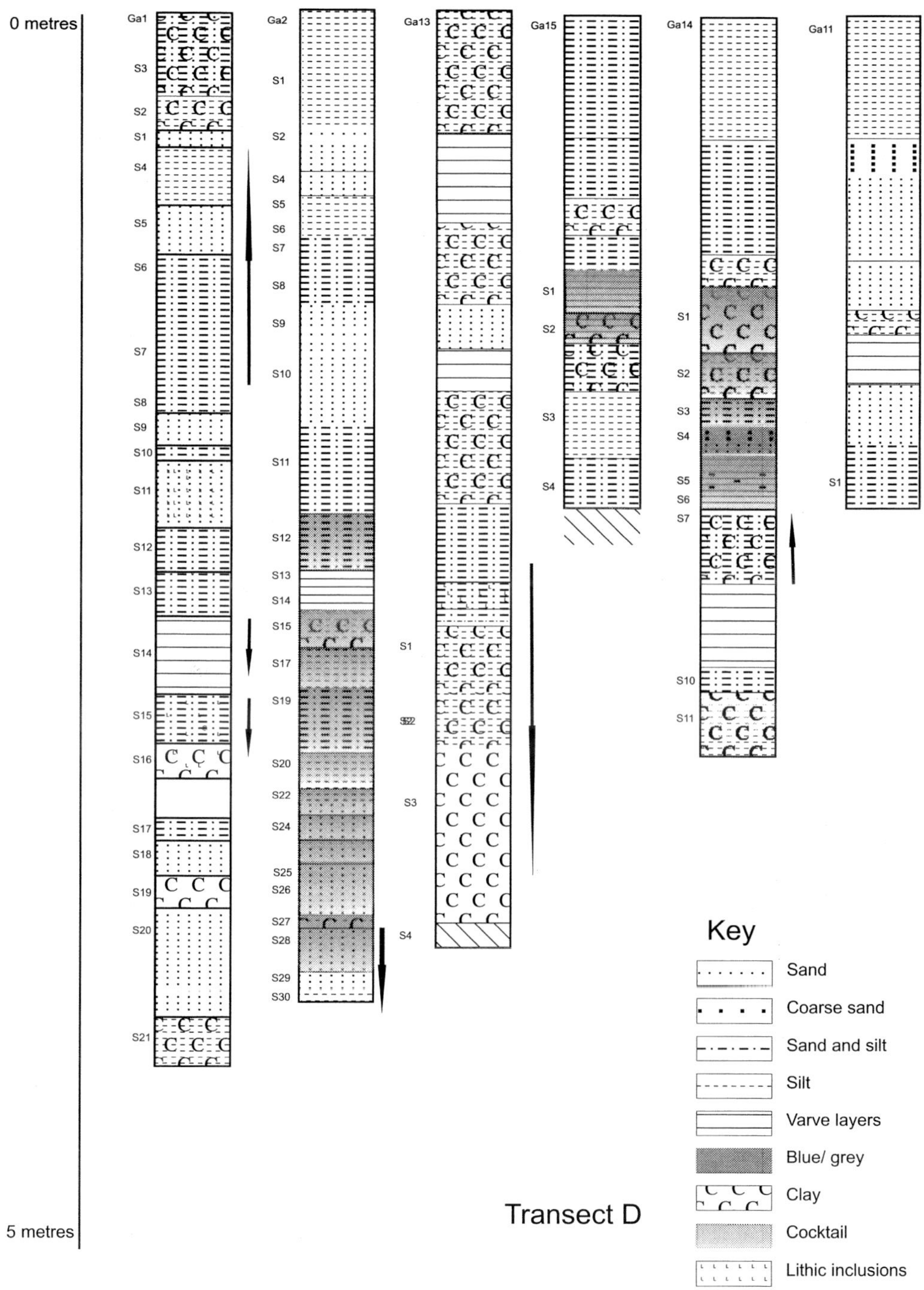

Figure 5.5e Sedimentological stratigraphy of auger cores around Galala Hills

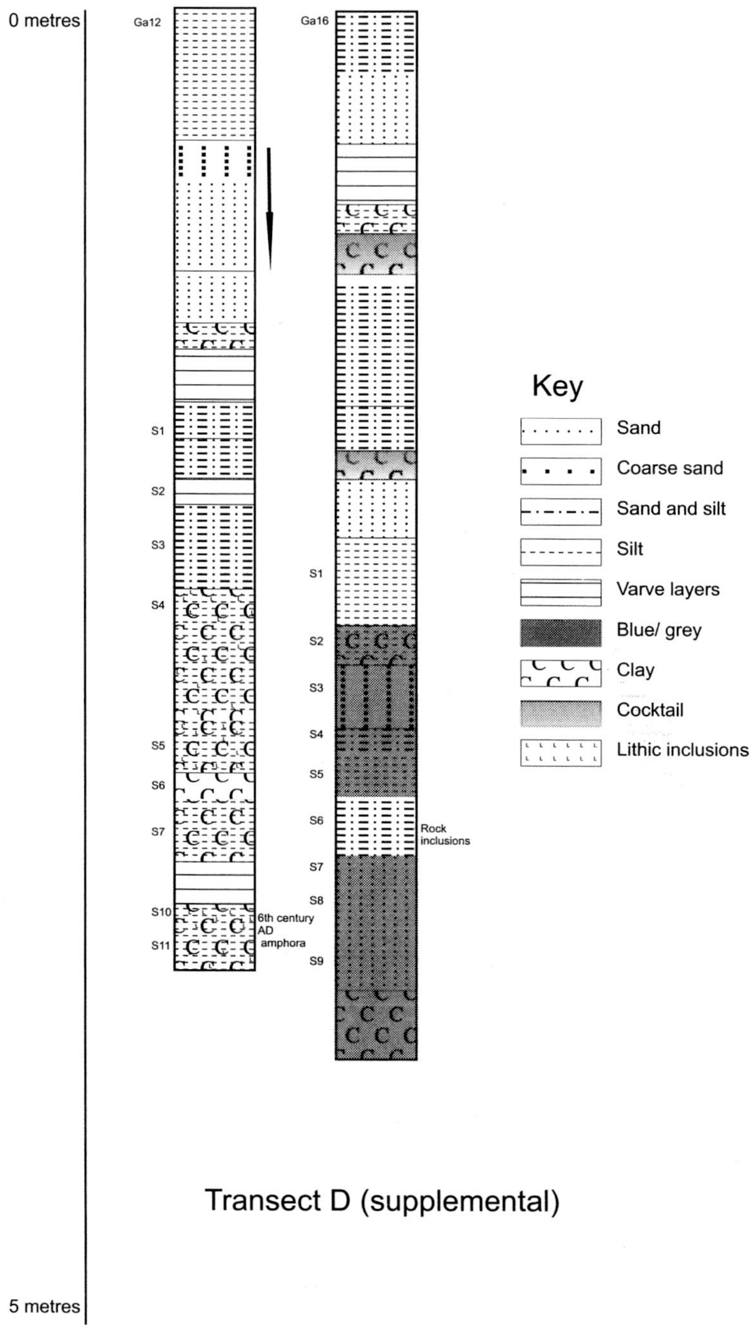

Figure 5.5f Sedimentological stratigraphy of auger cores around Galala Hills

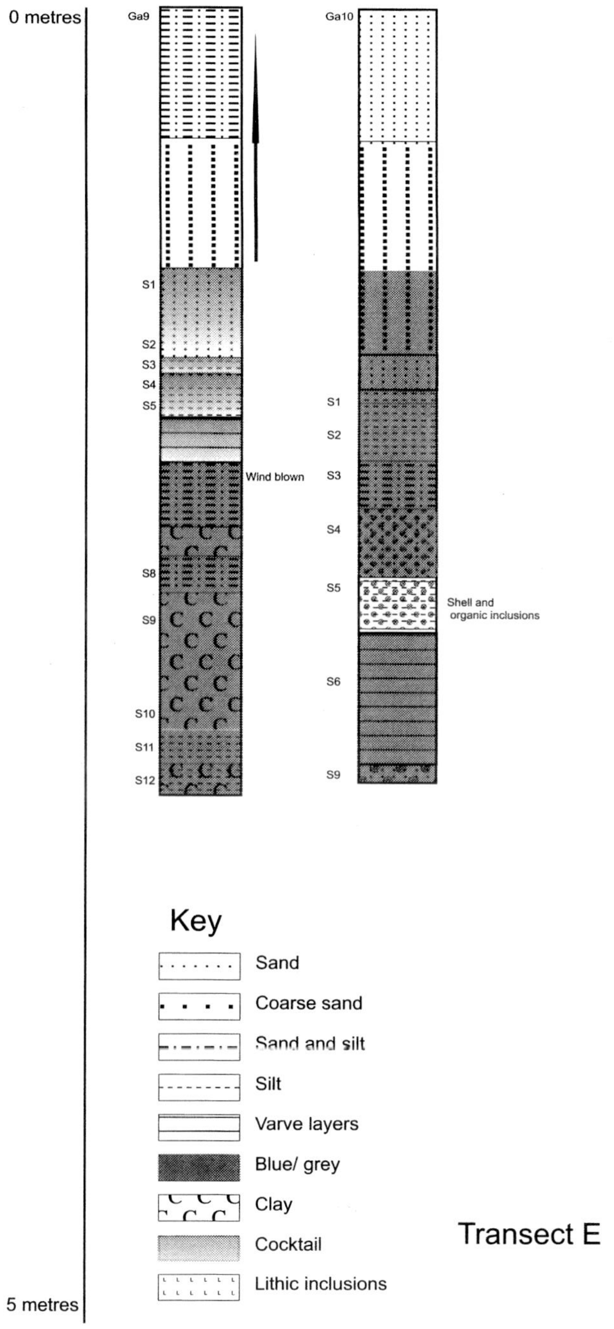

Figure 5.5g Sedimentological stratigraphy of auger cores around Galala Hills

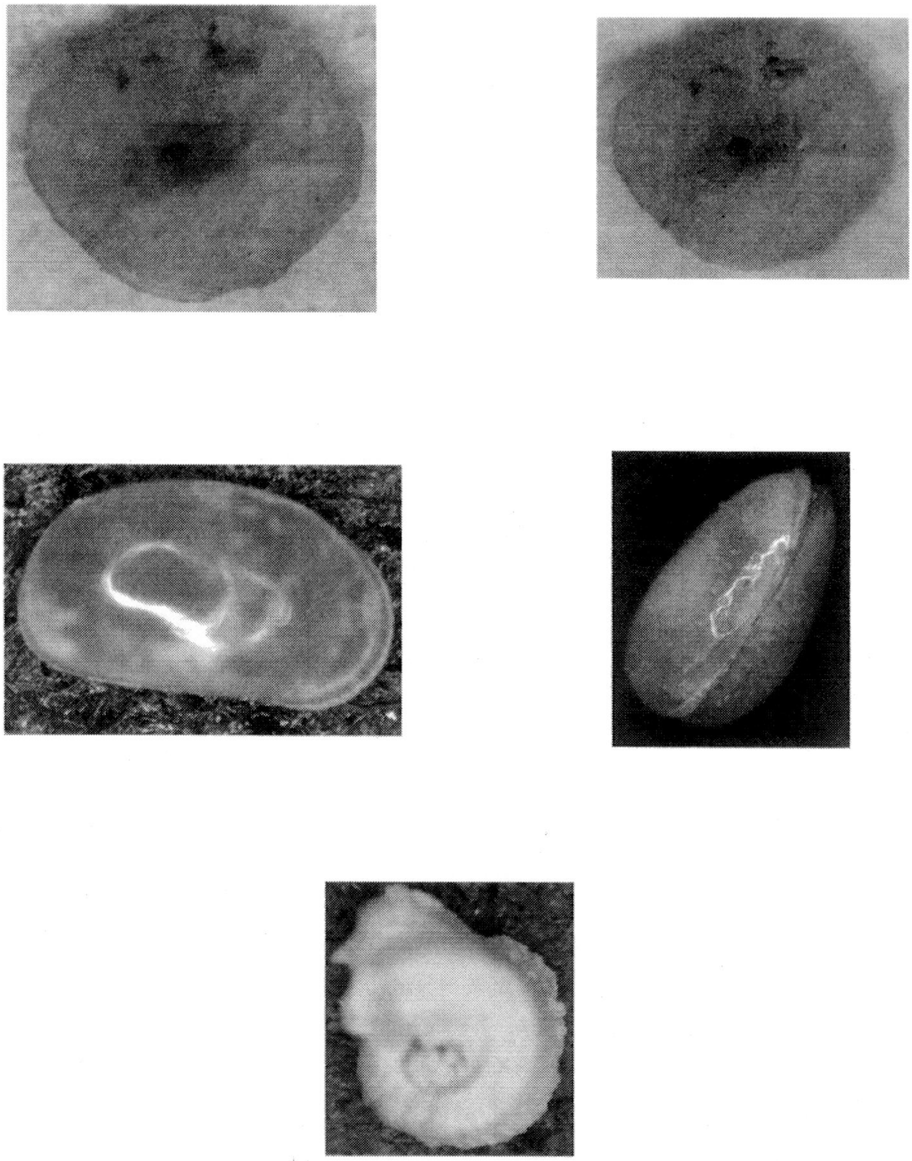

Figure 5.6 Material recovered from analysised sediment samples. Top: gypsum; Middle:ostracod; Bottom: seruplid

Chapter VI
Survey on the island of Dese

Lucy Blue and David Peacock

The island of Dese lies at the entrance to the Gulf of Zula about 25 km south-west of Dahlak Kebir (Fig. 1.3). It thus stands apart from the main archipelago from which it is separated by the Massawa Channel. It is also geologically distinct as it is made up of metamorphic rocks similar to those comprising the Ghedem Massif on the mainland to the west. This results in a hilly topography contrasting with the flat landscape of the Dahlak Islands and the adjacent Bure Peninsula (Fig. 6.1).

It is the nearest island to Adulis, which lies 24 km to the south-west on a bearing of 203 degrees. There can be little doubt that this is Orienê, the hilly island of the *Periplus*, as there are no other contenders (see also Chapter II, above). In view of this it was included in the Adulis project and was visited in 2004 and again in 2005. Both visits were limited to a single day, but in 2005 it was systematically examined by a team of 11 people, permitting a good proportion of the surface to be walked, albeit cursorily.

The island forms a long thin strip oriented roughly north-south, about 7 km long and about 100 m wide (Fig. 6.2–3). The modern settlement of about 20 houses lies on the middle of the island on the eastern side, where there is a superb, sheltered, sandy bay, ideal for anchoring and beaching boats. Behind the settlement is a high hill, part of the chain which forms the backbone to the island. In the middle of the island this bifurcates into two, forming a central valley running north-south and terminating in a large sea water lagoon to the north. The modern settlement is built on a slightly elevated sand bar to the north of which is an arc of salt marsh, suggesting that at one time the bay would have been much larger and would have extended more deeply into the island. Water is sparse and believed to be somewhat saline, but there is a well at the north end of the island connected by a path to the settlement.

To the west of the settlement is a prominent hill, which would have been a good vantage point with commanding views around much of the island. On its crest is a circular stone structure, said to be the tomb of a Sheik, but it could equally be a much ruined skopelos or look out point (Fig. 6.4). At the foot of this hill are ruined stone-built houses, some with wooden lintels still in place (Fig. 6.5). They are surrounded by many shell middens which stretch around the south-western edges of the salt marsh behind the modern village (Fig. 6.6). A few sherds of Aqaba amphorae and one piece of Late Roman 2, suggest that they

Figure 6.1 A beach at Dese showing hilly topography behind

may be Aksumite in date. The stone buildings may be more recent and some glazed Islamic pottery was found near them.

Field survey of the northern part of the island produced much Aksumite pottery, but no trace of anything which could be ascribed to the Roman period. However, in the central valley to the west of the settlement the situation was very different (Fig. 6.7). We did not have time to study this area in detail, but at locality A (Fig. 6.3), we found many fragments of Dressel 2–4 amphorae and some Eastern Sigillata A, dating to the 1st century AD (see below p.82). It was mixed with a little Aqaba pottery and some Late Roman 1 and 2 amphorae suggesting that the area was occupied in both Roman and Aksumite periods. Traces of buildings could be seen, but we had no means of surveying them in detail. To the north of locality A, lies locality B where we found more Roman period pottery and it may well be that much of the central valley was occupied during Roman times.

Most intriguing of all is the north end of the valley where there is a lagoon opening to the sea to the west. Today it seems to be shallow with mangroves growing in the middle, but before silting, it would have been an excellent sheltered harbour. We did not have time to explore it, but the Quickbird satellite image reveals an underwater linear structure at the northern end and possibly another on the western shore opposite (Fig. 6.8). If this is not geological, it might be the remains of an artificial mole. Another linear structure, this time on land connects the lagoon with the well. It is possible that this is an ancient path used to obtain water for replenishing ships: there are no habitations in the area and as it resembles the tracks connecting the modern village to the well, it could be ancient equivalent.

The whole area deserves much more detailed study than we were able to give it and it is matter of regret that we could not return to complete this work in 2006.

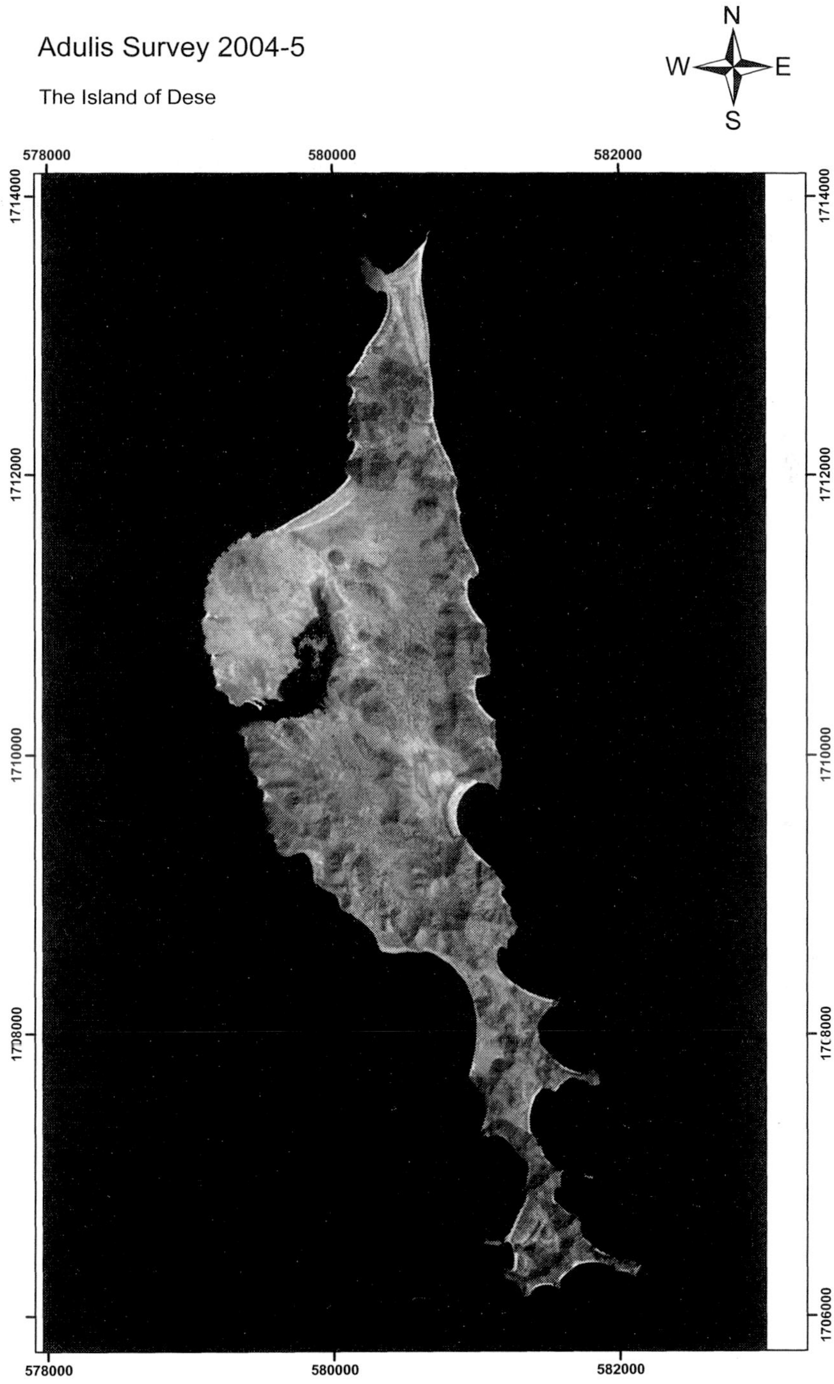

Figure 6.2 Quickbird satellite image of Dese.

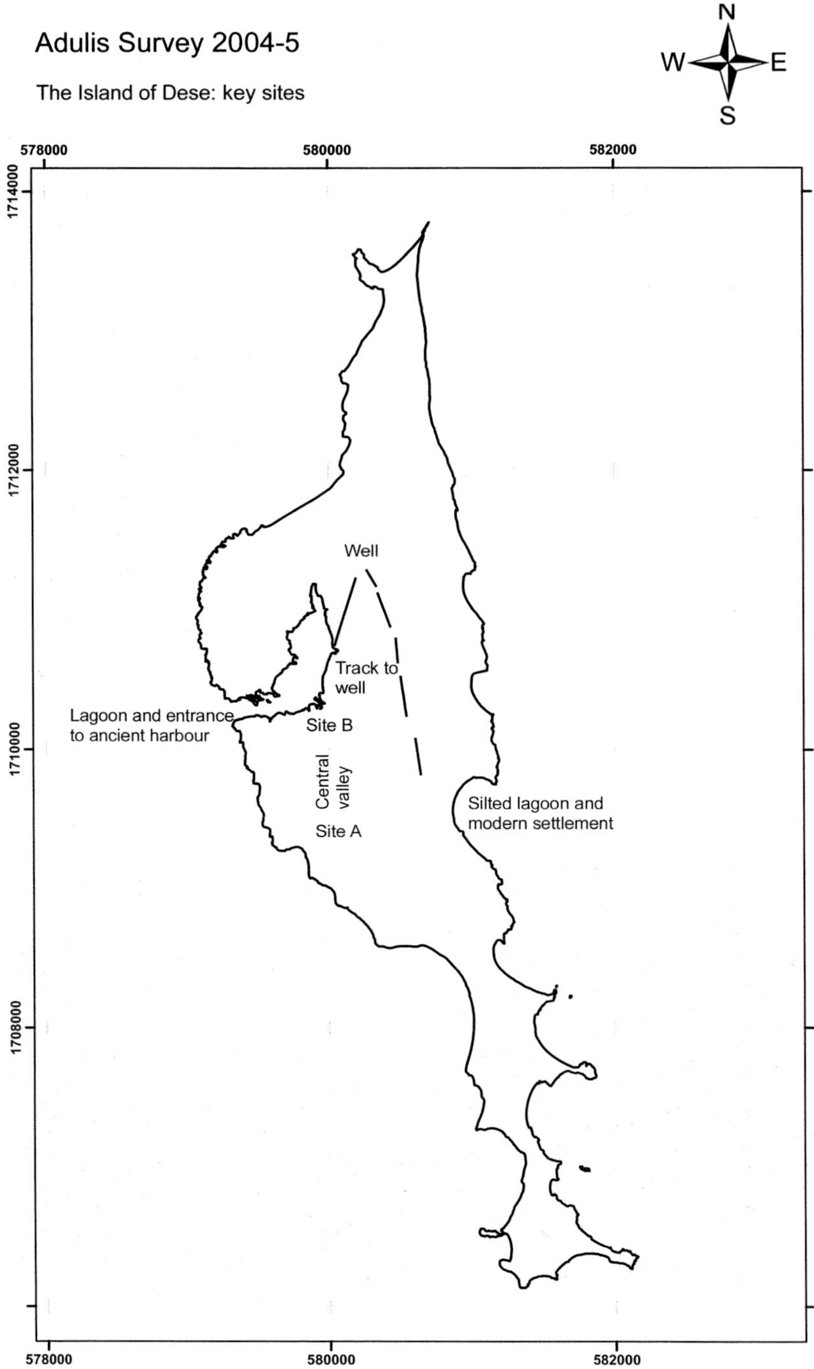

Figure 6.3 Map of Dese showing localities mentioned in the text

Figure 6.4 The modern settlement from the sea, with hills behind and location of sheikh's tomb or possible skopelos

Figure 6.5 Stone buildings, Dese

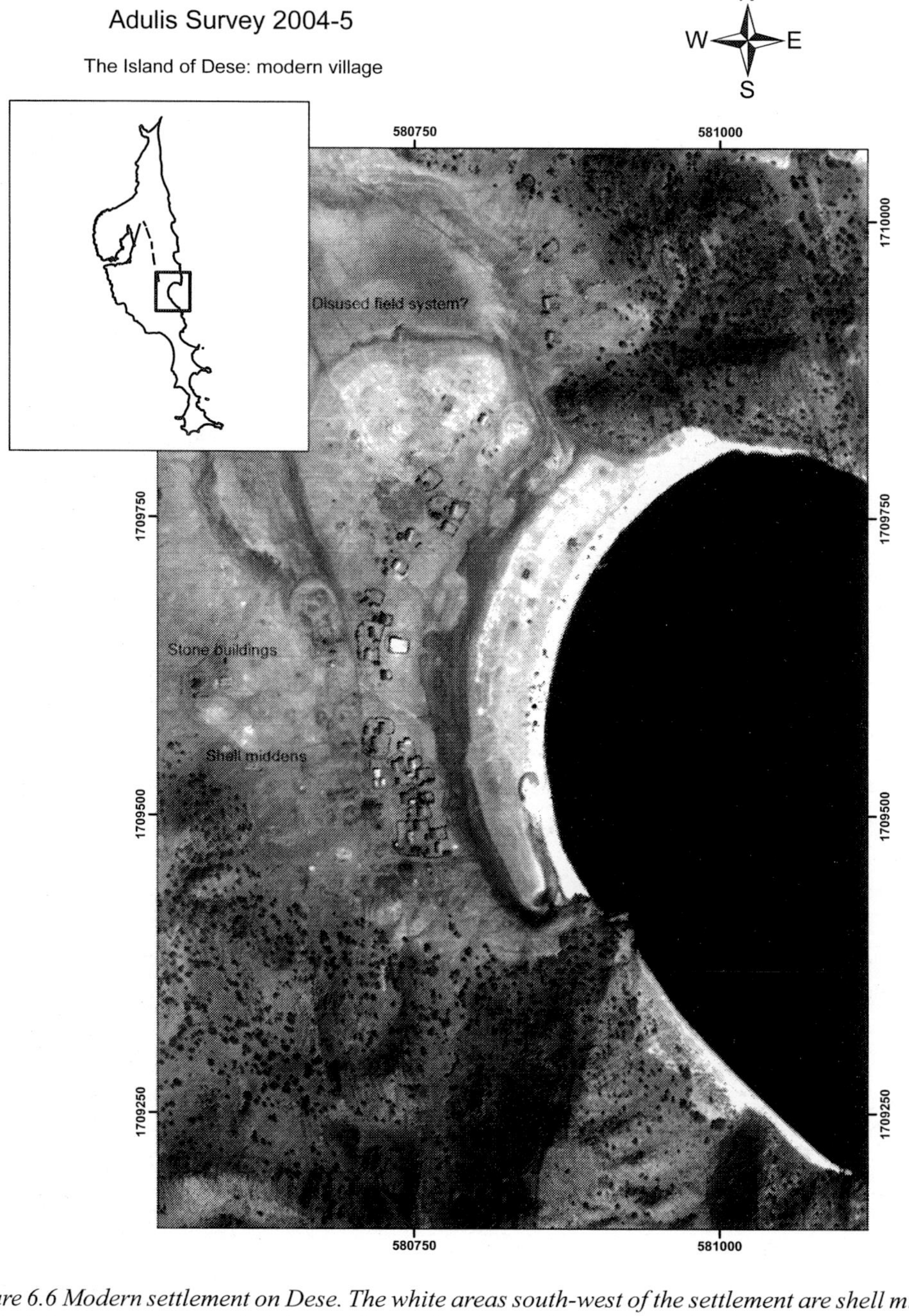

Figure 6.6 Modern settlement on Dese. The white areas south-west of the settlement are shell middens, the dark linears modern tracks. Note evidence of earlier settlement immediately west of current houses.

Figure 6.7 Central valley, site A.

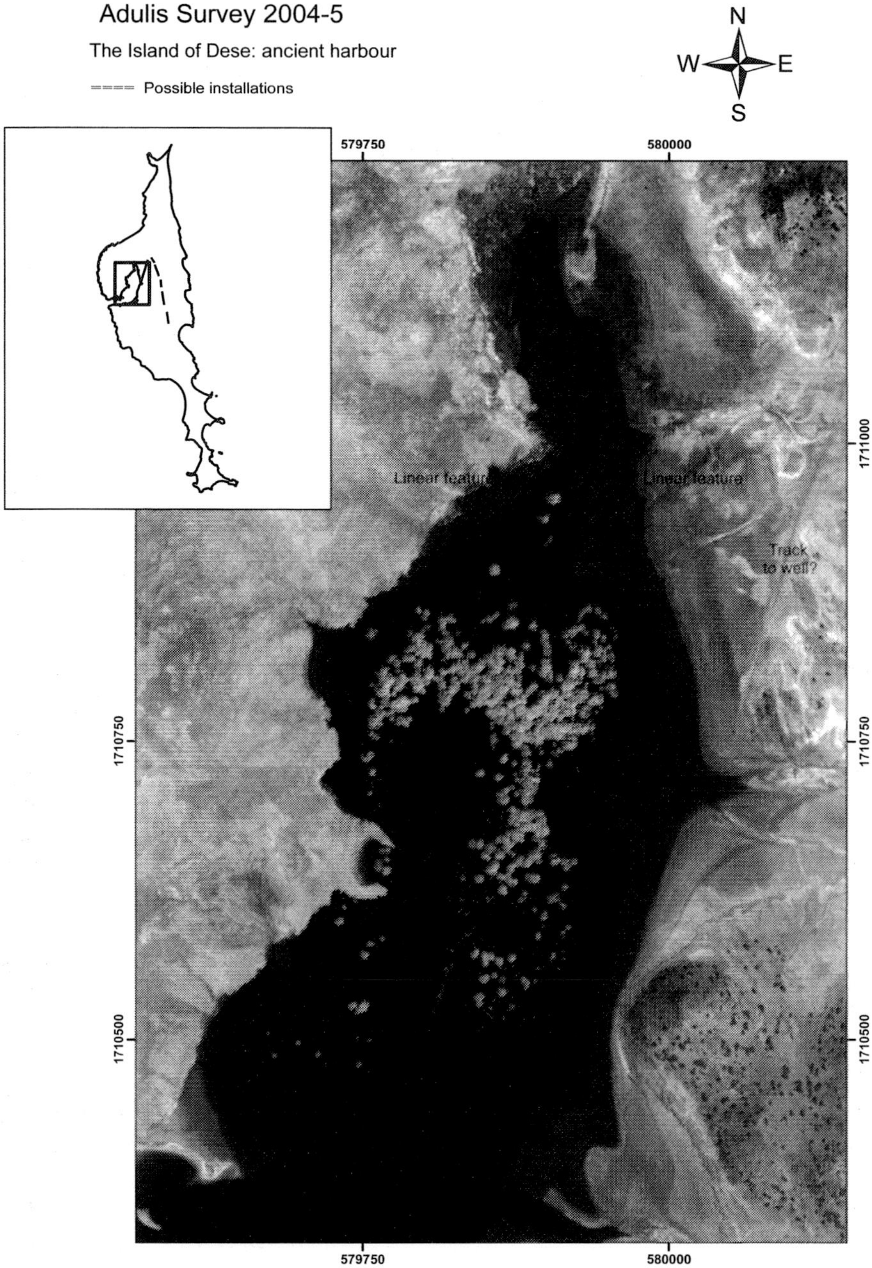

Figure 6.8 Enlargement of the satellite image showing linear features in the region of the lagoon.

Chapter VII
Samidi

Darren Glazier, Julian Whitewright and David Peacock

with a contribution by Sonia R. Zakrzewski and Sarah A. Inskip

An attempt was made to locate the ancient site of Samidi, featured in the 6th century map of Cosmas Indicopleustes (Fig. 2.1). The map marks the location of three different coastal sites in the region – Samidi, Adulis and the customs house of Gabaza – although Samidi itself does not appear in any other source. It is nevertheless suggested by Munro-Hay (1996, 403) that Ptolemy's Sabat, located to the north of Adulis, may be Cosmas' Samidi, an 'otherwise completely unknown' coastal city, though others equate Sabat with the Saue of the *Periplus* (*e.g.* Huntingford 1980, 100), or the modern site of Girar, close to Massawa (*e.g.* Tamrat 1972, 14). There is no indication of the size or extent of the site in the work of Cosmas and it is therefore argued by Munro-Hay (1996, 403) that Samidi may have been a major coastal city, an alternative port of Aksum. The lack of other references to the site, and its apparent proximity to Adulis, renders such a hypothesis implausible. Investigations in the region have, however, revealed the presence of two substantial mounds of stone 7 km to the north of Adulis, some 500 m apart (Fig. 7.1). Explorations continued to a distance of 30 km north of Adulis yet no further archaeological sites were found, whilst the region to the south of Massawa yielded only ruins dating from the Ottoman period at Arkiko (see Chapter V), likely to be the Turkish military post marked on Von Heuglin's map of 1857 (Heuglin 1860). Given the lack of other suitable contenders, there can be little doubt that these mounds are the Samidi of Cosmas Indicopleustes.

Survey at Samidi

A complete survey of the mounds was conducted, using the Leica Total Station previously utilised for the topographic survey at Adulis. The survey plotted the topography of the individual mounds, labelled Samidi South and Samidi North, traces of extant architecture and the location of architectural features relative to each mound. A decision was taken to survey each mound within its own arbitrary grid, independent of the main site grid, thus allowing for easier manipulation of the data. Station 1 was therefore established at Samidi South with the grid co-ordinates 1000 m East, 3000 m North, with a vertical datum of 25 m (1000, 3000, 25). An orientation point was established 44 m east of Station 1, with a height of 24.6 m. The grid at Samidi North was established around Station 1 with an Easting

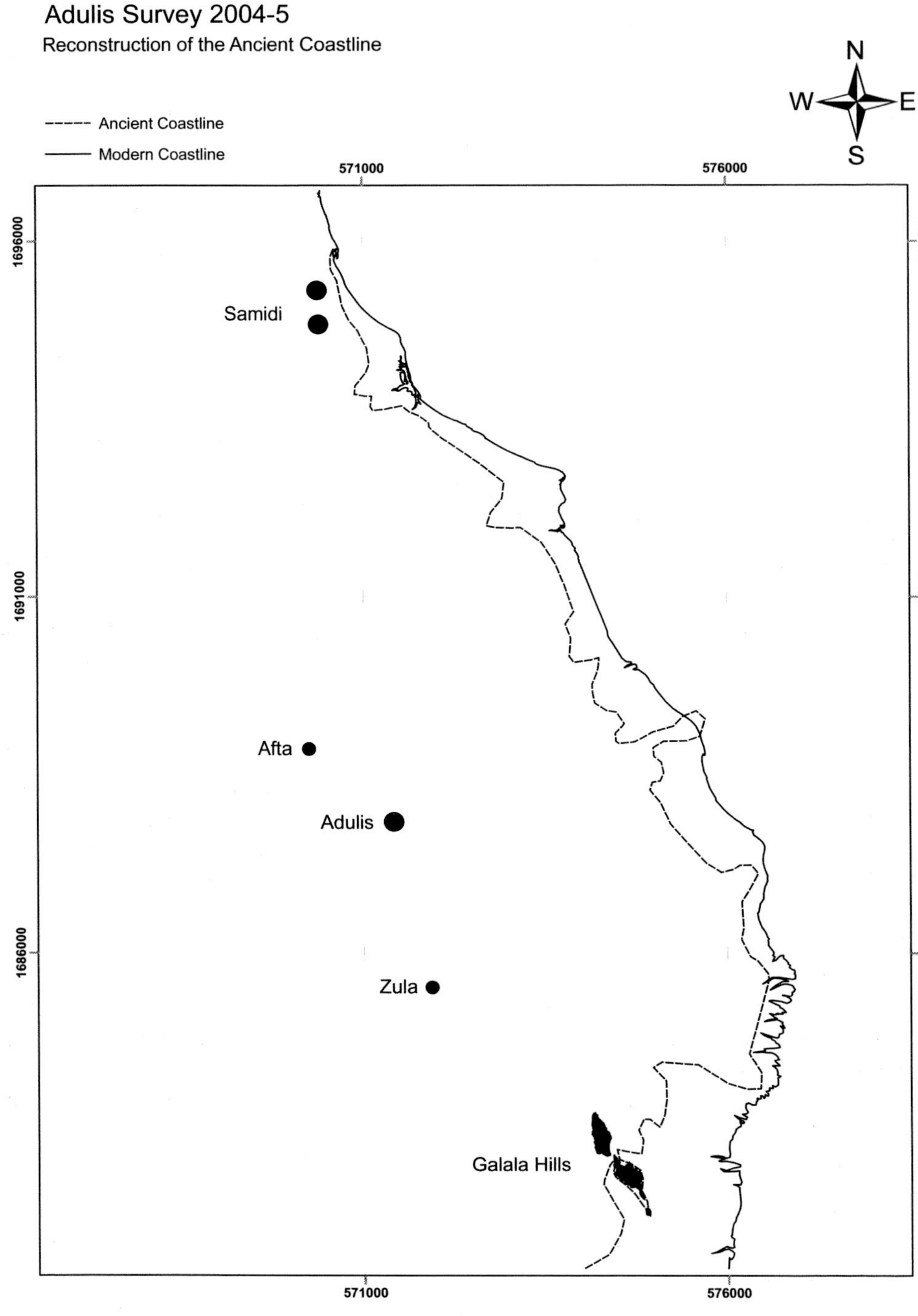

Figure 7.1 The location of Samidi

of 3000, a Northing of 6000 and a height of 25 (or grid co-ordinates 3000, 6000, 25). An orientation point was created at co-ordinates 3035, 6000, 24.28 (Station 2).

Both surveys were conducted with two staff mounted prisms set at a constant height of 1.3 m. As with the survey at Adulis, the sites were traversed east-west following a course plotted with handheld compasses, thus ensuring maximum site coverage. Readings were taken approximately every 2 m in the areas surrounding the mounds, every 50 cm on the mounds themselves. Architectural features were plotted following the completion of the topographic survey. Data was processed in Eritrea using Leica Liscad Software, later re-processed using ArcGIS in the Digital Archaeological Laboratory, University of Southampton. Unfortunately, the quantity of surface material made geophysical survey unpractical.

Results

The results of the survey of Samidi South are shown in Fig. 7.2, Samidi North in Fig. 7.3. These figures represent the first topographic and architectural survey of Samidi to be produced. Samidi South, the larger of the two mounds, is approximately 40 m long and 25 m wide and composed largely of schist (Fig. 7.4). It is possible that it was once stepped – traces of what appear to be steps are visible on its flanks, though these are much eroded. A number of ornate basalt architectural blocks are found both on the plateau of the mound and close by (see below); their locations are marked on Fig. 7.2. Also apparent are a number of linear features on the mound itself. Of these, two are associated with several blocks that appear to form a semi-circle; another outlines a rectangular structure. The latter is, however, so eroded, that it is difficult to trace with any degree of certainty. Fragments of human bone can also be seen on Samidi South (see below).

Samidi North is located some 500 m from Samidi South and appears to be independent of the southerly mound. In contrast to Samidi South, no architectural blocks are visible, though a circle of upright but unworked stones are found atop the mound (see below). Two 'satellite mounds' are shown in the survey; considerably smaller mounds with associated unworked stones lying flat. Also marked are two possible grave sites. The mounds are composed of schist mixed with numerous carefully selected white quartzite boulders, which give the mounds a strikingly white appearance (Fig. 7.5–6)

Architectural fragments from Samidi

Seven architectural fragments, all in black basalt, were found on and around the southern mound. It seems likely therefore that the mound was crowned with a monumental structure. The fragments are illustrated in Fig. 7.7.

A. A fragment of a column base or possibly capital. The podium has two steps and the column has been worked to give the appearance of a cluster of nine conjoined smaller columns

B. A smaller fragment almost identical in size and conception

C. A complete base or capital identical to the above, but taller

D. A fragment of a column drum which would fit with the above

E. A cube with a simple square hole in one face, perhaps to hold a wooden door jamb

F. A cube almost identical to the above

G. A rectangular block with a rectangular hole and a square one at the bottom. The use is uncertain, but it seems to be a socket for a jamb

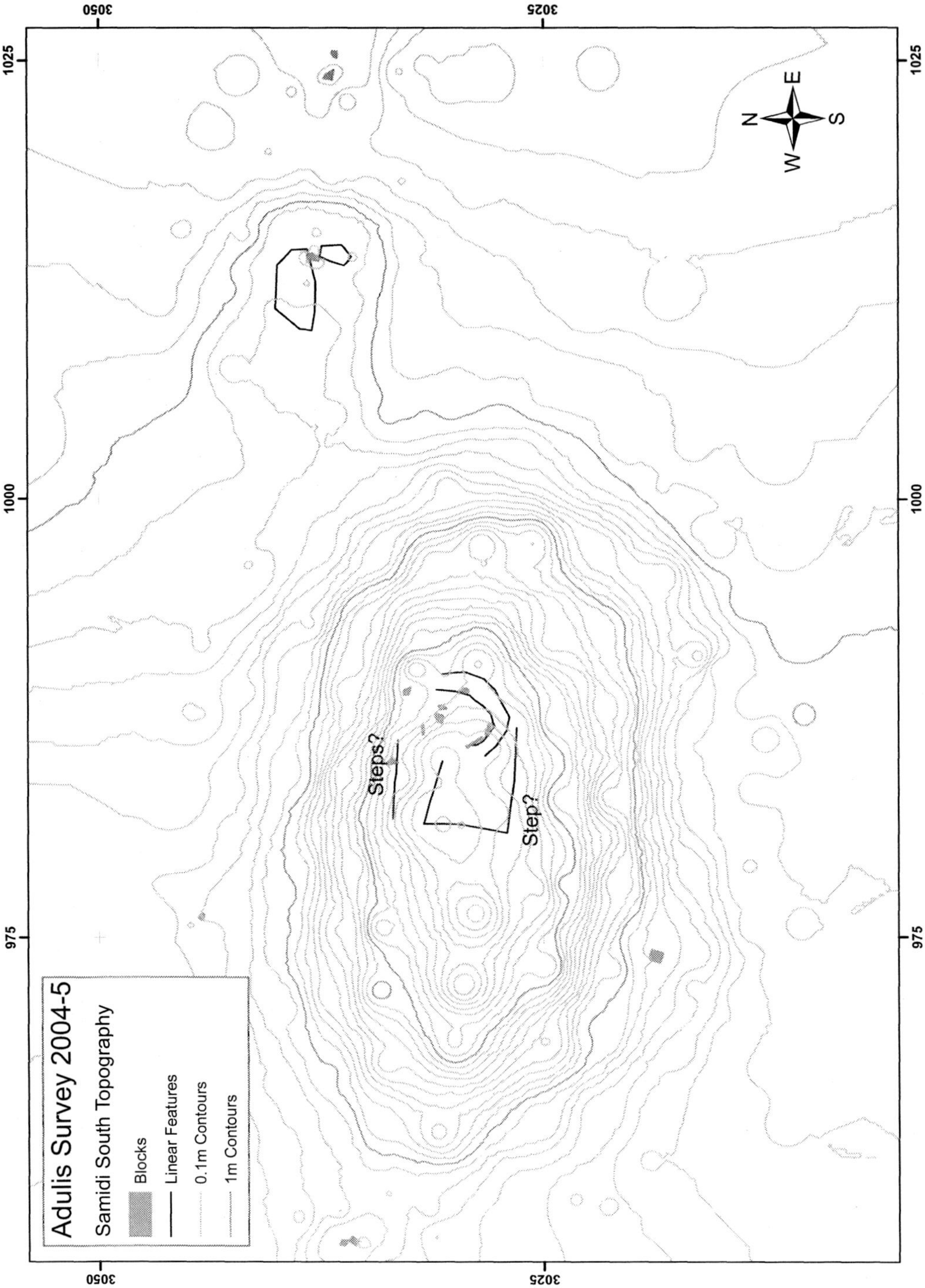

Figure 7.2 Survey of Samidi South

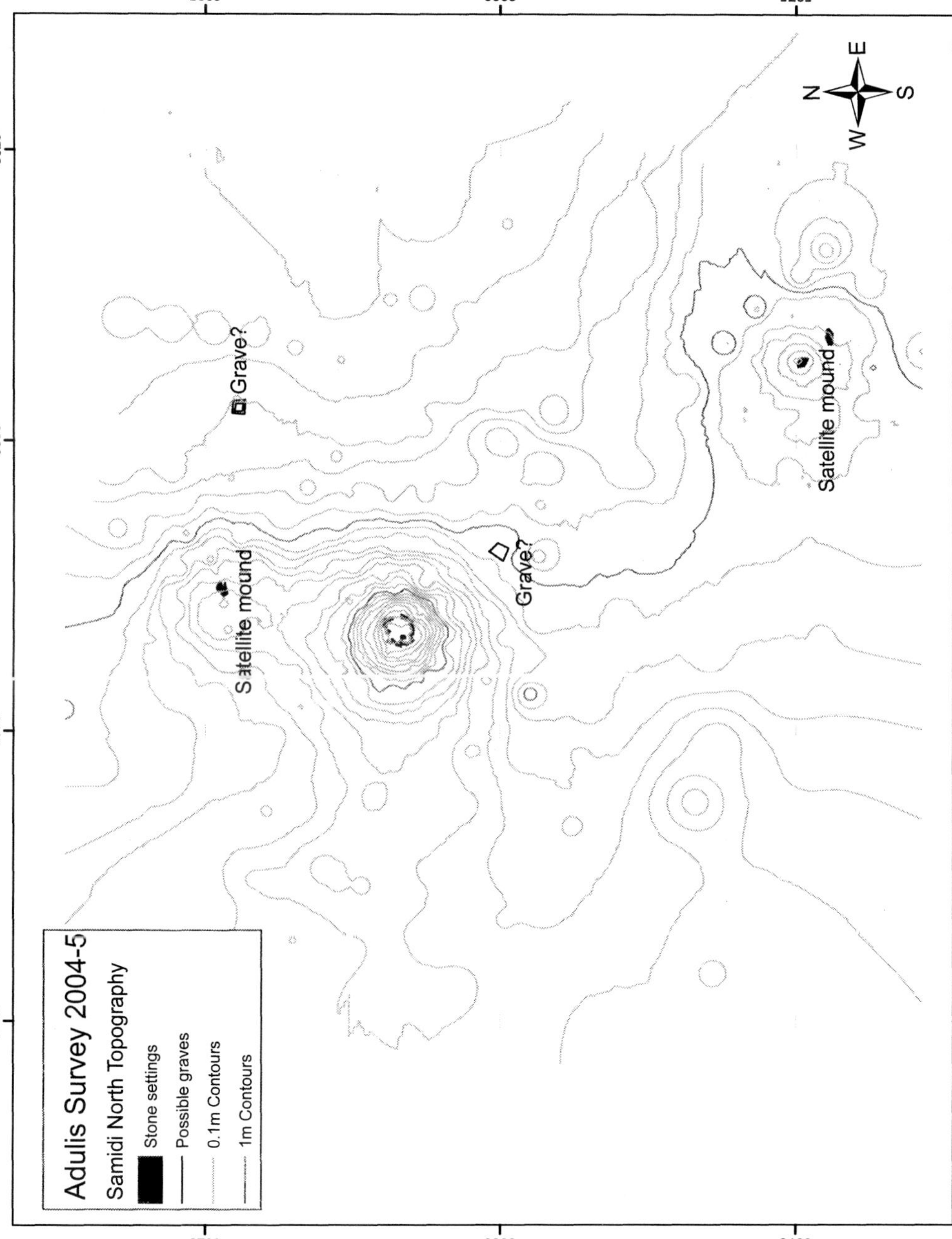

Figure 7.3 Survey of Samidi North

Figure 7.4 A view of the mound of Samidi South

Interestingly, the body of the columns at Samidi exhibit significant differences from those at the main site of Adulis. Although roughly square, the pillars were carved to resemble three circular, upright rods, when viewed from the side (*e.g.* Block D), in marked contrast to the roughly octagonal pillar bodies found at Adulis itself. It is difficult to ascertain what purpose these blocks served in the architecture of Samidi, though they are clearly monumental.

Samidi North has a circle of unworked, upright stones on top. Many of these bear markings, which do not seem to correspond to any known script (Fig. 7.8–9). It is possible that they are *wasms* used by tribes to mark their territory, perhaps placed there by different groups of Rashaida nomads. As with any rock art, dating is exceptionally difficult. There is, however, no indication that the markings are contemporaneous with the construction of the mound or stone setting. Little is known of such markings in this part of Africa, but remarkably similar symbols are still used by different groups of Bedouin in the Eastern Desert of Egypt as territorial markers (Hobbs 1989, 109). Clearly the site has retained relevance within the landscape over many generations.

The skeletal material, by Sonia R. Zakrzewski and Sarah A. Inskip

Photographs of six bone fragments were studied in July 2006. Of these, one fragment was definitely human and three were definitely non-human. The other fragments could not definitively be assigned as human or non-human due to difficulties in interpreting the photographs.

Fragment 1 is a human left parietal bone. The lateral lower margin (articulating with the temporal) was well preserved.

Fragment 5 appears to be a scapula, most likely deriving from sheep/goat. This specimen is

Figure 7.5 A view of the mound of Samidi North

Figure 7.6 A view of the mound of Samidi North

Fragment 2 appears to be a frontal bone portion (potentially human), including the roof of one orbit and part of the calotte. It is weathered at the margins.

Fragment 3 appears to be an occipital fragment (potentially human), including the internal occipital crest. The fragment shows some signs of weathering.

Fragment 4 is a portion of a non-human skull, with lateral damage to the temporal bone. The species of origin could not be determined.

highly weathered.

Fragment 6 appears to be an ungulate phalanx, most likely deriving from sheep/goat.

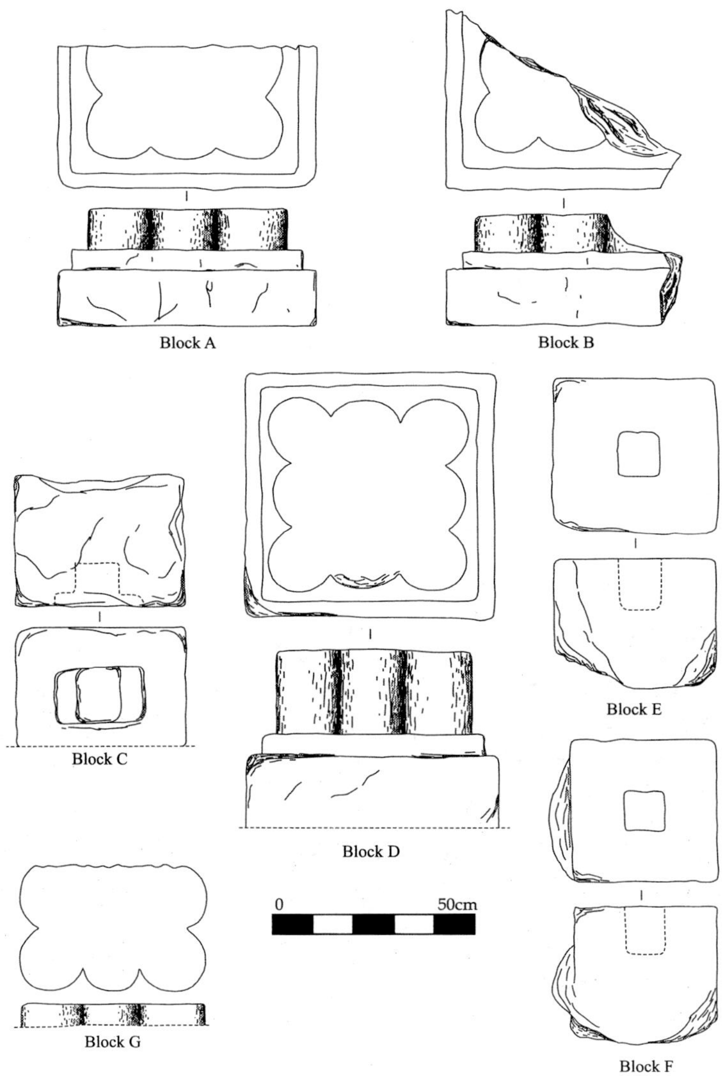

Figure 7.7 Architectural fragments from Samidi South

Figure 7.8 The stone setting on Samidi North showing markings

Figure 7.9 Markings on the stones of Samidi North

Discussion

Although the surveys have been conducted seperately, the lack of other archaeological sites in the region, coupled with the proximity of the two mounds to each other, demands that they be treated as a single archaeological site. The exact nature of the site is unclear in the work of Cosmas, but our surveys indicate a funerary function: the presence of fragments of human bone at Samidi South, combined with the lack of any evidence of continued, domestic use of the area, would suggest that both mounds are tombs, with the architecture at Samidi South indicative of a substantial mausoleum. Surprisingly little pottery was recovered from either site during the survey, though a sherd of an Aqaba amphora and particularly one of a Late Roman 1 amphora from Samidi North suggest a date of the early 6th century, which accords well with Cosmas' *Christian Topography*. It is tempting to speculate that this is a royal burial site, commanding a prominent position on the headland with sweeping views across the Gulf of Zula. Without excavation this must remain only a hypothesis, albeit a tempting one.

The Massawa airport mounds

There are few comparanda for these tumuli, but during our stay at Massawa, we were asked to comment on a group of mounds, 3 km south-west of the end of the runway of the new airport at Massawa, and about 15 km west of Massawa itself. We were only able to make two short visits which permitted us to examine the main central part of the mound clusters. However, examination of an incredibly detailed, high definition Quickbird satellite image of the region dated 6th October 2006, combined with our brief field analysis has facilitated further comment.

The central cluster of mounds lies at N 15° 38′ 40.23″, E39° 20′ 08.77″. In all there are about 100 mounds over a distance of *c.* 2 km, arranged in a line striking north-west – south-east. There appears to be five clusters on low ridges. The distribution is clearly controlled by topography as they are placed on high ground with none in valleys (Figs 7.10–7.12).

The mounds themselves are round and vary in diameter between 10 and 15 m, while some are up to 10 m high. Occasionally stone work can be seen within them and it appears that they were originally square or rectangular and may have been stepped (Fig. 7.12). If so they were very different from the Samidi mounds.

It is very hard to date these mounds as no pottery was found securely embedded in them, but a few sherds of Ayla-Aksum amphorae were found on the ground surface at the central cluster. This suggests that they may be Aksumite in date, although an earlier date is not precluded.

There is no sign of a settlement in the area, but the neighbouring satellite images on Google Earth are of low resolution so this could not be pursued further. The main valley bottoms show evidence of cultivation, some recent, some more ancient, but these could not be satisfactorily dated.

It is difficult to find parallels, but there is something of a resemblance to the tumuli of the 'Ballana or X-group culture' in Nubia, which dates between the 4th and 6th centuries AD. If the structures were originally square in plan they could have resembled the pyramids in the Meroe cemetery, which continued to be built up to the beginning of the fourth century

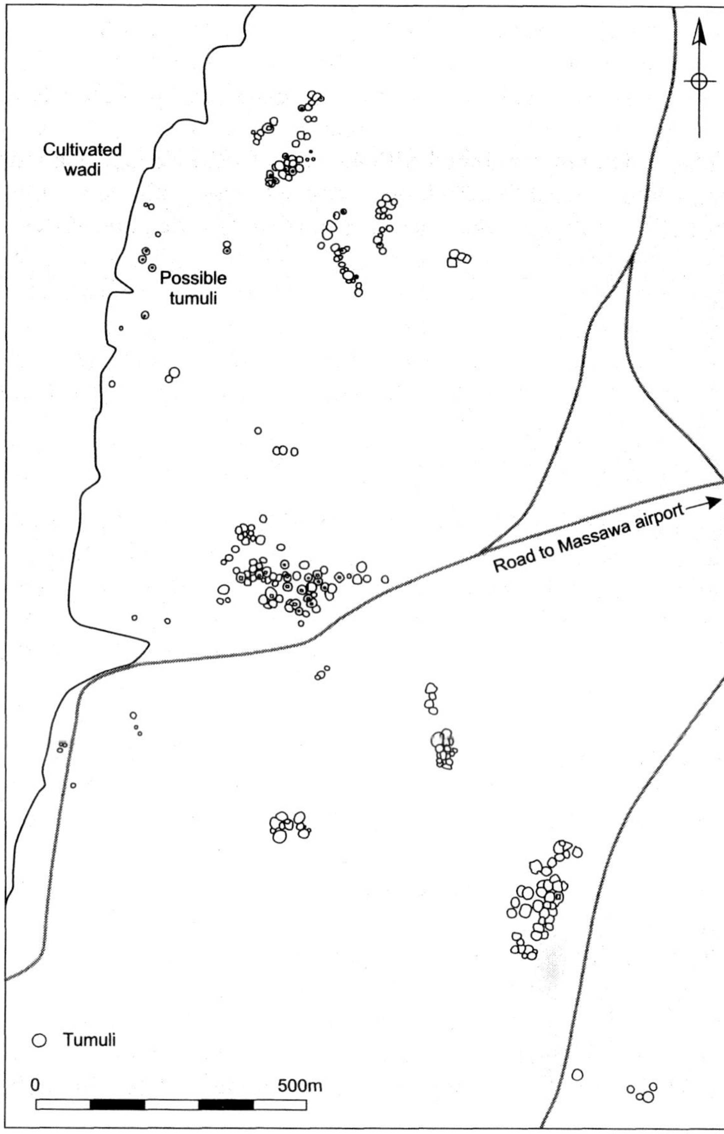

Figure 7.10 Distribution of mounds south-west of Massawa airport based upon Quickbird satellite image

(see Emery 1948, Edwards 1996, Török 1997). It is worth noting that a considerable amount of quarrying seems to have occurred around and among the mounds between our visit in February 2005 and October 2006, the date of the satellite image.

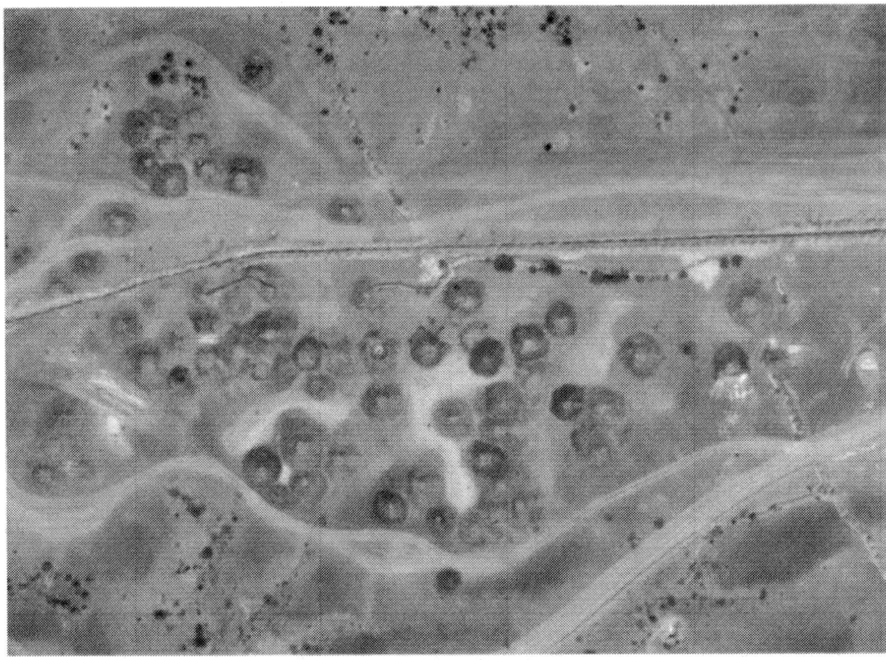

Figure 7.11 Detail of central cluster of mounds. ©Digital Global Inc.

Figure 7.12 Detail of mound in main cluster

Figure 7.13 Detail of mound in main cluster

Chapter VIII
Pottery from the survey

David Peacock

with contributions by Ismini Nina, Philip Kenrick, Jeroen Poblome, Roberta Tomber and Kerlijne Romanus

Introduction

Surface pottery was collected from six different sites in the region of Adulis: Diodorus Island, Galala, shoreline deposits, two sites on Dese and at Adulis itself. Each is considered separately. The material has been deposited in the Northern Red Sea Regional Museum at Massawa.

Methodology

The sites were sampled in different ways. All featured sherds that could be found on Diodorus Island were collected. A small sample of the featured sherds to be found on the main Dese site (A) were retained and a few representative pieces were taken from the other Dese site (B). As time on Dese was limited, this played an important part in determining how much was collected. The material from Galala comprised sherds from the easternmost hill and pieces from its foot which had washed down from it; the westernmost hill had been heavily mined by the Ethiopians and was not available for study. Small accumulations of worn and rolled pottery marked the ancient shoreline, and these beach deposits are described as an entity. Pottery abounds at Adulis itself and an attempt was made to study distributions across the site, the results of which are presented below. As the quality of the evidence varies from site to site, each of these assemblages will be considered separately below.

Diodorus Island

The pottery from this locality is particularly important as it is a diverse assemblage, seemingly accumulated over a short period of time. It can be dated by the presence of Mediterranean amphorae and fine-ware, and is intimately associated with local wares. From these imports it is reasonable to extrapolate dates for the local wares, thus giving, for the first time, rather precise chronological implications. The amphorae comprise Dressel 2–4 from Italy and should date from the late 1st century BC to the 1st century AD. However, the few sherds of Eastern Sigillata A are dated from sometime in the 1st century BC to the Augustan period. The assemblage would therefore be comfortable in the early part of the 1st century AD or the latter part of the 1st century BC, which accords well with the historical evidence of the *Periplus*: if it was written in the mid 1st century AD, as is generally accepted, the pottery should pre-date this, as by this time Diodorus Island had become unsafe and the harbour moved to the island of Dese.

The amphorae would not be out of place at Quseir al-Qadim in Egypt or in India, reinforcing the role of Diodorus Island as a port of trade on the haul between Egypt and India. However, interestingly only two sherds in the 'black sand' fabric were noted. It has been argued that the main production area for this fabric was the bay of Naples and it seems probable that production would have been devastated by the eruption of Vesuvius in AD 79 (Williams and Peacock, 2005). However, it is now apparent that this fabric is easily confused with that of Laodicean amphorae, although the examples here seem to be closer to the Campanian fabric (see below p.83).

Catalogue

Fig. 8.1. The amphorae

1. Rod handle in a fine pale buff fabric. Type not determined.
2. Rod handle. Sandy red fabric with grey core. Some volcanic inclusions.
3. Bifid handle Dressel 2–4. Red brown fabric with fine sand and volcanic grains.
4. Rod handle. Red brown fabric with grey core and fine sand.
5. Rod of a split bifid handle Dressel 2–4. Buff fabric with paler surface. Fine ?volcanic sand.
6. Rod of a split bifid handle Dressel 2–4. Black sand fabric.
7. Bifid handle Dressel 2–4. Reddish fabric with quartz, feldspar and volcanic grains.
8. Rod of a split bifid handle Dressel 2–4. Reddish buff fabric with pale surface. Red volcanic inclusions.
9. Rod handle in a fine pale buff fabric as no1.
10. Rim and neck Dressel 2–4. Sandy red buff fabric with paler surface.
11. Rim and neck in orange-red ware with grey outer surface. Probably Dressel 2–4.
12. Rim and neck in fine red-buff clay. Dressel 2–4
13. Rim in red ware with white surface. Dressel 2–4
14. Rim in black sand fabric. Dressel 2–4

Fig. 8.2. The coarse-wares

1. Flagon neck. Wheel made in pale brown fabric with a white outer surface. ?Imported.
2. Wheel made rim in coarse micaceous red brown ware.
3. Strap handle. Fine buff fabric with smooth surfaces.
4. Rim and handle of ?two handled jar. Incised roughening of outer face of handle. Hand-made in fine buff clay with black core.
5. Body sherd with incised decoration. Buff brown sandy ware with black surfaces.
6. ?Hand-made rim with pierced lug. Diameter uncertain. Coarse brown ware with grey core.
7. Hand-made handle fragment in coarse red micaceous ware.
8. Hand-made handle in coarse brown micaceous ware.
9. Hand-made rim, with tooled wavy line, uncertain diameter. Fine micaceous buff ware.
10. Body sherd decorated with roller impression and incisions. Fine micaceous buff ware. *c.f.* Paribeni, Tav III, 34; Fattovich, XXXI, 13
11. Handle fragment in fine brown ware.
12. Coarse hand-made lug with 1 mm quartz and feldspar grits.
13. Body sherd with incised decoration.

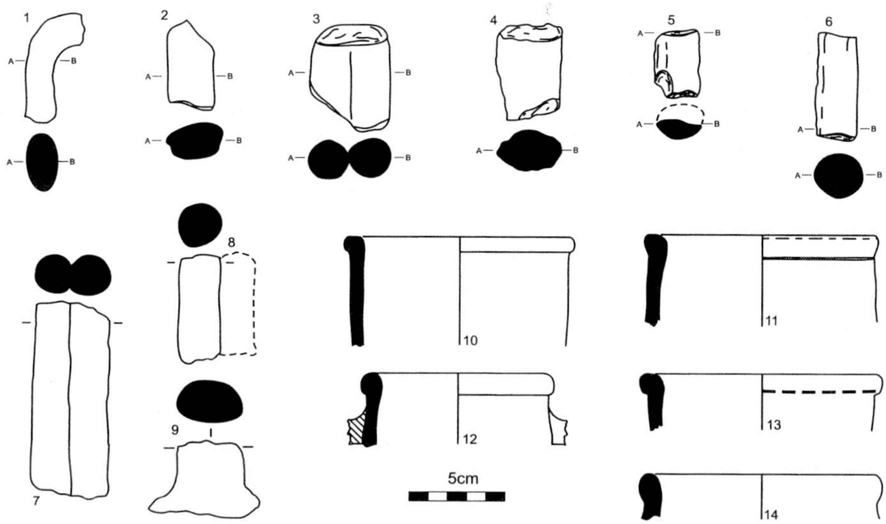

Figure 8.1 The amphorae from Diodorus Island

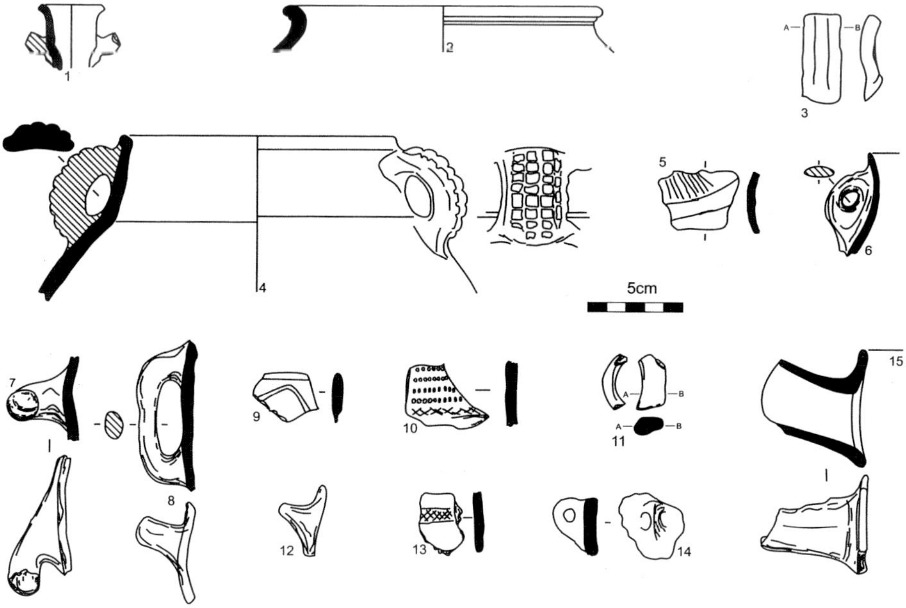

Figure 8.2 The coarse-wares from Diodorus Island

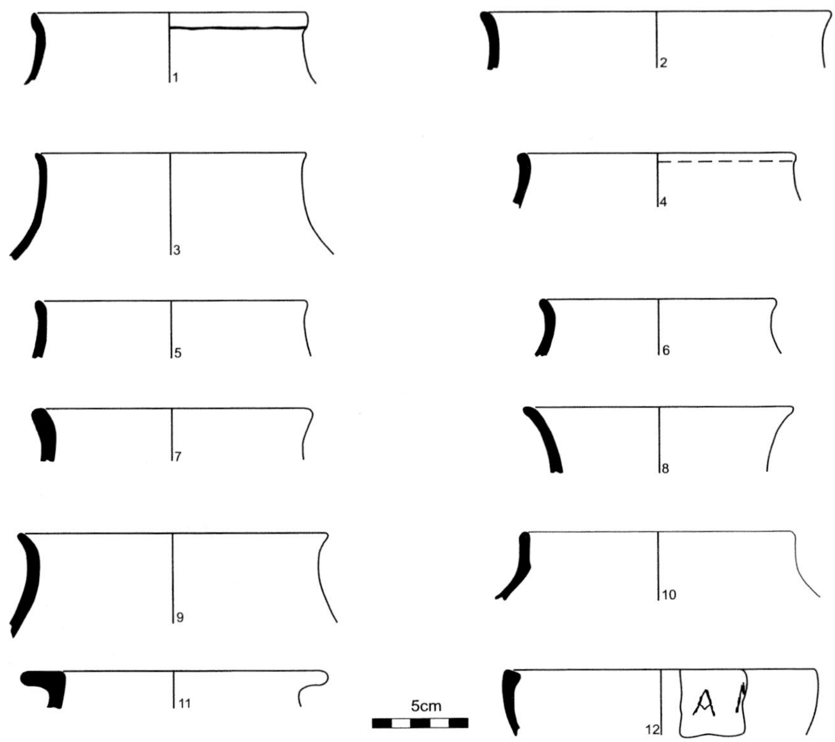

Figure 8.3 Hand-made jars and bowls from Diodorus Island

14. Hand-made pierced lug in red-brown sandy micaceous ware.
15. Spout in coarse micaceous red-brown ware.

Fig. 8.3. Hand-made jars and bowls

1. Neck of jar in fine micaceous red brown ware with polished surface
2. Jar neck in micaceous buff ware with black core
3. Jar neck in coarse micaceous buff ware. *c.f.* Fattovich, IV, 1,23
4. Jar neck in fine buff ware.
5. Jar neck. Coarse sandy micaceous fabric. Buff with black core.
6. Jar neck in coarse buff ware with black core.
7. Jar neck in coarse micaceous red brown ware.
8. Jar neck in coarse red-brown ware with black core.
9. Jar neck in highly micacous red brown ware with black core.
10. Jar neck with internal carination. Fabric as no 5.
11. Flat everted rim. Fine red buff ware with white surface.
12. Bowl in fine polished ware with black interior and reddish burnished exterior. Letter A followed by part of an M or N, scratched on outer surface.

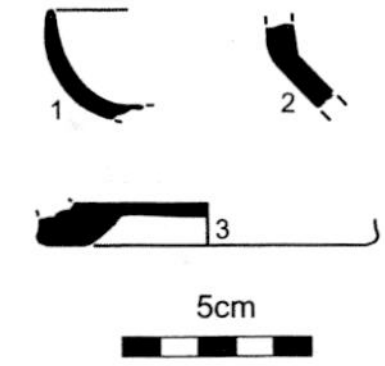

Figure 8.4 The fine-wares

Fig. 8.4 The fine-wares

These sherds have been examined by Professor Jeroen Poblome, Dr Philip Kenrick and

Dr Roberta Tomber. All agree in assigning a date in the range late 1st century BC to Augustan.

1. Eastern Sigillata A dish in a pale buff fabric with a slightly orange red slip.
2. Carination from a bowl in Eastern Sigillata A. Pale buff fabric with a slightly orange red slip. Diameter about 380 mm?
3. Foot ring in Eastern Sigillata A. Buff fabric with a darker red slip.

Dese

Aksumite pottery is to be found all over Dese but particularly around the modern settlement on the eastern side. However Roman pottery is restricted to the central valley connected with the large natural harbour, accessed from the west. The area was not studied in detail, but two sites, labelled A and B were sampled. The assemblages here were dominated by amphorae, with, in the case of Dese A two minute sherds of Eastern Sigillata A and in the case of B one of Eastern Sigillata A and one which could be Italian. These are probably datable to the Augustan period. The presence of a potential Gauloise 4 handle from the South of France from Dese A, suggests the date range extending further into the 1st century AD. If this is correct the assemblage should continue later than that of Diodorus island and corroborates the information in the *Periplus*.

On this site six sherds were in the 'black sand' fabric, which is a very high proportion considering the more limited size of the collection. The black sand fabric is characteristic of Campania, but is easily confused with that of Laodicea (Tomber 1998) and the *Periplus* refers to the importation of the wines of Italy and Laodicia.

In the museum of Lattakia, Syria, is a complete amphora of the eastern variant of Dressel 2–4, Dressel 5 (*c.f.* Martin-Kilcher 1994, fig.120, 10). The paste is pale buff in colour in contrast to the much redder Campanian fabric, but it contains numerous black grains of pyroxene and a little golden mica. This may be typical of Laodicean amphorae. The form is usually ascribed to Kos, but in this fabric it is unlikely as the geology does not correspond. A similar but coarser fabric was produced at the only known pottery production site in the area Ras al Basit, although the forms are different. In thin section the fabric of the latter contains abundant pyroxene, derived from the local ophiolite, a little shell or limestone and some serpentine. It lacks the lava fragments so frequently seen in the Campanian fabrics.

Reynolds (2005, 565) has argued that amphorae of the Dressel 2–5 type may have been made in the adjacent Yumurtalık area of Turkey and filled in Laodicea. This is possible, but the geology of northern part of Laodicea and of the upper reaches of the el Kebir river valley is identical. In the absence of systematic survey, it is impossible to rule out Laodicean production.

On the basis of visual inspection supported by a limited number of thin sections, it appears that most, if not all, of the Adulis 'black sand' amphorae are from Campania. However, it would be surprising if more detailed research in the future did not reveal that there was some importation from Laodicea.

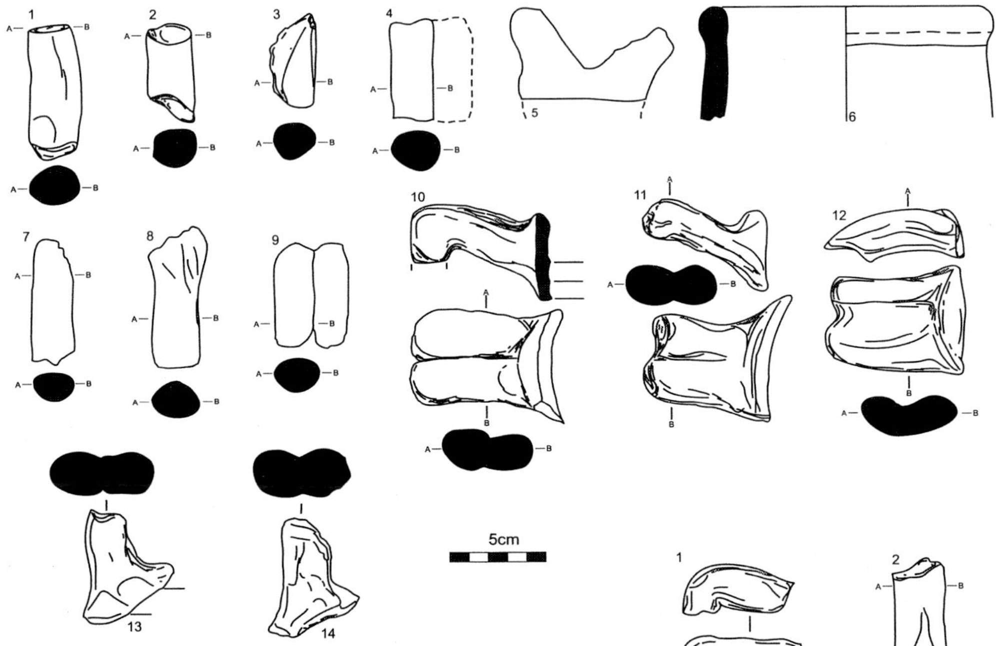

Figure 8.5 The amphorae from site A

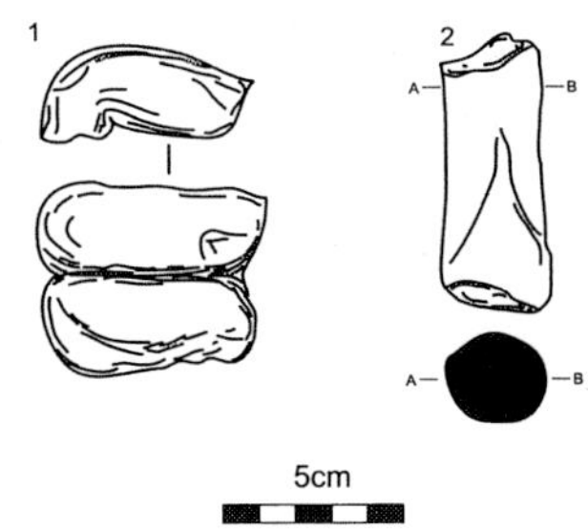

Figure 8.6 The amphorae from site B

Catalogue

Fig. 8.5 The amphorae from site A

1. Rod of bifid handle in fine brown buff ware.
2. Rod of bifid handle in black sand fabric.
3. Rod of bifid handle in black sand fabric.
4. Rod of bifid handle in black sand fabric.
5. Fragment of spike in black sand fabric.
6. Rim of Dressel 2–4 in red buff ware.
7. Rod of bifid handle in black sand fabric, broken at angle.
8. Rod handle. Red buff ware with volcanic grains.
9. Fragment of bifid handle in black sand fabric.
10. Angle of bifid handle in red brown fabric with volcanic grains.
11. Angle of bifid handle in buff fabric with volcanic grains.
12. Strap handle, almost certainly Gauloise 4. In fine pale clay, but slightly redder than normal for this type.
13. Handle stub of Dressel 2–4 in black sand fabric.
14. Handle stub of Dressel 2–4 in pale buff fabric with volcanic inclusions.

Fig. 8.6 The amphorae from site B

1. Angle of bifid handle in black sand fabric.
2. Rod of bifid handle in reddish fabric with white outer surface. Volcanic inclusions.

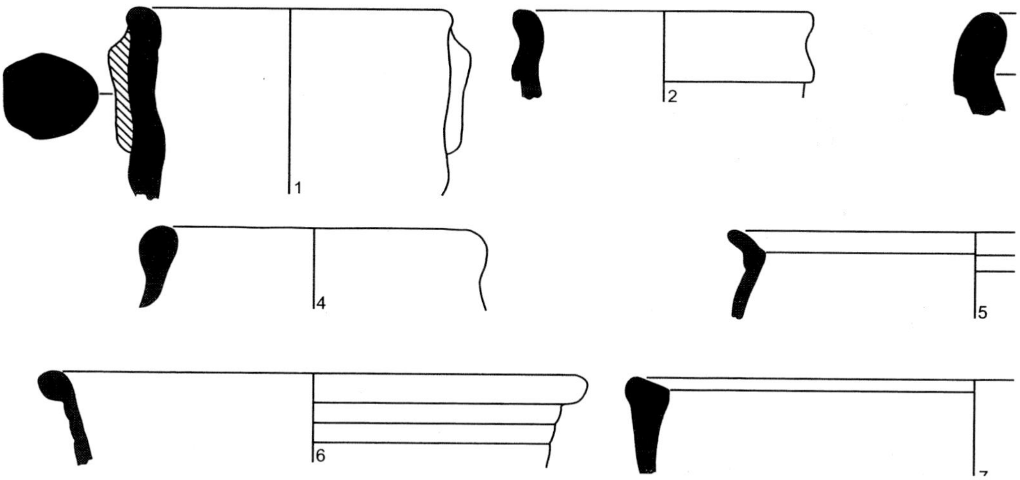

Figure 8.7 Pottery from the Galala hills

The Galala Hills

Body-sherds of Ayla-Aksum amphorae abound in this locality, both on the eastern hill and at its foot. Sundström (1907) correctly notes its similarity to material from Adulis itself. Only featured sherds are illustrated.

Catalogue

Fig. 8.7. Pottery from the Galala hills

1.Rim and handle stub of Late Roman 1 in typical fabric with limestone and pyroxene.
2. Rim of Late Roman 1 in typical fabric with limestone and pyroxene.
3. Rim of Africana amphora in fine reddish clay with whitish grey outer surface. Also stub of Africana base (not illustrated).
4. Hand-made coarse-ware rim. Red brown sandy ware.
5. Hand-made coarse-ware rim. Red brown highly micaceous fabric with some voids ?due to vegetable matter. Black core.
6. Coarse-ware rim. Grey sandy ware with voids ?due to vegetable matter.
7. Hand-made coarse ware rim. Red brown sandy fabric with black core. Some vegetable matter visible on surface.
8. Coarse-ware base with foot-ring. Grey sandy ware.
9. Handle with incised decoration on top. Highly micaceous red brown ware with black core.

The Shoreline deposits

Body sherds of Ayla-Aksum amphorae (not illustrated) are present on Beaches 2 and 3. They suggest that these deposits are Aksumite in date.

Catalogue

Fig 8.8. Pottery from the shoreline deposits

1. Beach 1. Coarse-ware rim, uncertain diameter. Red brown ware with black core. Much mica and some fine sand.

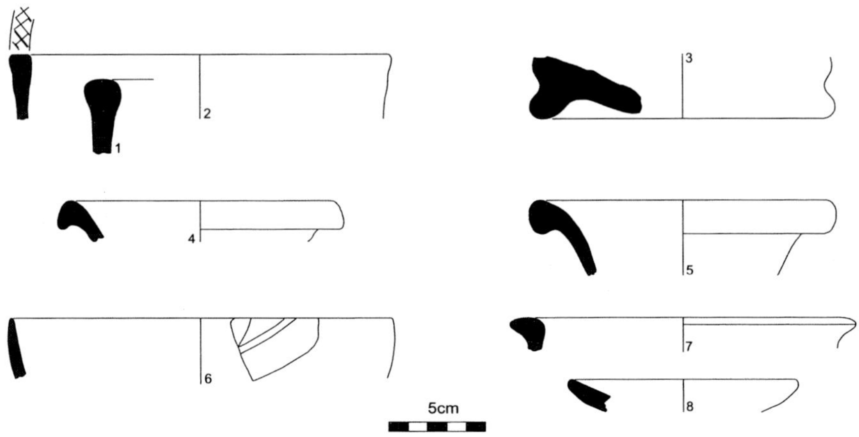

Figure 8.8 Pottery from shoreline deposits

2. Beach 1. Rim of scratch top bowl. Fine micaceous red brown ware with black core.
3. Beach 1. Base with foot ring. Coarse red brown ware with large ?limestone inclusions up to 2mm across.
4. Beach 2. Coarse-ware rim. Red brown ware with many white limestone inclusions up to 1mm across.
5. Beach 3. Coarse-ware rim. Fine red brown ware with some mica and fine sand.
6. Beach 3 Bowl with incised lines on outer surface. Inner and outer surfaces burnished. Hard red brown ware with sand and a little mica
7. Beach 3. Coarse-ware rim. Fine red brown ware with grey core. Many voids ?due to vegetable matter.
8. Beach 3. Open bowl or lid. Fabric as no 7.

The ceramic survey of Adulis

As pottery is so common at Adulis, the site was subjected to a systematic ceramic survey. A series of 20 m squares were laid out across the site on the same axis as the geophysics grid, but separate from it, and 5 people collected all featured sherds they could find in the square in 7 minutes. These were then classified and counted. New types were put aside for drawing and fabric study, the rest being returned to the grid whence they came. In this manner it was possible to build up a typology and to examine the distribution of different types across the site, with minimum disturbance of the archaeology.

Fig. 8.9 shows the location of the 47 squares studied in this way. The transects ran roughly east-west, but were expanded in the south-west corner of the site because of the exceptional interest of this area (see below). In addition to pottery, obsidian was collected and this clustered markedly in the south-west corner. This suggests that it might be largely indicative of pre-Aksumite activity, because otherwise it might be spread across the whole area more evenly (Fig. 8.10). Wares which were considered likely to be pre-Aksumite also clustered in this area (Fig.8.11).

Figs. 8.12–14 show the distribution of imports attributable to the Aksumite period. It is

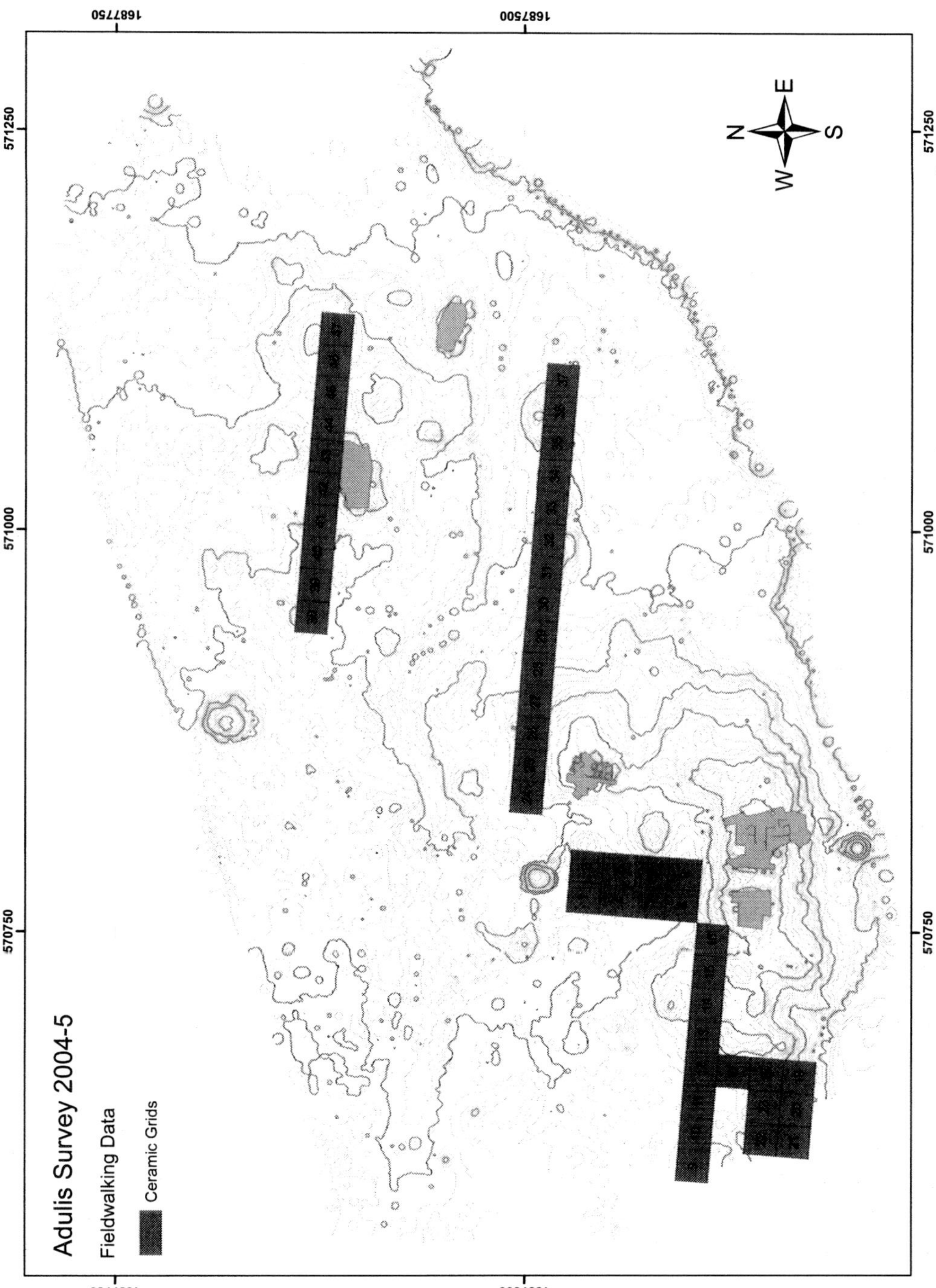

Figure 8.9 Location and numbering of squares used in gridded survey

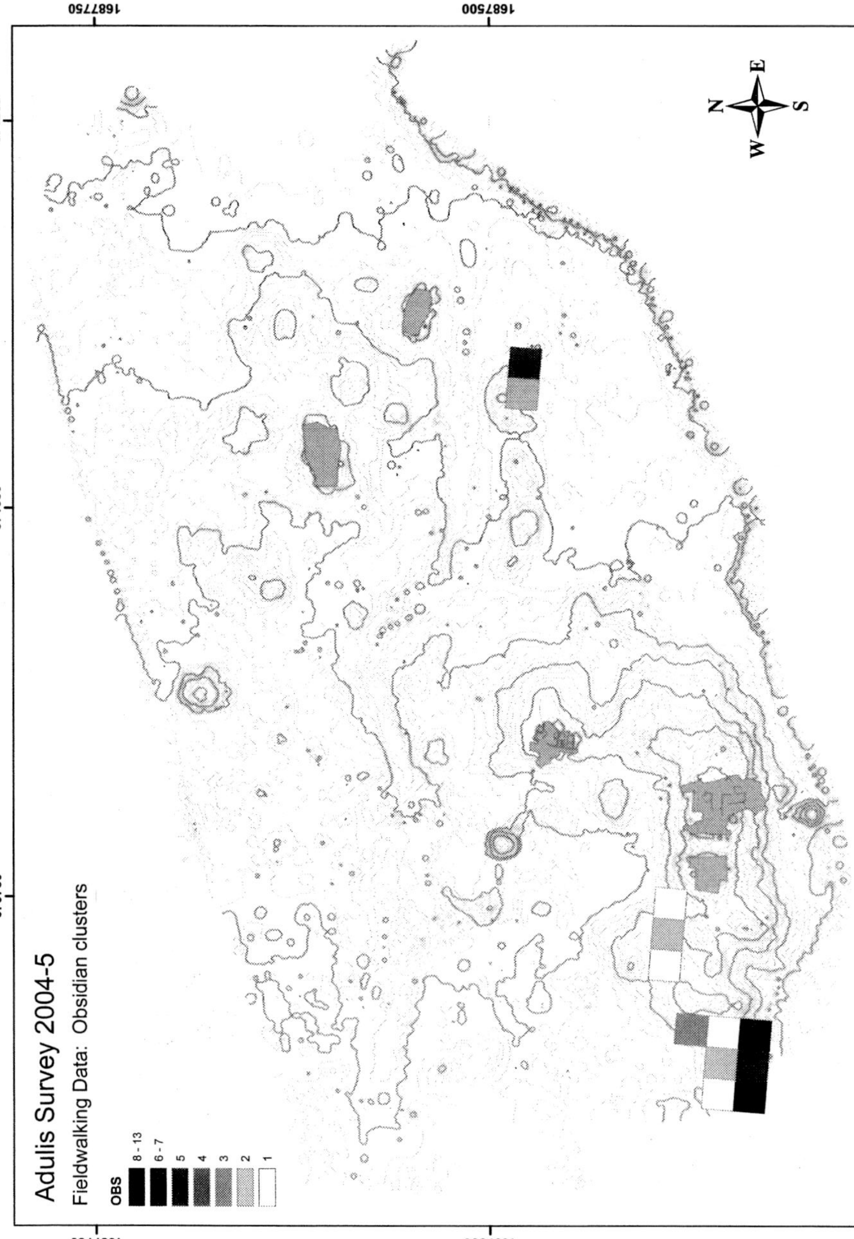

Figure 8.10 Distribution of obsidian

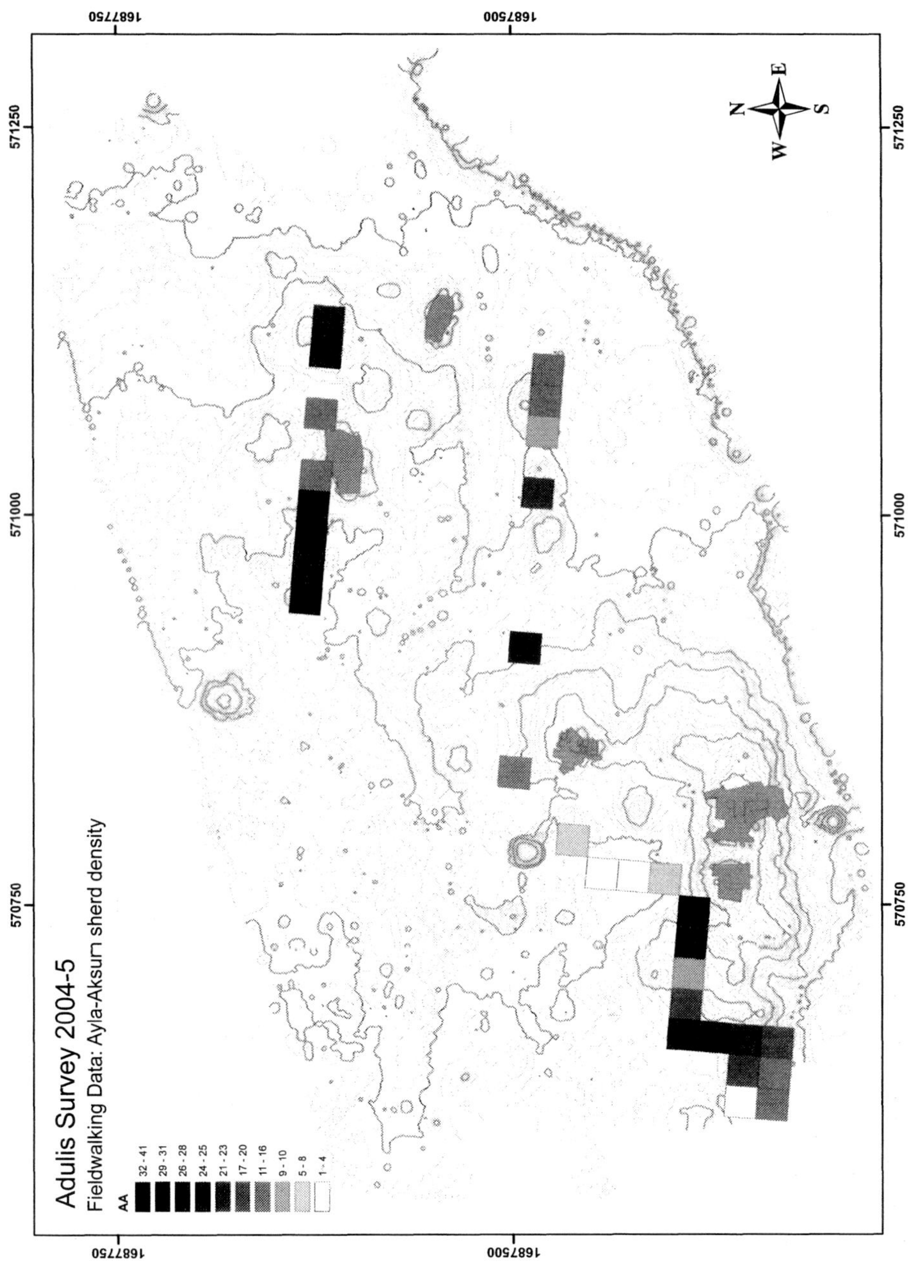

Figure 8.11 Distribution of pottery regarded as possibly pre-Aksumite

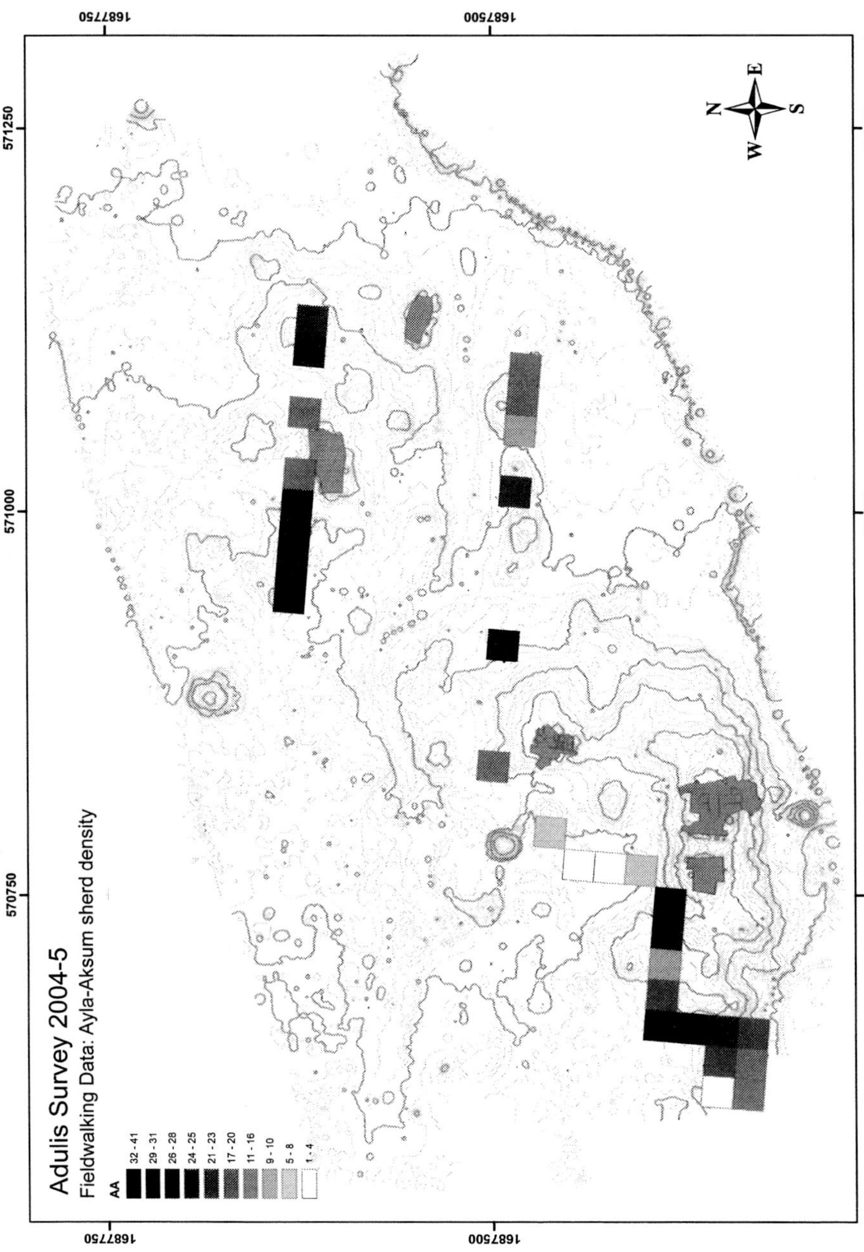

Figure 8.12 Distribution of Ayla–Aksum amphorae

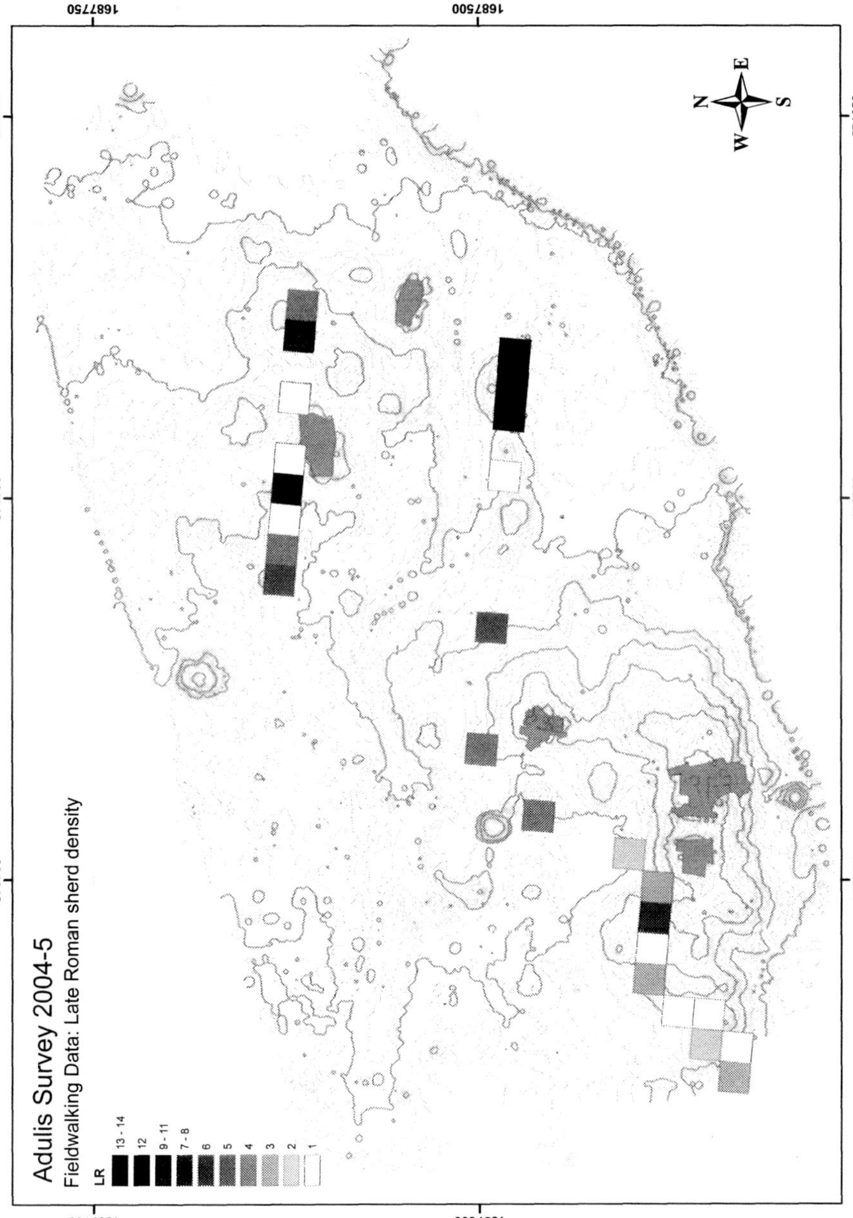

Figure 8.13 Distribution of Late Roman 1 and 2 amphorae

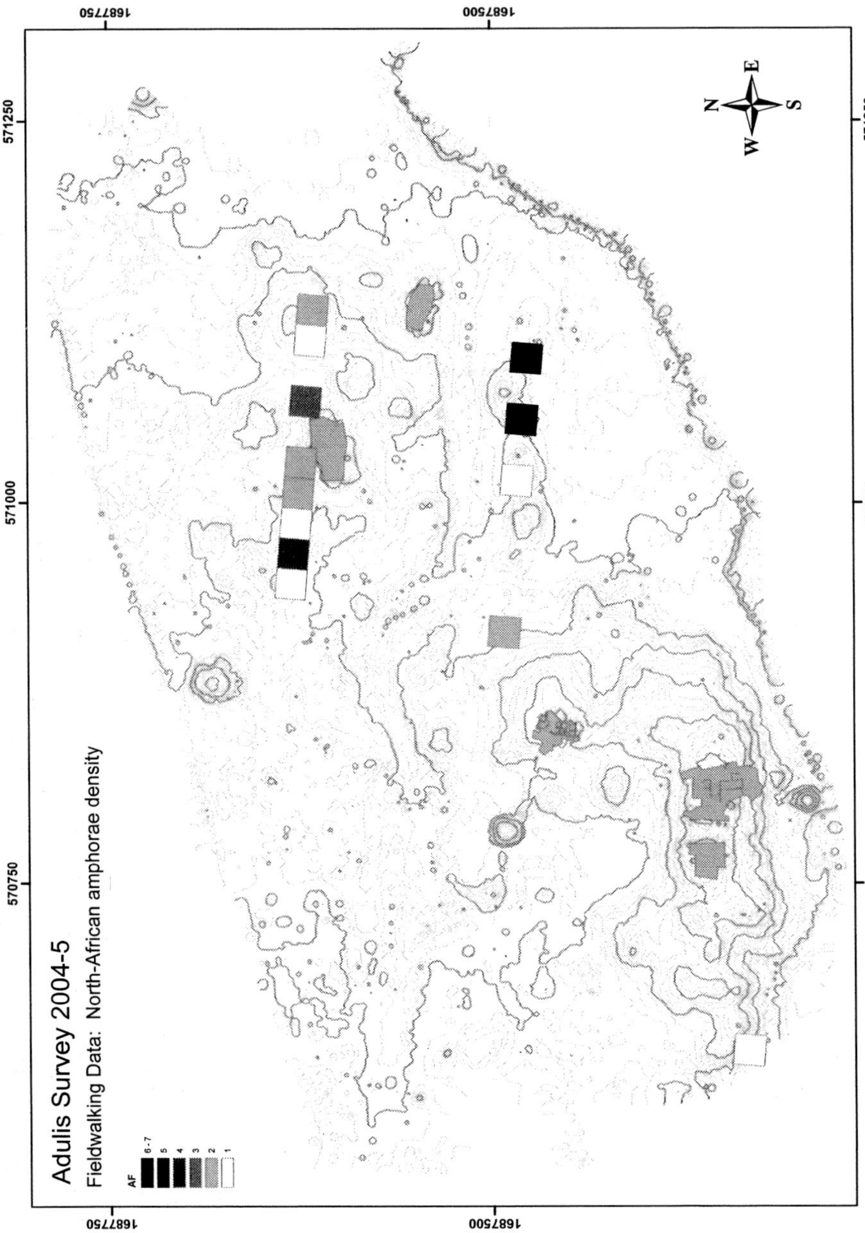

Figure 8.14 Distribution of African amphorae

clear that they are more widely spread across the whole area of the site, with particularly rich concentrations in squares C38–42, west of the palace and in squares C35–37. The latter suggests that the grid may have be placed over a warehouse area, but without excavation and further sherding it is impossible to be certain.

Supposed Pre-Aksumite pottery from Adulis

The pottery from Adulis is broadly similar all over the site, with the exception of the south-west corner, which produced wares not encountered elsewhere. It was in this general area that Paribeni (1907, 446) placed his trench 1 in which he claimed to have found archaic deposits predating the main Aksumite settlement. An attempt was made to date this earlier occupation by carefully studying surface sherds and collecting apparently associated shell fragments which were then subjected to radiocarbon dating.

Four shell samples were collected from the south-west corner of the site, where they were intermingled, on the surface, with pottery which appeared to be pre-Aksumite in date, although lesser quantities of the later Aksumite pottery were also present, as might be expected. While later pottery was found in this area (and in square C21), the shell was taken from patches where no late material was present, but where there were sherds of potentially pre-Aksumite date associated with concentrations of obsidian flakes. ADU 1 and 2 comprised a marine gastropod (too large to have been imported by birds) and a small fragment of a cockle shell. They came from ceramic grid C21, an area believed to broadly correspond, as far as can be ascertained, with the location of Paribeni's trench 1. ADU 3 and 4 comprised a large oyster shell and small fragments of bryozoa respectively. ADU 3 is unlikely to have been transported by birds in view of its size and the bryozoa, though small, would have had limited food value. This location lay outside the ceramic grid, but there were traces of a building which seems to correspond with that brought to light by Paribeni (1907, 458) in his trench 3.

The samples were dated by Beta Analytic Inc. of Miami, Florida, using their standard methods of preparation for shell and their results are summarised below. Samples ADU 1 and 3 were dated using the normal radiometric technique, while ADU 2 and 4, were dated using AMS because of their smaller size.

Sample no	**Measured ^{14}C age BP**	**^{13}C / ^{12}C**	**Conventional Age BP**	**Cal. date BC/AD** (95% confidence)
ADU 1	1170 ± 60	+2.4	2230 ± 60	10 BC – 260 AD
ADU 2	1870 ± 40	–0.8	2270 ± 40	10 BC – 150 AD
ADU 3	1810 ± 60	+0.7	2230 ± 60	10 BC – 260 AD
ADU 4	1650 ± 40	+3.2	2110 ± 40	150 – 360 AD

As this is surface material the results must be treated with caution, but the fact that they are so tightly grouped within the Roman period, strongly suggests that these sites correspond to the Adulis of the *Periplus*, and that the 'fair sized village' was located in the south-west part of the site under the Aksumitic town. It is possible that some of the material is even more archaic, as Paribeni and others have supposed, but equally it is possible that most of

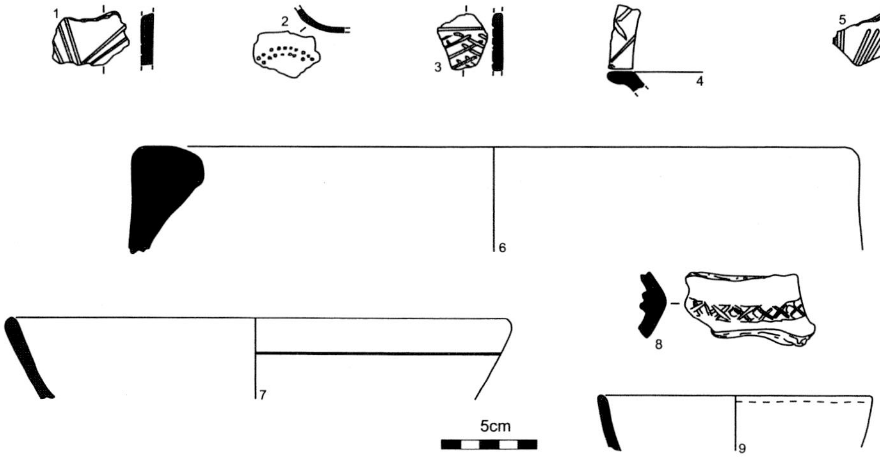

Figure 8.15 Pottery from the areas radio-carbon dated

the material belongs to the Roman period and has not been recognised as such because of a dearth of Mediterranean imports. It is interesting to note that Paribeni found, apparently at a depth of 2 m, *una lucernetta di un tipo che è largamente rappresentato in tutto il mondo romano.* It is a Dressel type 30 or Bailey (1980) type R, which the latter dates between the 3rd and 5th centuries AD. It is difficult to know what to make of this, as the date range is too late for the *Periplus* and a little too early to correspond with the main Aksumite occupation, but the overlap with the date of ADU 1 is suggestive.

Catalogue

Fig. 8.15. Pottery from areas radiocarbon dated.

1. From C21 ('associated' with ADU 1–2). Hand-made body sherd with tooled decoration. *c.f. e.g.* Paribeni, 1907, Tav. IV, 11.
2. From C21 ('associated' with ADU 1–2). Hand-made body sherd with dotted decoration. Polished red brown ware. *c.f. e.g.* Paribeni, 1907, Tav. III, 27.
3. From C21 ('associated' with ADU 1–2). Hand-made body sherd with tooled decoration. *c.f. e.g.* Paribeni, 1907, Tav. IV, 15.
4. From C21 ('associated' with ADU 1–2). Hand-made body sherd with tooled decoration.
5. From C21 ('associated' with ADU 1–2). Hand-made rim of bowl with tooling on top. Diameter unclear (? *c.* 30 cm). *c.f. e.g.* Paribeni, 1907, Tav. IV, 11.
6. 'Associated' with ADU 3–4. Heavy rim of large bowl or jar. Coarse red-buff fabric with some mica. Hand-made.
7. 'Associated' with ADU 3–4. Hand-made bowl with tooled line on outside. S3.
8. 'Associated' with ADU 3–4. Hand-made jar with cordon around neck. Incised decoration. Sandy buff to red brown ware with buff outer surface.
9. 'Associated' with ADU 3–4. Hand-made bowl in coarse buff ware with black core and red polished exterior.

Petrology of sherds 1–5 by Ismini Nina

1. Medium hard, well fired, hand-made with fine clay.
2. Hard, well fired, hand-made, with fine clay. Red burnished. Moderate quantities of quartz with traces of limestone, iron ore chert and ? quartzite can be seen in the hand specimen. Thin sections reveal poorly sorted, rounded quartz (<0.4 mm) with a little limestone, metamorphic rocks, chert and quartzite.
3. Soft, well-fired, hand-made with fairly fine clay. Quartz in common, mica sparse with occasional feldspar visible in the hand specimen. Thin sections reveal moderate amounts of poorly sorted, rounded quartz (<0.4 mm) much mica (<0.3 mm) and traces of limestone.
4. Medium hard, with oxidised core and fine clay. Evidence of coil building. Hand specimens suggest common quartz, sparse mica and rare feldspars, with a few granitic inclusions. Thin sections reveal sparse poorly sorted rounded quartz (<0.5 mm), common mica (<0.1 mm) and rare poorly sorted feldspars, together with a few granitic rock fragments.
5. Soft, well fired, hand-made with fairly fine clay. Hand specimens reveal sparse quartz, sparse mica and a few sandstone and metamorphic rock fragments. Thin sections reveal sparse poorly sorted, fairly angular quartz (<0.4 mm), sparse mica (<0.3 mm) and occasional fragments of sandstone and metamorphic rock.

These sherds are broadly similar and were compared with hand-made material from Diodorus island and from Aksumite contexts at Adulis and Galala. They were all similar with quantities of quartz, mica and material of metamorphic origin, probably deriving from the local Ghedem massif. They can be regarded as typical of local production, with the exception of no. 2 which lacks mica and is more probably an import.

Aksumite Period Pottery (including potentially residual material)

The imports afford the best chronological indicators. The commonest imported material on the site emanates from the kilns in Aqaba. It is found mainly as ribbed body sherds, largely from amphorae and costrels with some coarse-wares. Here we illustrate a selection of different types. The Aqaba kilns were excavated by Melkawi *et al* (1994) and produced wares which were considered part of the Jordanian Byzantine/ Umayyad tradition with a probable 7th century date. The distribution of Aqaba amphorae has been studied by Tomber (2004b). The earliest firm dating evidence comes from Berenike where it is found in contexts dating from the 4th century continuing into first while at Abu Sha'ar and Ayla the type occurs from at least the 5th century – clearly earlier kilns await discovery. At Qana they appear in the 'Upper Period' dating to the 6th and 7th centuries (Sedov 2007).

The distribution of these amphorae is interesting and very much focussed on the Red Sea, with Adulis clearly the most prolific site. The distribution list currently reads as follows: Adulis, Aksum, Abu Sha'ar, Berenike, the Black Assarca wreck, Iskandil Burnu and Bodrum (Turkey), Dese, Kamrej (India), and Qana. It is notable that only two of these sites (Bodrum and Iskandil Burnu) lie in the Mediterranean (See Alpözen *et al.* 1995; Gupta 2007; Tomber 2004b, 2005a for further references).

The content of these vessels is unknown and hence we are unable to gauge the nature of the trade they represent. Ayla is surrounded by desert where the only conceivable products would be marine food or dates from the oasis. However, as Whitcomb has suggested, they might be containers for produce grown elsewhere in Palestine and brought to Ayla as an object of trade (Melkawi *et al.* 1994, 463). The new analysis by Kerlijne Romanus, below, points firmly, but not conclusively towards wine or date products.

However, the trade was not restricted to amphorae and the costrels could have been containers for another, although equally unknown, commodity. The bowls may have been traded for their own sake, but it is not impossible that they too were containers.

Imported fine-wares are scarce at Adulis, although a few sherds of African Red Slip Ware were found. In only one case could the form be determined – part of the body of a Hayes 72 dating from the early 5th century, found in the spoil from Paribeni's excavation in the southern part of the site.

Other imports from the Mediterranean region include amphorae of the forms Late Roman 1 and 2. Late Roman 1 was made along the southern Turkish coast (particularly Cicilia) and also Cyprus, although at present it is difficult to decide between the two regions. It was once considered to be a container for oil, but now the argument has swayed in favour of wine (Pieri 2005; Brun 2004). Late Roman 2 seems to have been made in the general region of southern Greece and the Aegean, but it is very difficult to be certain of its contents (Pieri 2005, 92). Both are characteristic of late 5th and 6th century AD deposits and usually occur together, as at Adulis. This might suggest that they were containers for different rather than competing commodities. If that is the case, oil would be more probable than wine.

Also present are Africana amphorae from Tunisia and Libya, which may have contained oil or in some cases fish sauces. All the material from Adulis comprises body sherds and it is hard to comment further on this material. Late Roman 3 from the Sardis region is present, but very scarce and represented by a very few body sherds.

If the Ayla-Aksum amphorae are disregarded the assemblage is typical of Byzantine contexts anywhere in the Mediterranean world. In this case it seems to date between the 4th or more probably early 5th centuries and the 7th. Without excavation it is difficult to refine the chronology further.

The local wares are more problematic. The most prolific area was the south-west corner of the site, where there is a mixture of late and early material, perhaps resulting from early excavations. Some types are spread over the site suggesting that they are Aksumite in date, but others are not and are chronologically equivocal. Only excavation will permit the sequence to be unravelled. In general sherds from C24 onwards are most likely to be Aksumite, those from lower numbered squares could be either. Sometimes the best (and hence illustrated) examples come from the south-west corner, but the type is found over the site. Such instances are noted below. Fabric might also be a chronological indicator as vegetable temper was not present on Diodorus island or in the supposedly early material from Adulis itself.

Catalogue

Fig. 8.16. Imported Aksumite period pottery

1. Rim and neck of Ayla-Aksum amphora from C21. Note the typical seating for lid. Hard reddish sandy fabric with white outer surface, typical of Ayla products. *c.f.* Melkawi *et al.*, 1994, 10e.

2. Operculum or lid from C13. Probably for sealing amphorae as no 1. Cream sandy fabric as no 1.

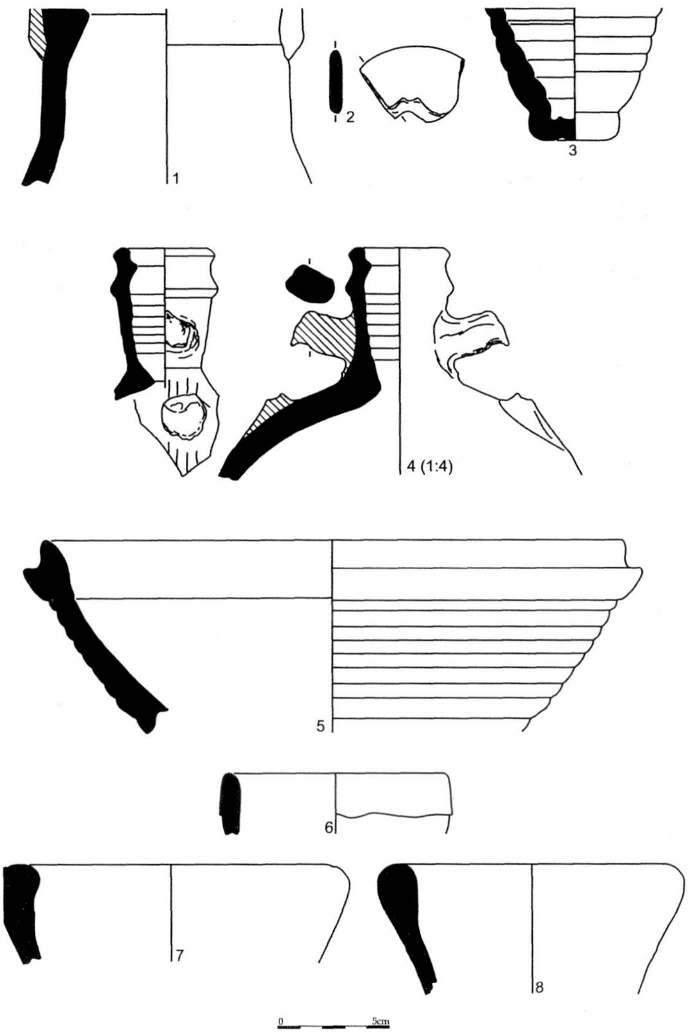

Figure 8.16 Imported Aksumite period pottery

3. Base of Ayla-Aksum amphora from C20. Fabric as no 1. *c.f.* Melkawi *et al* 1994, 10,m.
4. Neck and upper part of ribbed costrel from C27. Note the lid seating suggesting use as a container. Coarse pale pink sandy ware with cream surfaces. *c.f.* no 1. *c.f.* Melkawi *et al.* 1994, 10,l.
5. Flanged bowl from C18. Fabric as no 1. *c.f.* Melkawi *et al.* 1994, 8k.
6. Rim of Late Roman 1 from C29. Typical fabric with limestone and pyroxene inclusions (see Peacock 1984, Bii).
7. Rim of Late Roman 2 from C30. Typical fabric, reddish buff with a few grains of limestone and very sparse mica (see Peacock 1984, Bi).
8. Rim of Late Roman 2 from C25. Fabric as no 7.

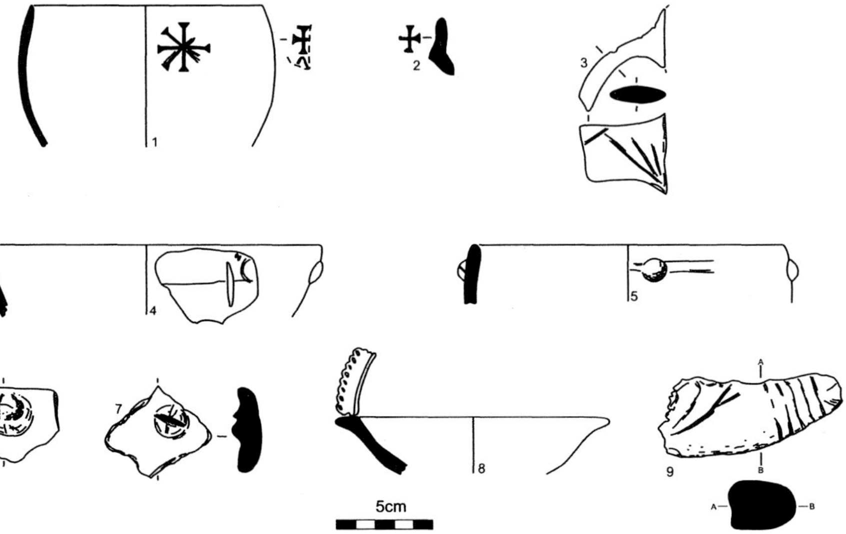

Figure 8.17 Hand-made Aksumite period pottery

Fig. 8.17 Hand-made decorated wares

Some of these sherds are certainly Aksumite in date (*e.g.* nos. 1–2), the remainder are less certain and as they come from the south-west corner of the site they might well be Pre-Aksumite in date. Where no ceramic square is quoted they came from outside the gridded area.

1. Bowl with two carefully incised cross motifs 83mm apart, from C21. *c.f.* Phillips, 2000, figs 273 and 341. Fine red buff ware with polished surfaces.
2. Body sherd with cross decoration as above, from C24. Sandy buff ware with smooth redder surface.
3. Handle with scratch mark decoration on top from C17. Red buff sandy fabric with a grey core.
4. Bowl with vertical incised line and a hemispherical appliqué from C18. In a grey buff ware with a grey core. Contains very fine sand a chopped vegetable matter.
5. Bowl with horizontal incised lines and hemispherical appliqué from C21. Red buff ware with fine sand and chopped vegetable matter.
6. Bowl with hemispherical appliqué decorated with an incised cross. Angle uncertain. Red buff micaceous ware with a black core. *c.f.* Fattovich, XXI,1 or XXIII, 9, Tomber 2005b, fig. 4, 2–4. The close resemblance of this motif as well as the fabric, to material from Quseir is striking and suggests a Roman date (found outside survey grid).
7. Body with hemispherical appliqué decorated with an incised cross. Fabric as no 6. See comments above (found outside survey grid).
8. Bowl with impressions around rim top. Red brown micaceous ware, with vertical burnished streaks on outer surface (found outside survey grid).
9. Horn from ?statue or figurine from C18. Alternatively could be a phallus. Coarse micaceous sandy ware. Red buff surfaces, black core.

Fig. 8.18 Scratch top wares

One of the most distinctive types of Adulis pottery are hand-made bowls and jars with

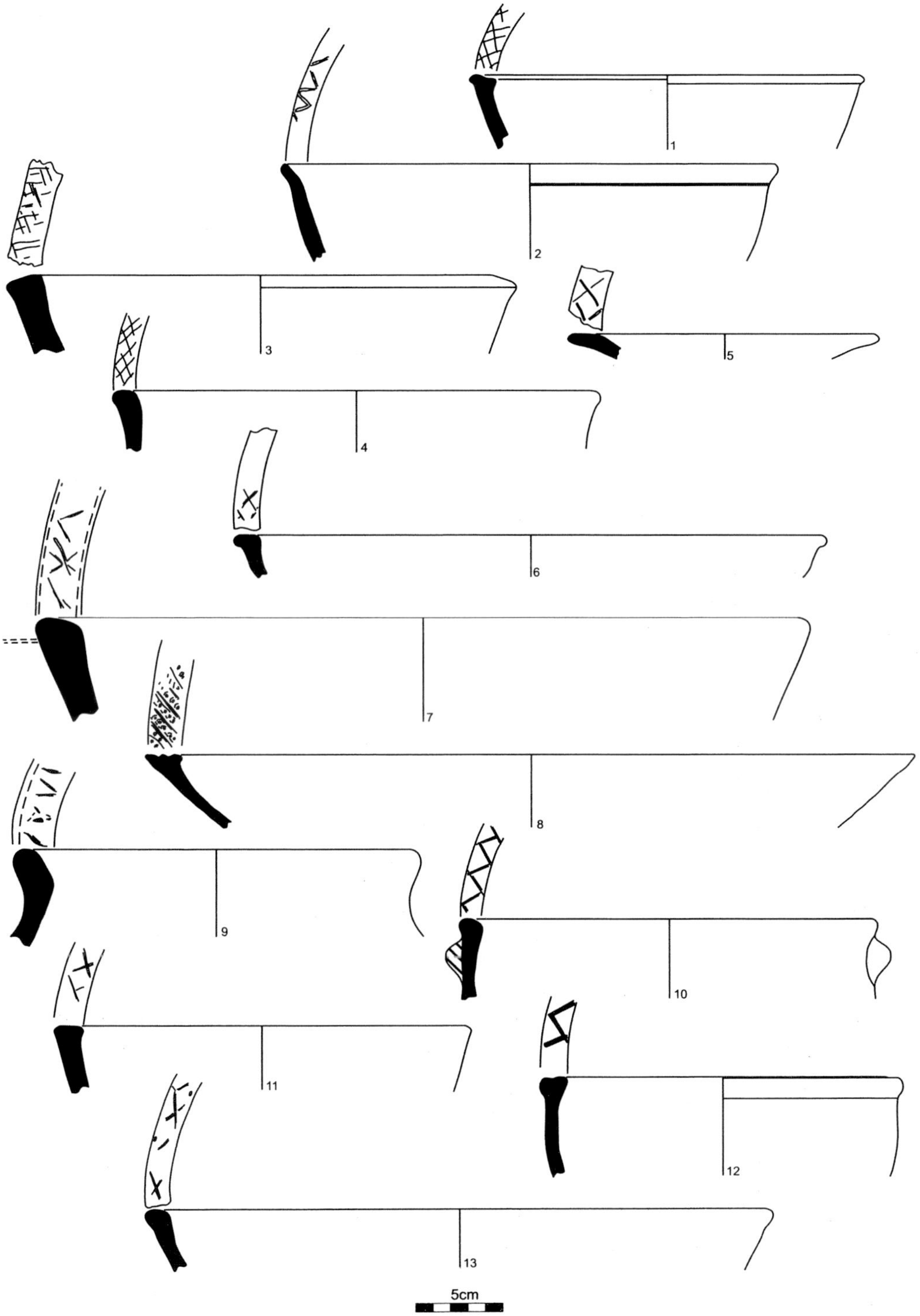

Figure 8.18 Scratch top ware

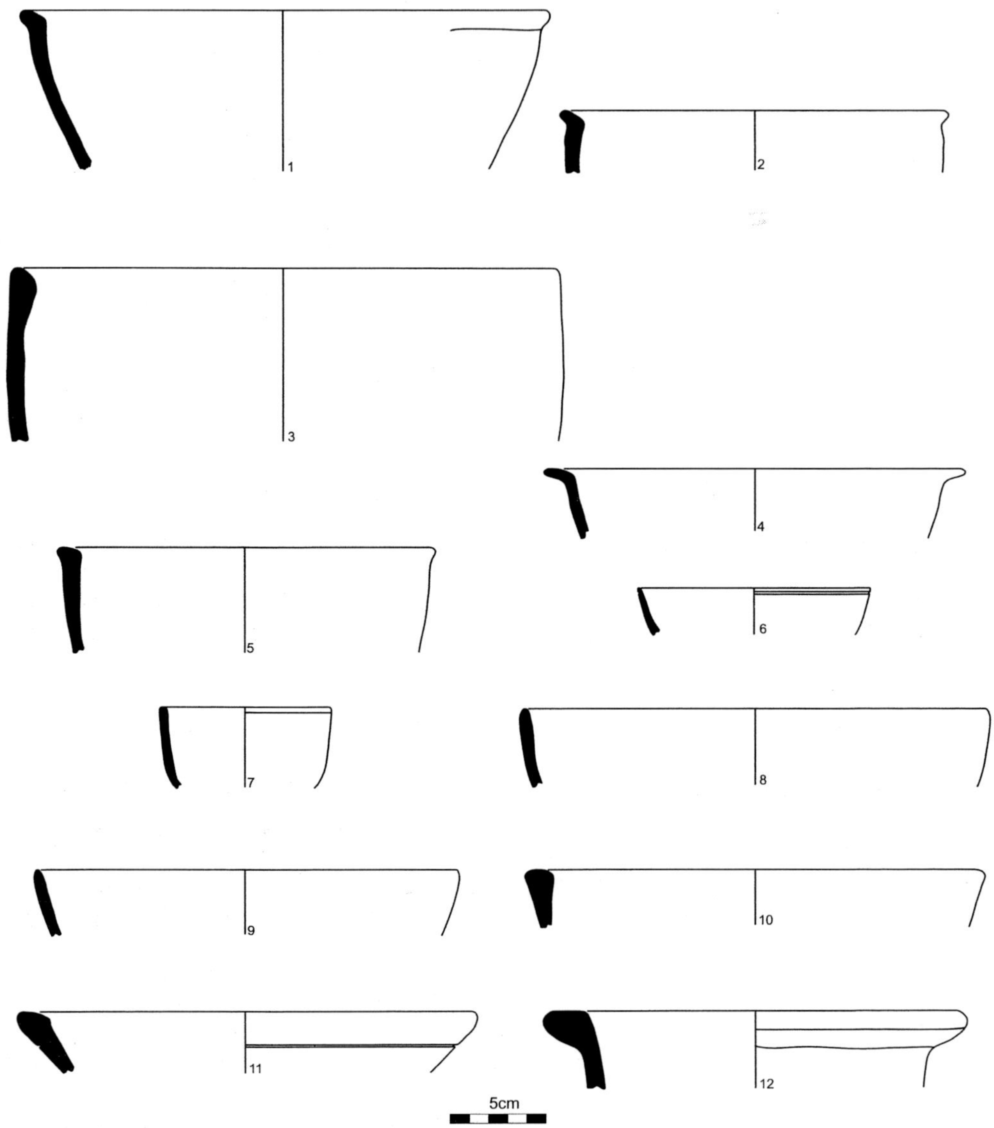

Figure 8.19 Hand-made open bowls

incised 'scratch' marks on the top of the rim. These usually take the form of chevrons or cross hatching and may be continuous around the rim or occur in intermittent patches. One example was included among the Pre-Aksumite wares above because it was found in close proximity to the decorated sherds described above, akin to those reported by Paribeni, and had similar tooled decoration. The illustrated examples of this ware were found in the south-west corner of the site and it may all be Pre-Aksumite. However, nothing of this nature was found in the assemblage from Diodorus island and sherds of this type are found all over the site so there is a good possibility that they are Aksumite. These wares resemble late Meroitic 'Doka' from Sudan in decoration, if not form (information Ross Thomas).

1. Bowl with thickened rim and intermittent hatching on top, from C20. Fine buff ware with black core.
2. Open bowl with intermittent chevron pattern on rim from C21. Fine micaceous red buff ware with grey core.
3. Heavy bowl with cross hatching on rim from C21. Coarse micaceous buff ware with grey core.
4. Bowl or jar with cross hatching on rim from C21. Fine micaceous red buff ware with grey core.
5. Open bowl or lid with cross hatching on rim from C19. Fine micaceous red brown ware with a grey core.
6. Expanded rim of bowl with intermittent cross hatching on top from C17. Fine buff ware with a grey core.
7. Large heavy bowl with incised marks on top of rim from C20. Red brown ware with black core. Some fine sand and vegetable matter.
8. Open bowl with expanded rim and incised oblique lines with dots in between from C18. Fine red buff ware with some fine mica. Burnished vertically on outside and horizontally on inner.
9. Heavy rim of jar with chevron pattern on bevel from C20. In a micaceous buff ware with some vegetable matter.
10. ?Cooking pot with hemispherical appliqué handle or decoration from C23. In a soft buff fine sandy fabric with a grey core.
11. Bowl with intermittent cross hatching on top from C16. In a fine sandy buff ware, reddish inside with a grey core.
12. Bowl with intermittent chevrons on rim from C12. In a soft orange brown micaceous fabric.
13. Large bowl with intermittent hatch marks on top from C10. Red buff fabric with vegetable temper.

Fig. 8.19 Hand-made open bowls

1. Bowl with slightly everted rim. Highly micaceous red buff ware with black core. Rare voids from ?vegetable matter.
2. Bowl with simple bead rim from C20. Buff micaceous sandy ware.
3. Slightly inturned thickened rim from C21. Red buff ware with grey core. Some vegetable matter as inclusions.
4. Markedly everted rim from C43. Red brown ware with black outer surface and black core. Sand and mica inclusions.
5. Bowl with thickened and flattened rim from C18. Micaceous red buff ware with mica. A few voids, possibly from vegetable matter.
6. Open bowl with external groove below rim from C14. Fine red ware with burnished surfaces inside and out.

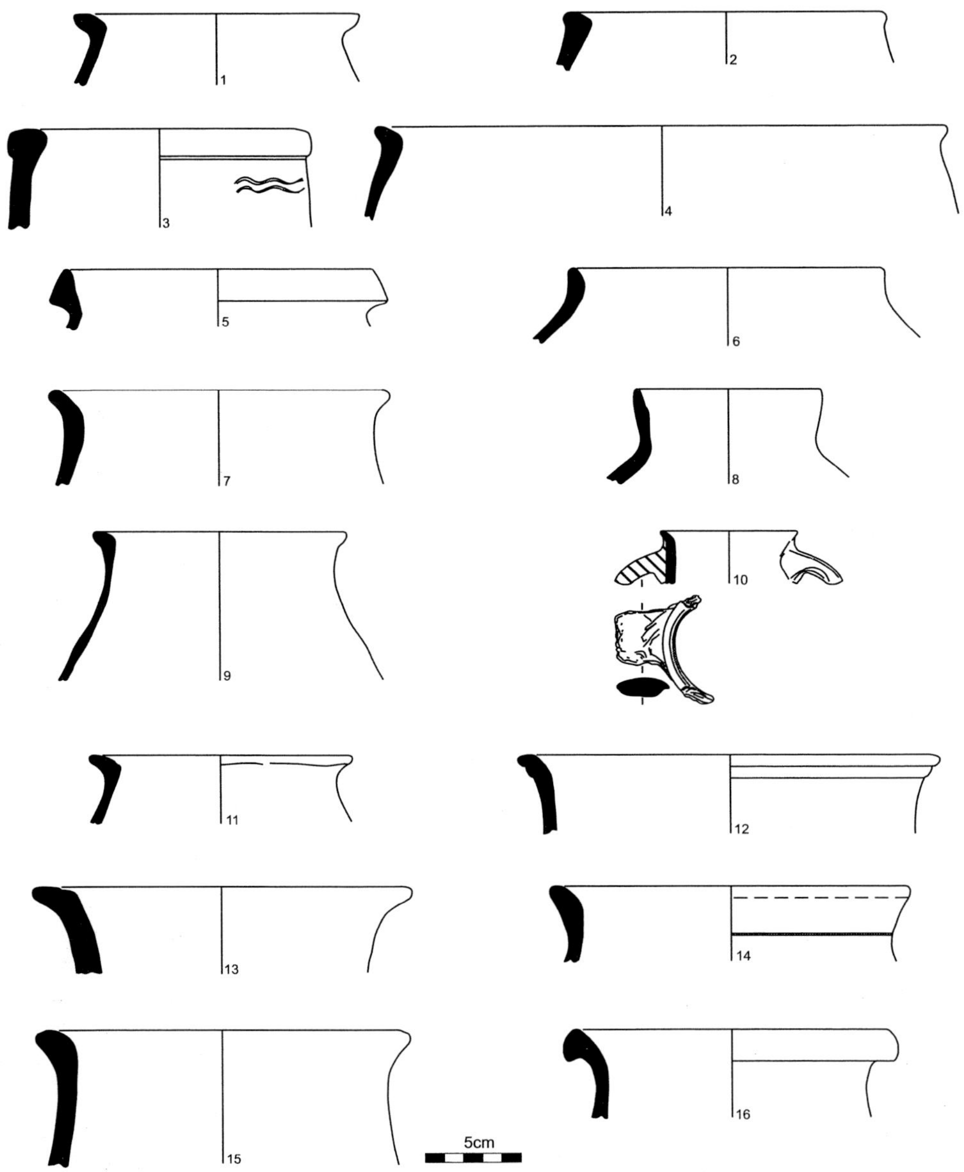

Figure 8.20 Hand-made jars with everted rim and necked jars

7. Small bowl or cup. Fine orange red ware with sparse inlcusions. Outer surface smooth with darker red skin (found outside of grid).
8. Open bowl from C16. Fine reddish brown ware with a pale grey core. Some quartz inclusions. Smooth inner surface, vertical burnishing on outer.
9. Bowl from C30 in fine buff ware with a black core.
10. Expanded rim from C23. Sandy red brown ware with black core.
11. Bowl or perhaps large lid from C30. In red buff ware with grey core. Tempered with vegetable matter and some sand.
12. Heavy rim of bowl or jar from C27. Finer micaceous red brown fabric with black core.

Fig. 8.20 Hand-made jars with everted rim and necked jars

1. Everted rim from C28. Highly micaceous red brown ware with dark core.
2. Thickened rim from C13 in orange buff ware with grey core. Inclusions of sand with some vegetable matter visible on outer surface.
3. Thickened rim from C23. Red brown fabric with grey black surface. Some sand but much vegetable matter as inclusions.
4. Everted rim jar from C23. Fine buff micaceous ware with grey core.
5. Triangular rim from C13. Fine red buff ware with grey core. Sand and some fine vegetable matter as inclusions.
6. Jar from C20. Red brown ware with buff surface. Sandy with much quartz up to 1 mm.
7. Thick jar neck from C22. Red brown sandy ware.
8. Jar rim from C35. Buff ware with very fine sand and no visible mica.
9. Upper part of jar from C18. Fine buff fabric with darker buff core.
10. Neck of handled jar, with one or two handles from C43. Buff clay with black core and vegetable temper.
11. Everted jar rim from C21. Reddish buff sandy fabric.
12. Jar rim with bead under from C20. Buff sandy ware with grey core.
13. Heavy everted rim from C21. Coarse micaceous black ware with buff surface.
14. Jar with heavy everted rim and groove below from C18. Soft buff micaceous fabric with grey core and some vegetable temper.
15. Heavy jar from C21 in fine red brown sandy fabric with grey core.
16. Expanded rim in red brown ware with grey core from C38

The contents of Ayla-Aksum amphorae

Adulis is, without doubt, the most prolific site for this type of amphora, with the exception of Aqaba itself. Cosmas (*Christian Topography*, 2) indicates that traders were coming to Adulis from the Elanitic Gulf (the Gulf of Aqaba), but he gives no indication of the commodities they brought. Clearly coarse pottery was among the imports, but the amphorae are likely to have been traded for their contents. It would therefore be of considerable interest to know what these vessels contained.

Tomber (2004b, 398) has recently reviewed the scant evidence. Melkawi *et al.* (1994, 463) suggested that they contained agricultural produce from the Palestinian hinterland, while Parker (1998, 37; 2000, 380) suggested they were for *garum* made from Red Sea fish. More recently Dolinka (2003, 95–6) suggested that the earlier vessels at least were containers for *garum*, dates and/or date wine. The only firm evidence however, is a sherd from Berenike bearing the titulus pictus *oinos*, wine. Some of the amphorae bear Christian monograms, suggesting that the contents may sometimes have had a role in church liturgy (e.g. Pieri 2007, figure 3). This accords with the frequency of finds from Adulis which was certainly a major centre of Christianity in the Red Sea area.

Aqaba is a desert port and the only food resources seem to be marine, or dates from a fairly extensive palm plantation around the oasis. However, it is possible that the desert was formerly more productive than it appears today. Work in the Negev desert has demonstrated the existence of remarkable evidence for cultivation dating between 5th and 8th centuries AD, precisely the date of Aqaba amphorae (Glueck 1959; Aharoni *et al* 1960; Mayerson 1962; Rothenberg 1967). There is thus a distinct possibility that the amphorae contained produce imported from nearby regions as originally suggested by Melkawi *et al*. Interestingly, much of this appears to be focused upon the production of wine. The 6th century church at Petra has a mosaic which shows a man apparently drinking from an amphora, which is clearly of the Ayla-Aksum type. If so this reinforces the view that this type carried wine.

The question of what these amphorae contained is an open one, and some sherds from southern Jordan were subjected to contents analysis by Kerlijne Romanus of the Universiteit van Leuven – her report is appended below. The sherds produced a weak fatty acid methyl ester (FAME) response which was hard to interpret (see Fig. 8.21). Animal fats can be eliminated as they would have given a clear signal. However, had olive oil or fish been present, it would have been recognised as would the resin coating normally associated with wine amphorae. Date products would have produced sugars which would have been lost during burial due to the action of the bacteria which feed on them.

At present the evidence favours either dates and date products or wine, if we assume that the hard firing would have obviated the need for a resin interior coating.

Report residue analysis on ceramics from Aqaba, Jordan by Kerlijne Romanus

Sample information

We received eleven amphora potsherds from Aqaba, Jordan. Five of them came from the site of Roman Aqaba, five from the Islamic site and one from the inland site of Humayma, in the desert north of Aqaba.

Extraction

The potsherds were crushed in a mortar with a pestle. After adding 0.5 mg of the internal standard n-heptadecane, 5 g of the milled sherd were submitted to a Soxtec extraction with 60 ml chloroform : methanol (2:1). The extraction consisted of boiling for 45 min followed by rinsing for 2 hours. The solvent was partially evaporated in the Soxtec apparatus and the remaining solvent was removed under a stream of nitrogen. The dried total lipid extracts were stored at –18°C until further analysis.

Derivation

Identical lipid extracts were used for the different analysis methods. The total lipid extract was used for preparation of the fatty acid methyl esters (FAME). A known method was applied for methanolysis of only the acylglycerols (AG) (Kimpe 2003). In this method, 300

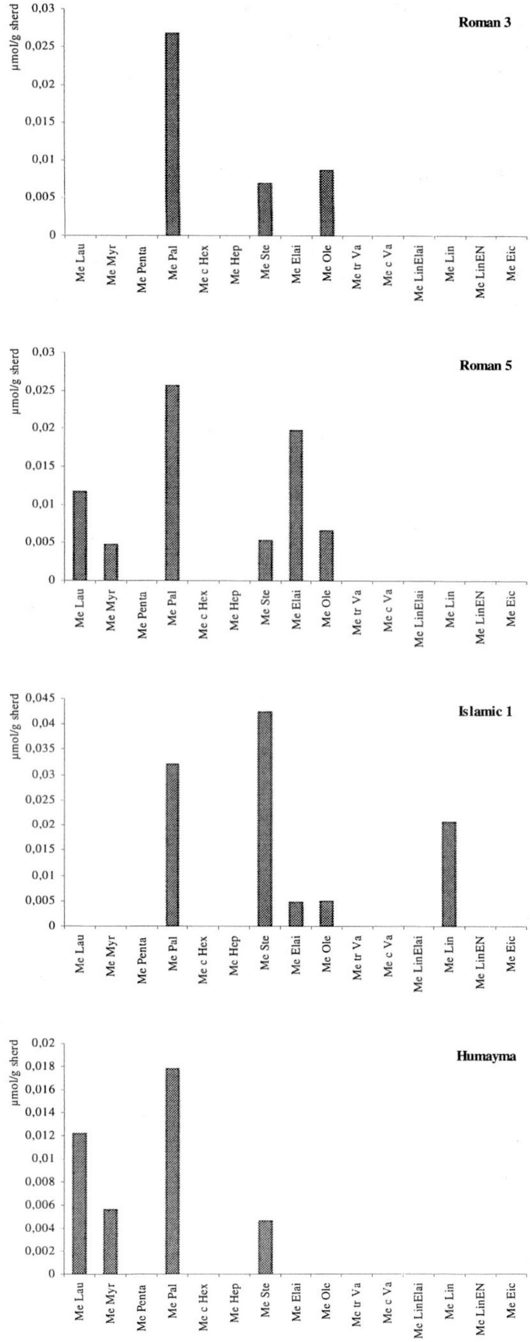

Figure 8.21 FAME content of selected Ayla-Aksum amphorae

μl of KOH in methanol (0.45g KOH in 8g methanol) was added to the total lipid extract dissolved in 200 μl diethylether. After shaking for three minutes, 1 ml cyclohexane and 200 μl bidistilled water were added. After centrifugation the cyclohexane phase was separated, washed with 200 μl bidistilled water and dried. The fatty acid methyl esters were dissolved again in 100 μl cyclohexane and analysed on a polar phase gas chromatograph (PPGC). For quantitative analyses 1 μl of the extract obtained by the method, mentioned above, was automatically injected on a Hewlett Packard 6890 GC with automatic integrator HP 3365. The instrument was equipped with a capillary 60 m fused silica column with an internal diameter of 0.32 mm, and with a polar BPX70 stationary phase (SGE, film thickness of 0,25 μm). The sample was injected twice at a split ratio of 1:100 at 250°C. The oven temperature was held at 180°C for 32 min, increased to 250°C at 3°C/min followed by an isothermal 5 min hold at 250°C. A flame ionization detector (FID) was used at 260°C. Compound identification was accomplished by comparison with retention times of known methyl esters. The individual FAME were quantified by using appropriate response factors.

The second dried total lipid extract was used for analysis on a gas chromatograph with mass spectrometer (GC-MS). Therefore a silylation was performed. The lipid extract was dissolved in 100 μl toluene and 50μl N-methyl-N-(trimethylsilyl)-trifluoroacetamide (97%) (MSTFA) was added. This mixture was held at 60°C for 1hour before the solvent was removed under a gentle stream of nitrogen. The silylated lipids were again dissolved in 50 μl toluene before analysis on a GC-MS. GC-MS analyses were performed on an Agilent 5973 Network Mass Selective Detector coupled to an Agilent 6890N GC with a 30 m HP5MS capillary column with an internal diameter of 0.25 mm. One μl of the sample was injected in the splitless mode at a temperature of 290°C. The oven temperature was held at 140°C for 2 min, increased to 325°C at 4°C/min followed by an isothermal 5 min hold at 325°C. Afterwards a second step of 1°C/min going to 340°C was programmed. The mass spectrometer was held at a temperature of 340°C. Spectra were taken between *m/z* 50 and *m/z* 800.

Results

The graphs with the fatty acid methyl esters (FAME) represent the quantitative results of the fatty acid content in the ceramic material. From these fatty acid profiles we obtain information about the similarity of the samples, the lipid concentration and in some cases about the origin of the lipids.

For the 8 samples analysed thus far, we can see that *only 4 contained a significant amount* of FAME and for those 4 amphorae *very low concentrations* were measured. From this observation we can conclude very few lipids were stored in the amphora or sustained preservation during burial. The latter possibility is less probable because of the arid climate in Jordan and consequently this would have been an ideal preservation context. Bearing in mind the very low concentrations and therefore a lesser trustworthiness of the results, we can see the diversity in the fatty acid profiles of the different samples indicating different commodities were stored in the amphorae. The concentrations are too low to claim, with enough confidence, the origin of the lipids.

		Aqaba Roman 1
		kr06okt08
RT	***prod***	**19.09.06/2**
3,69	butanedioic acid bisTMS	*
4,23	nonanoic acid TMS	*
4,63	? 3-acetobutyric acid TMS	*
5,65	decanoic acid TMS	*
6,82	? butanal 2,3,4 triTMS	*
7,66	C12 alcohol (243)	*
8,3	?	*
8,83	dodecanoic acid, 1 methylethylester	*
9,03	a sugar	*
9,46	dodecanoic acid TMS	*
10,45	*IS*	*10,46*
11,91	C14 alcohol (271)	*
13,32	a sugar	*
13,75	a sugar	*
13,92	tetradecanoic acid TMS	*
14,36	phthalate	*
14,43	a sugar	*
14,54	a sugar	*
14,98	alkane	*
15,38	a sugar	*
15,62	a sugar	*
15,84	a sugar	*
16,18	pentadecanoic acid TMS	*
16,47	phthalate	*
17,22	alkane	*
17,79	C16:1 acid TMS	*
17,8	a sugar	*
18,55	hexadecanoic acid TMS	*
19,53	methyloleate	*
20,85	C18 alcohol (327)	*
22,13	C18:1 acid TMS	*
22,31	C18:1 acid TMS	*
22,73	octadecanoic acid TMS	*
27,41	a sugar	*
27,8	alkane	*
28,67	phthalate	*
29,43	a sugar	*
30,61	a sugar	*
31,02	a sugar	*
31,53	a sugar	*
31,73	a sugar	*
32,34	C24 alcohol TMS (411)	*
33,63	squalene	*
34,8	een alkaan (408 -> C29)	*
37,46	3beta, 5beta cholestan 3yl oxy TMS	*

Table 8.1 FAME content of Roman 1

Silyl derivatives

The results of these analyses provide information about specific chemical compounds which may be characteristic for the food being stored in the vessel. For example, if we can trace cholesterol, we can assume animal fat was present in the ceramic. We call these compounds biomarkers. These analyses confirm the results of the FAME indicating low concentration of lipid material. Only in one amphora, Roman 1, we were able to trace a high amount of sugars (the results of this amphora are presented in Table 8.1). A cholesterol oxidation product was found, but together with the presence of squalene it indicates the potsherd was touched by human hands. This analysis needs to be confirmed to give surety about this result. For the other amphorae, no significant amount of lipids was detected. This indicates that these amphorae did not contain greasy products in the past. One important remark is that no pitch biomarkers were found which excludes also the storage of wine. This calls for a more elaborate research.

Conclusion

The results of the standard lipid analyses, here performed, show that hardly any lipids are preserved in the ceramics from Aqaba. Bearing in mind the ideal preservation conditions of the arid climate in Jordan, we can assume no greasy products were stored in these vessels. A few other approaches need to be investigated to reveal which compound classes we are dealing with.

Chapter IX
Stone artefacts from the survey

David Peacock

with a contribution by Keith Matthews

Introduction

The mounds of Adulis are made up largely of heaps of stone representing destroyed or decayed buildings. Two types of stone are present in considerable quantities: black vesicular basalt and mica schist, both of which were certainly obtained locally. Cenozoic basalt flows outcrop near the village of Foro, only 4 km from the site, and they are probably the major source of building materials. Basalt was used as unshaped blocks in much of the architecture and as shaped blocks for column drums and capitals.

It has often been supposed that the inscriptions recorded by Cosmas were on basalt, as the Greek word βασανίτου has been translated thus (*e.g.* Wolska-Conus 1968, 364), but this is unlikely as the rock is usually so vesicular and rough it would be unsuitable for such purpose. It is possible that a fine-grained non vesicular facies would have been purposefully selected, but it is probable that a quite different rock was used. In early Greek usage the term βάσανος was employed for touchstone, which is characteristically a fine-grained, homogeneous, black rock (Caley and Richards 1956, 157). It is difficult to know what rock is meant, but it is could have been a meteoritic stone (like the Kabaa' in Mecca) as might befit an important inscription.

The other common material, mica schist, probably came ultimately from the Ghedem massif, which dominates the site less than 10 km to the north. It is unclear how much was quarried in the mountain and how much was obtained at its foot as material washed down. Mica schist is a fissile rock which can be split into flat slabs for making string courses, to keep rubble building level or possibly even for roofing, although no pieces were found drilled for nail holes. The usage of basalt and schist in building is well illustrated in Fig. 9.1–3, a characteristic stepped and coursed wall, exposed in the Anfray trench, but hitherto unpublished. It is interesting to note, however, that there appears to be an absence of steps in the building's interior. Interior walls are dressed with basalt and run vertically down past the level of steps on the exterior face. Nor are there any openings for doors or windows in any of the rooms excavated by Anfray. Entry must therefore have been from the first floor above and they may be cellars. This is further suggested by a flight of steps running up the exterior wall near to the area surveyed. Such an arrangement may well have served to create a cool room at the base of the building, either for storage of food, or simply to

Figure 9.1 View of Anfray trench in 2005

Figure 9.2 View of the main wall exposed in Anfray's trench

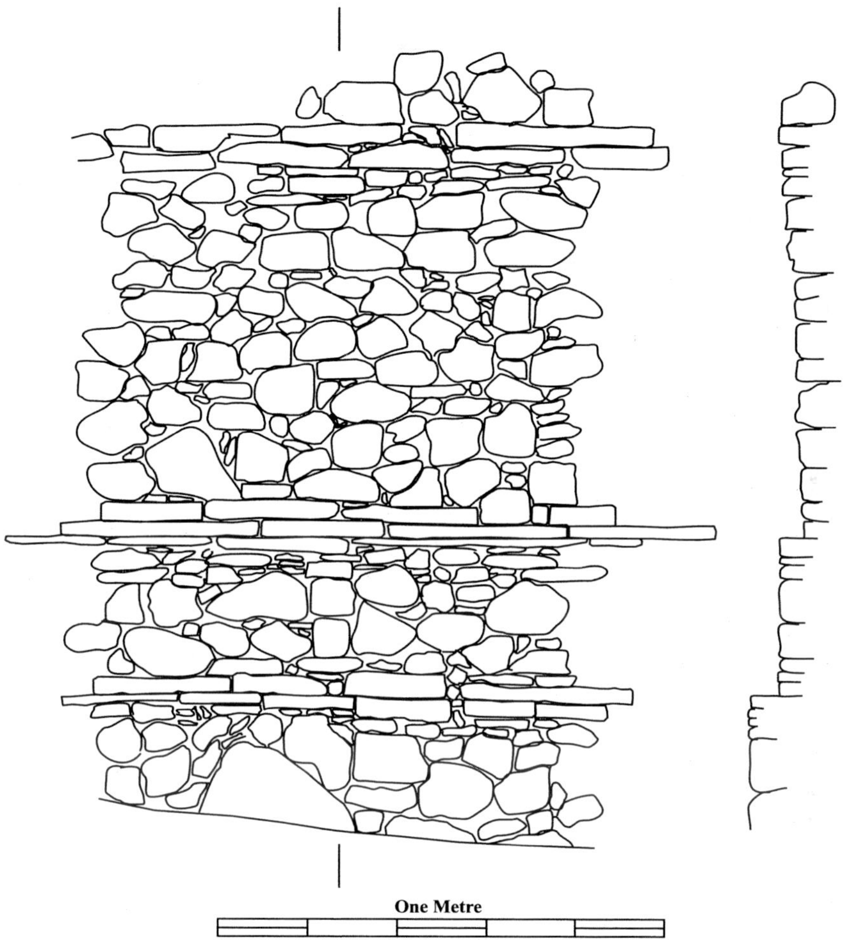

Figure 9.3 Profile of the wall

escape the searing heat of the plain of Zula. One metre of mud and basalt would certainly have provided a significant degree of insulation against the elements. The first-floor entry and height of the surviving walls suggests that the structures must have been at least two stories in height. The stepped style seems to have been typically Aksumite and has been noted at Aksum, Matara and Safira (Wenig 2002, Abb. 12–14, 34).

More exotic are small flakes and rarely cores of obsidian, which occur over the site but are concentrated in the south-west corner. In addition marble fragments of types well known in the Mediterranean were found on and around the British Museum church site and the palace site. Cosmas tell us that the throne found outside the town to the west, now lost, was made of excellent white marble. He mentions that it was not Proconnesian and it is interesting to note his familiarity with this stone (Wolska-Conus 1968, 364).

Each of these materials will be discussed below.

Architectural fragments from Adulis in basalt

Architectural fragments in basalt have been found at Samidi and at Adulis itself. Despite the lack of upstanding architectural remains at Adulis, several examples of ornamental architecture are still to be found on the site. These occur at two main locations; 'the palace' excavated by Sundström in 1906 and the church excavated by the British Museum in 1867–8.

The Church

Although the site has been much degraded through time, several of the architectural elements excavated by the British Museum expedition are still to be found on the surface of the trench. These take the form of large scale, worked basalt blocks, presumably from the same source as the rest of the basalt present on the site, and include the remains of pillars, plinths and bases (Fig. 9.4–5, A–F). The column drums are square in form with corners cropped and fluted to leave an irregular octagonal shape (blocks A, C, D); the column bases mirror the shape of the drums before terminating in a series of steps, the corners of which are not cropped (block B). This is mirrored in the one capital which was seen. Also still *in situ* was a large stone threshold from the western end of the church, although this was not in basalt, but an unidentified greenish marble. This block had been carved and notched, presumably to house the door frame which it would have supported.

Miscellaneous Blocks

Three other pillar fragments were located on the site during the course of the topographic survey (Fig. 9.6). All three blocks correspond with existing styles of architecture identified at Adulis during the recording of architectural elements from the church. One is the corner of a pillar base, characterised again by steps leading up to the main pillar drum. The two remaining blocks are both body elements which also exhibit the irregular octagon shape. One of these is remarkably well preserved, measuring 1.2 m in length with a square cross-section of 0.48 x 0.49 m. The cropped corners terminate before the end of the pillar suggesting that it was located towards the upper or lower part of the overall pillar. This differs somewhat from the architecture observed at the church, where cropped corners are found throughout the length of the pillar. There appears therefore to have been minor differences in the architecture found across the site, albeit within a broadly similar overall tradition.

Theodore Bent (1896, 228) identified similar architectural styles at Aksum, and Koloe (Qohaito):

> [w]e undertook the journey to Zula more from curiosity than in the hope of finding anything, and the net result of our expedition to the ruins of the ancient Adulis was the discovery, sufficiently important in itself, that the columns and capitals of Adulis, Koloe, the village below it, and Aksum, all belonged to the same order of architecture…

To this we can now add the architectural fragments from Samidi discussed above (pp.67–70). Taken with the stepped walls, it appears that the Aksumite kingdom developed its own characteristic building style. Basalt is a somewhat rough rock and it is reasonable to suppose that it would have been plastered, the vesicles aiding adherence.

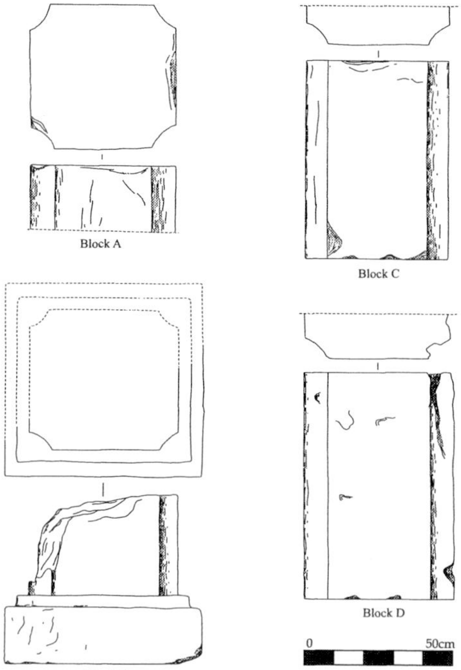

Figure 9.4 Blocks exposed in the British Museum church

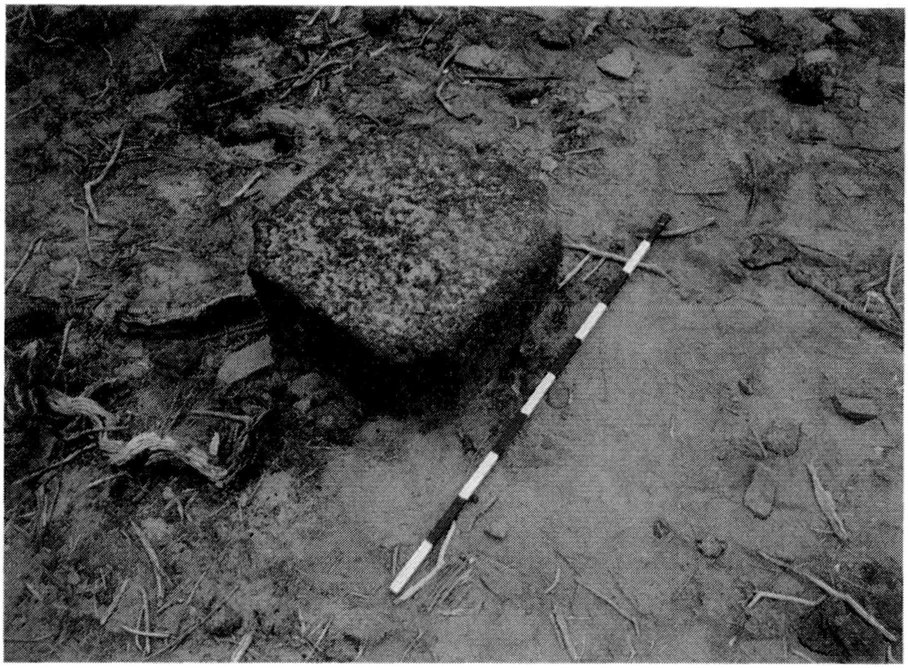

Figure 9.5 Block exposed in the British Museum church

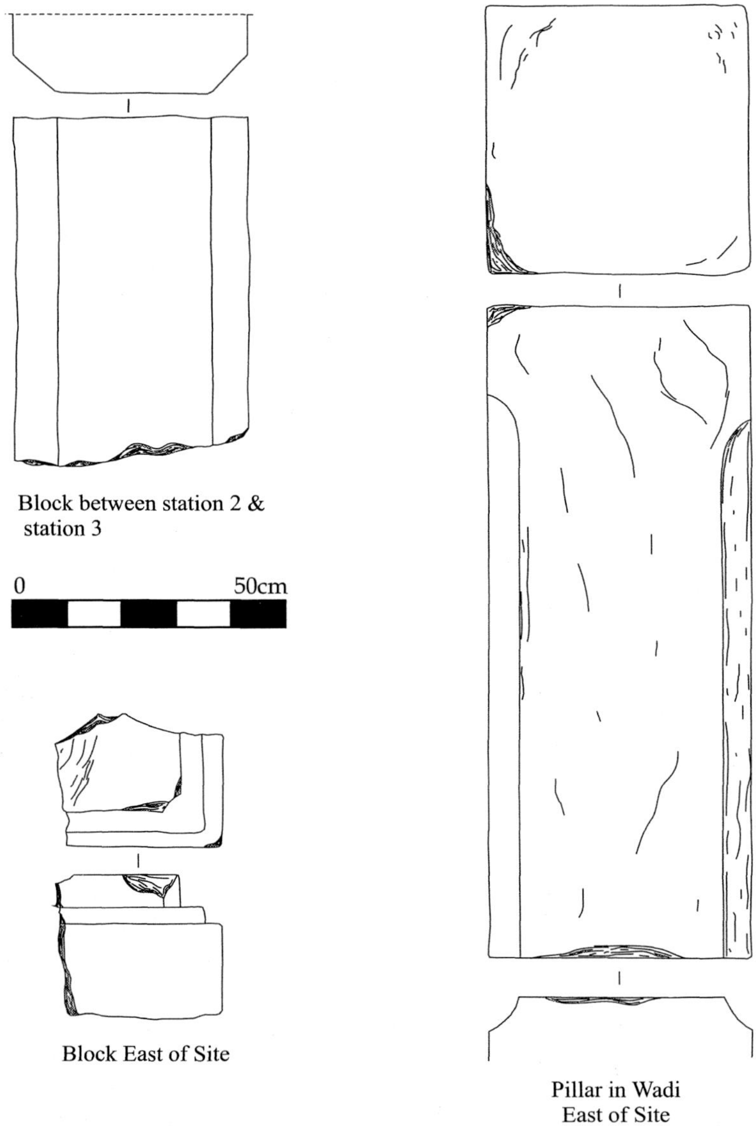

Figure 9.6 Blocks from other parts of Adulis

Marble

Marble fragments are to be found at both the church and the palace site. As these were scattered amongst the spoil from the excavations, they were collected and significant pieces drawn and photographed.

The proportions of marble from the palace are:

White marble (probably Proconnesian)	16 fragments
Travertine	1
Alabaster	12

From the church:

Pseudo *Rosso Antico*	Numerous fragments
White marble (Proconnesian)	4
Brilliant white (?Turkish)	1
Alabaster	10
Coloured alabaster	2
Bianco e nero antico	10

In addition a single piece of *porfido verde* was found 50 m south-west of the palace.

True *Rosso antico* comes from Tenaro in the southern Peleponese of Greece, but although the material from Adulis seems to broadly match that from the quarry, the large quantities on the church site suggest caution. Careful comparison suggests differences, even in the hand specimen. The Adulis rock is slightly paler, slightly softer and evenly bedded in contrast to the true *Rosso antico* which displays 'braided' bedding planes when seen in section. There is little doubt that it was used as a substitute for the true Greek material, but the source is at present unknown. It is possible that a similar material existed in Eritrea, although further geological and petrographic study would be needed to confirm this. Such a suggestion is, however, lent support by its frequent occurrence at a possible Aksumite burial site to the north of Massawa, where there are numerous tumuli associated with occasional Ayla-Aksum sherds (see above, pp.74–5).

The remaining decorative stones are less contentious. The travertine would come from the banks of the Tiber near Rome, the alabaster is probably Egyptian and the *porfido verde* was quarried near Sparta in southern Greece. It was particularly favoured in early Byzantine churches, such as those in Ravenna, Poreč etc, and small fragments have been found as far afield as Scotland, Ireland and the Czech Republic (Lynn, 1984). The crossed feldspars may have been seen as holy stigmata.

It is not possible to determine the origin of the brilliant white marble, but the isotopic analysis below suggests that it might be from Dokimeion.

The black and white veined marble visually matches the *Bianco e nero antico* (Grand Antique) from near St Girons in the French Pyrenees, although large quantities from the church are surprising. The quarries seem to have been opened in the 4th century and it is not clear how long they persisted (Borghini 1997). Paul the Silentiary mentions the presence of this material is S. Sophia in Constantinople, so its presence at Adulis, via an eastern Mediterranean intermediary, is not quite as exotic as it might seem at first sight.

The white marbles are certainly from the eastern Mediterranean and the dominance of Proconnesian need occasion no surprise. The quarries were active well into the 6th century and it is very common on Byzantine sites in the Eastern Mediterranean and it is the one marble that Cosmas mentions by name. Dodge and Ward-Perkins (1992) give a date range of 6th century BC to 6th century AD, while Gnoli (1971) cites an 8th century sarcophagus in Constantinople, although the material could have been quarried much earlier.

Most of the marble is found as slabs with one smoothed face, suggesting that it was used as wall sheathing or flooring. Those with moulding or grooving are almost certainly for walls rather than floors However, two fragments of spiral columns were found and these are invariably in Proconnesian marble. Similar columns, probably from the excavations are to be seen in the National Museum in Asmara.

Figure 9.7 Alabaster moulding from the palace site

Catalogue of drawn material from the palace site

Fig.9.7 Alabaster moulding from the palace site

1. Alabaster moulding
2. Alabaster moulding
3. Alabaster slab with tooling on reverse
4. Alabaster with groove

Fig. 9.8 Spiral column fragment

1. Column fragment in Proconnesian marble.

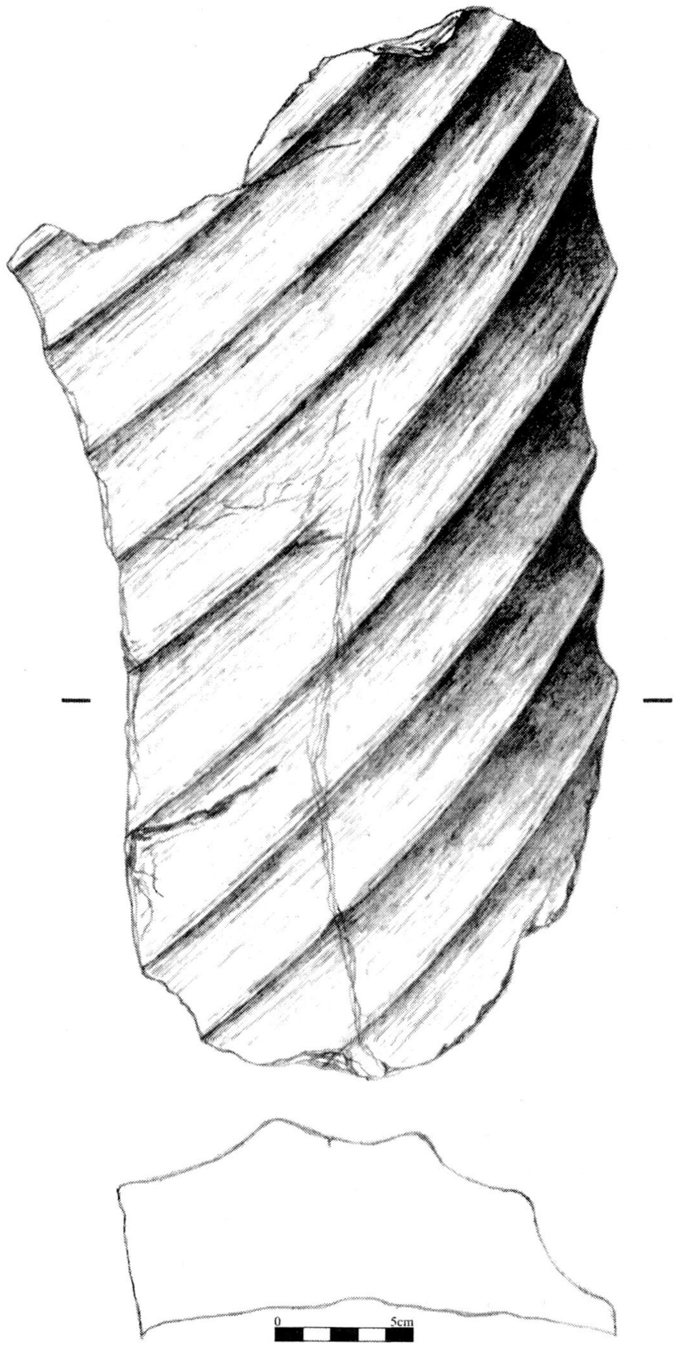

Figure 9.8 Spiral column fragment in Proconnesian marble

Obsidian

Small flakes and sometimes cores of obsidian are found all over the site. These are often prehistoric in date, but this is not necessarily always the case and two small pieces were found in Roman contexts at Quseir al-Qadim in Egypt (Peacock and Blue 2006). Obsidian can be characterised by chemical analysis and material from Adulis, Quseir, Dahlak Khebir, Mersa Fatma, Aliko and Bera'esoli was analysed by the ICPS at the NERC facility, Royal Holloway College, University of London. The specific question was to determine whether the material from Quseir came from Adulis, thus furnishing direct evidence of a link between the two sites. Unfortunately only a single piece from Adulis was available at the time of this study, but clearly the matter would be worth pursuing in greater depth. The results have been reported by Peacock, Williams and James (2007) and an edited version is reiterated here for ease of reference.

Two samples of obsidian were found in the excavations at Quseir al-Qadim. They both came from trench 7A where they were associated with late Augustan or early 1st century AD amphorae many of which were Italian Dressel 2–4 wine jars. A few pieces of pumice were found in the same deposit.

Obsidian is referred to in the *Periplus* (5:2.16–18) where there is mention of a source in a very wide bay, almost certainly Howakil Bay to the south-east of Adulis. Henry Salt (1814, 190) landed on the northern shore of the bay at Aréna:

> Near this spot I was delighted with the sight of a great many pieces of a black substance, bearing a very high polish, that lay scattered about on the ground at a short distance from the sea; and I collected nearly a hundred specimens of it, most of which were two three and four inches in diameter. One of the natives told me that a few miles further in the interior, pieces are found of much larger dimensions. This substance has been analyzed since my return to England, and proves to be the true opsian, or obsidian, stone, which answers most exactly to the following description given by Pliny: "Among the different sorts of glass may be enumerated the obsidian found by Obsidius in Aethiopia, of a very deep black colour, sometimes a little transparent (on the edges) but opaque in its general appearance, (when in a mass) and reflecting images, like mirrors placed against a wall. Many make gems of it, and we have seen solid images of the divine Augustus cut out of this substance; who ordered four obsidian elephants to be placed, as curiosities, in the Temple of Concord, &c."

It is very tempting to suggest that this was the source of the obsidian from Quseir. However, the association with Mediterranean, specifically southern Italian, amphorae could indicate an alternative source. Within this area, the sources closest to the area of origin of the amphorae would be Pantelleria, Lipari or the Pontine Islands. The obsidian of Pantelleria is very scarce even in the outcrops on the island, but invariably has a distinctive green colour (Peacock 1985). It can be eliminated as a potential source.

Williams-Thorpe (1993) has published a useful review of obsidian characterisation studies and sources in the Mediterranean. Francaviglia (1995) has also attempted to define parameters for discriminating between obsidians of Mediterranean origin. Obsidians are often classified chemically on their content of the oxides of aluminium, calcium and the alkalis, sodium and potassium. On this basis the samples from Quseir would be described as subalkaline, as Al_2O_3 is slightly in excess of Na_2O plus K_2O. The typical compositions given by Williams-Thorpe (1995, Table 1) suggest that the obsidians of the Pontine Islands and Lipari are also subalkaline, but more strongly so as aluminium is substantially in excess of alkalis. The obsidian from Pantelleria is strongly peralkaline.

The trace element distributions also show marked differences. The Italian sources have markedly lower Zr, higher Y, higher Sr, lower Rb, higher Zn, and lower V. The contrast is complete and convincing suggesting that these sources are highly improbable.

The eastern sources in the Aegean and Turkey are less probable as there is no evidence of a trade connection between these areas and Quseir. Equally it is possible to detect chemical differences with the Quseir samples (*c.f.* Francaviglia 1995).

As a Mediterranean source is improbable, it seems that the Quseir obsidian should originate further south in the Red Sea. A piece from Adulis was available, but as this is not a source area it must have been imported from elsewhere presumably in Eritrea. We were able to obtain 15 samples from north of Gela'elo. These took the form of pebbles from a recent gravel deposit which was almost certainly contiguous with the one from which Salt took his samples. Flakes were obtained from Mersa Fatma, Dahlak Khebir and Aliko in the same general region, while from the south of the country we had flakes from the beach at Beylul and near Bera'esoli. All of the samples hover around the subalkaline – peralkaline boundary, a majority just falling into the subalkaline field. This seems to be a regional characteristic.

Amongst the trace elements, Zr:Ba, Zr:Nb and Zr:Rb were adopted by Cann and Renfrew (1964) and more recently by Francaviglia (1995). In this case the Ba:Zr plot is least satisfactory. There seem to be two groups, one with high Ba and generally lower Zr, the other with minimal Ba and high Zr (Fig. 9.9). The former is typical of northerly sources, the latter of southern. One of the Quseir samples, the piece from Mersa Fatma and the Aliko samples fall in the first group, the other Quseir sample, that from Adulis and the piece from Dahlak fall into the second group. However plots of Nb:Zr and Rb:Zr show a clear break between northern and southern sources (Fig. 9.10), with only one sample from the south falling within the plot for Gela'elo. This is however a waste flake rather than an outcrop sample and may have been imported to Bera'esoli from the north.

The sample is a very small one and it is hard to judge from single analyses, but it is only possible to argue from the data available. The results tentatively suggest the Quseir pieces, that from Adulis, and that from Dahlak originated in the Gela'elo area. It seems entirely probable that Adulis was a distribution centre though which material from different parts of Eritrea reached Egypt and the more local places.

Early records of stone artefacts

In the Islamic cemetery on the site are a number of worked blocks of basalt, but none could be identified as finished works apart from pieces obviously used a door thresholds. However, in the 19th century, this was clearly a source of rich architectural pickings. Lefebvre (1845) records a number of pieces in white marble, some of which are reproduced here in Fig. 9.10:

1. the trunk of a spiral column.
2. a Corinthian capital.
3. a hexagonal column drum, apparently with a slot in one side.

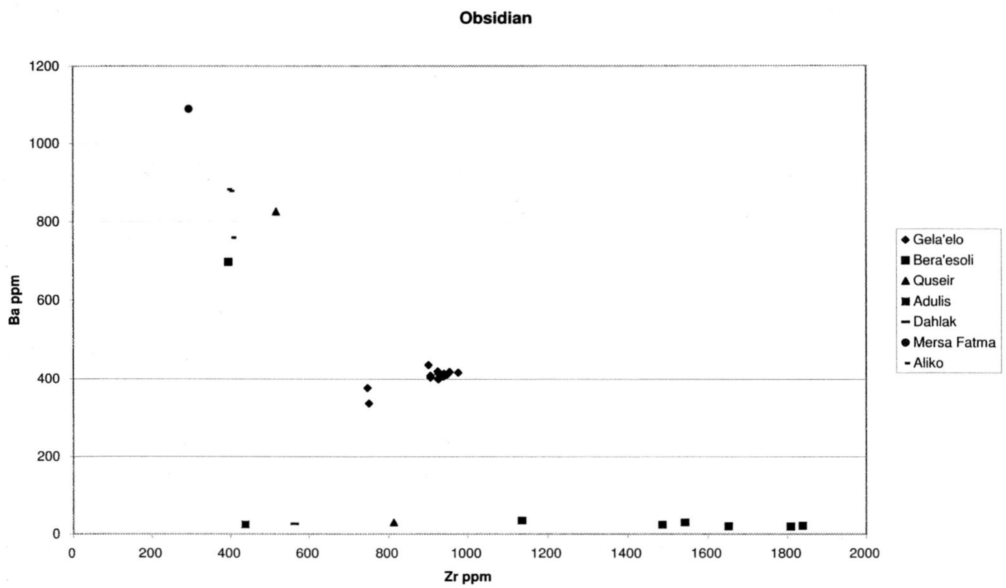

Figure 9.9 Obsidian Ba:Zr ratio

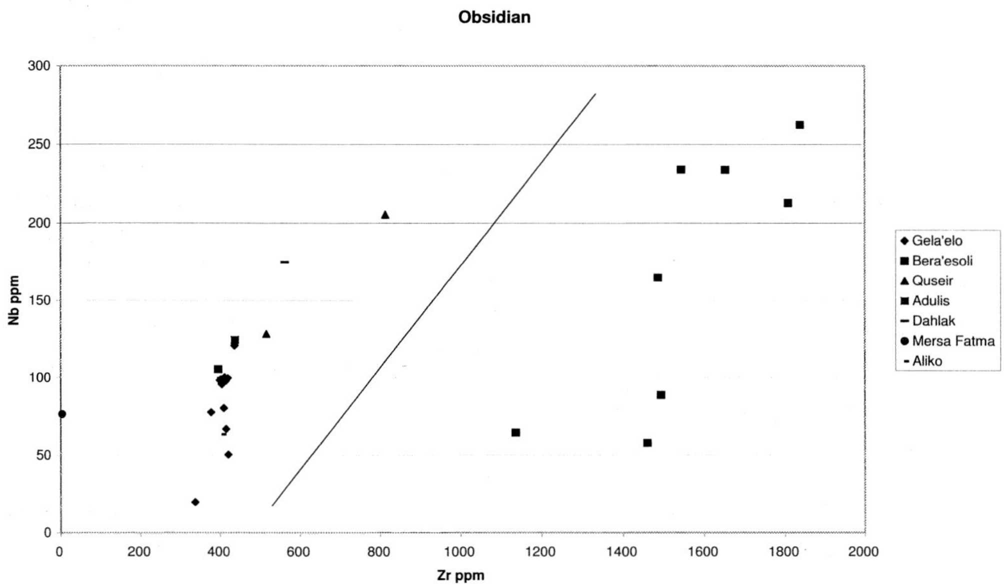

Figure 9.10 Obsidian Nb:Zr ratio

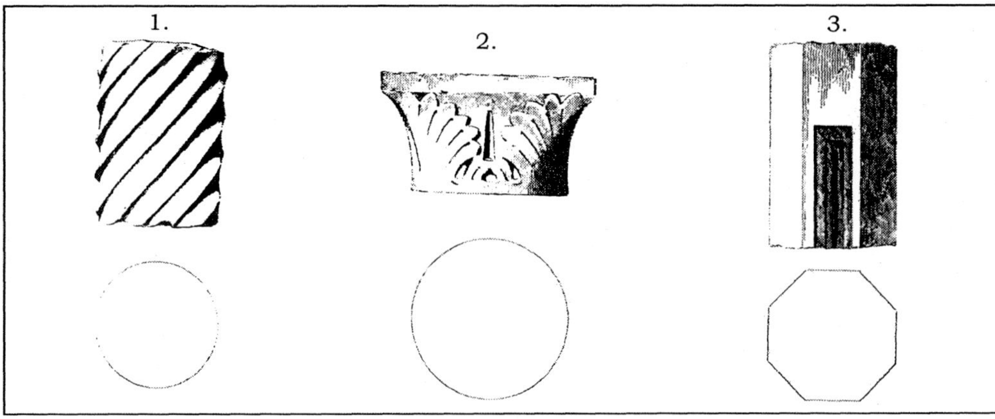

Figure 9.11 Marble recorded by Lefebvre

Similar artefacts from the British Museum church excavation appear in Captain Goodfellow's notebook (Munro-Hay 1989a, Pl IVa, b). Here the octagonal slotted column appears is similar although probably not identical, but the capital is very close, and possibly identical to the one illustrated by Lefebvre. Unfortunately, some of this material can no longer be found and it seems to be split between the Prehistoric and Europe Department and the Ethnography Department (information Dr J.D. Hill). Some years ago five marble fragments were examined by Dr K Matthews of the British Museum Research Laboratory, who was of the opinion that three were Proconnesian and of the other two, one is likely to be from Dokimeion and the other is either from a hitherto uncharacterised source or from Sardis. We are privileged to include his unpublished report at the end of this section.

Munro-Hay (1989a, PlVIb) also illustrates three square columns with ovoid pine-cone finials and decorated with groves in the form of one rectangle inside another. Also illustrated are two slabs with star shaped monograms. The pieces are now in Asmara Museum and the columns were examined by the writer. They appear to be Proconnesian marble. According to Munro-Hay (1989a, 50) they

> came from near the so-called 'Ara del Sole' cleared during Paribeni's excavations..... They appear to have come originally from the church which Paribeni found to have been constructed on top of the older building. Possibly belonging to the same structure were two panels bearing a star-like motif....which Paribeni thought represented the sun, and which encouraged him to designate the building in which they were found 'Ara del Sole'.

Munro-Hay (1989a) also illustrates some decorative fragments shown in Fig. 9.12.

These pieces were almost certainly from screening around the sanctuary or the *Ciborium* and are probably Christian rather than earlier. Everything points to exotic marbles being imported during the 6th century for church ornamentation, although some was used for important structures such as the so-called 'palace'.

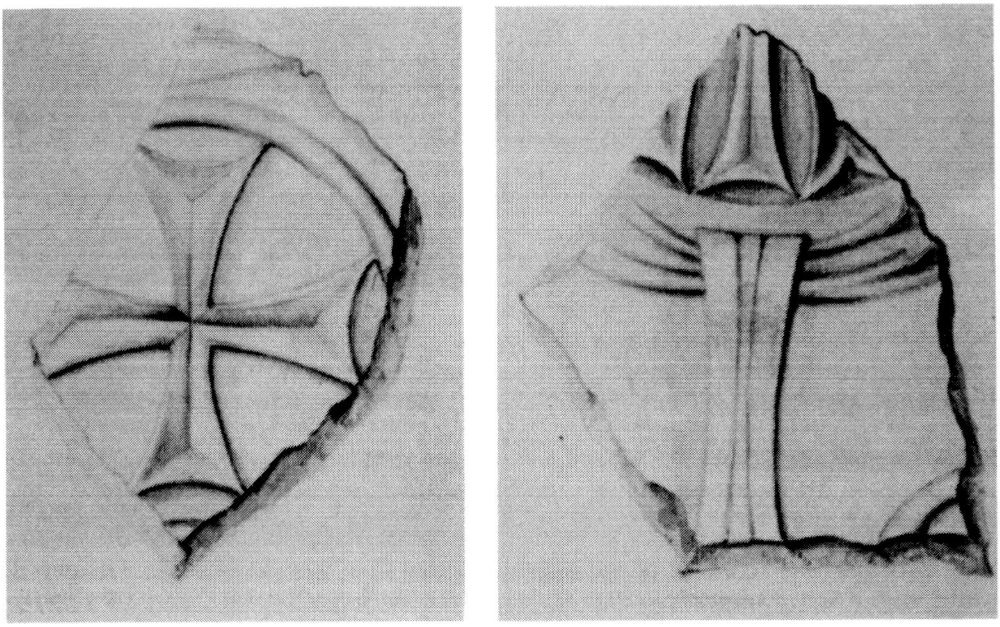

Figure 9.12 Marble from the church recorded by Munro Hay (1989)

Report on the stable isotope analysis of marble fragments from Adulis, now in the British Museum, by Keith Matthews

Introduction

The five marble fragments that were isotopically analysed and reported here, are in the collections of the Department of Prehistory and Europe. They were acquired for the British Museum in 1868 by its representative, Richard Holmes. He had, during General Napier's Magdala Expedition, encouraged the soldiers to excavate at Adulis on the Red Sea coast, and during this dig they found a church. It is known that it was a bishopric from at least the 5th century A.D. and subsequent Italian excavations discovered other churches. In the Museum's archives there are very detailed accounts by Captain Goodfellow of the finds from Holmes' excavation.

Experimental Procedure

The experimental procedure is based on the work of McCrea (1950), although it was not applied to the provenancing of classical white marble until the early 1970s (see for example, Craig and Craig 1972; Coleman and Walker 1979). The samples were obtained from the objects by drilling into surfaces of the sculptures that had previously suffered damage, using a 3/16 inch tungsten carbide tipped masonry drill. The initial drillings were discarded in order to remove any effects of weathering or conservation. From this powder, 10 mg was reacted with 100% orthophosphoric acid under vacuum. The carbon dioxide thus obtained was isotopically analysed using a VG Micromass 602D mass-spectrometer. The isotopic ratio (δ) obtained is given in parts per mil (‰ *i.e.* per thousand) relative to the PDB standard (Craig, 1957), where

$$\delta = \frac{(Rsample - Rpdb) \times 1000 ‰}{Rpdb}$$

and R= $^{13}C/^{12}C$ or $^{18}O/^{16}O$.
The standard error on these measurements is typically ± 0.05 ‰.

Results

The results are shown in the table overleaf, and are also plotted graphically as the carbon isotope ratio $\delta^{13}C$ versus the oxygen isotope ratio $\delta^{18}O$. Also on the plot are the 90% ellipses (Leese 1988) of isotopic signatures obtained from quarry data very kindly made available by Professor Norman Herz of the University of Georgia, and supplemented by Carrara data from quarry samples measured by the British Museum Research Laboratory. The ellipses selected include those for some of the more important marble quarrying areas in antiquity, and for which data are available, albeit limited.

Discussion

The plot of the results shows that several different sources of marble were exploited to produce these five objects. It had been suggested that the Proconnesian quarries on the island of Marmara were a probable source. This appears to be true for just three of the objects (numbered 1, 3, & 5) and although they fall within an area of the plot where there are isotopic overlaps with other quarries *i.e.* Dokimeion and Carrara, Proconnesus is the only one common to these particular three samples. Furthermore, none of these three objects are likely to be of Carrara marble as the grain size was fairly coarse. Sample number 2, an octagonal screen post has an isotopic composition that seems to indicate the Dokimeion quarries in Asia Minor. Although the result does not fall within the ellipse itself, it is nevertheless very near to it, and several Phrygian sarcophagi held in the collections of the Department of Prehistory and Europe at the British Museum are carved of marble with similar isotopic ratios.

The only fragment not considered so far is the small fragment depicting leaves (number 4). Reference to the plot shows that its oxygen ratio is such that it is too negative to appear within the confines of the axes used for isotopic measurements on marble. There are data available for only two classically exploited marble sources, Naxos and Sardis, that exhibit ratios similar to those of this fragment. Also, recent analysis by this laboratory of a few specimens from the island of Kos, has demonstrated that marble from this island shows oxygen ratios that are very negative. However, the visual appearance of the fragment (number 4) indicated that it was not coarse grained enough to be from either Naxos or Kos.

Synopsis

The five results reported here have shown that although they are for a group of objects from the same site in Eritrea, at least three different sources of marble are involved. The notion that they were all Proconnesian marble has not been substantiated, although there would appear to be three items from that source. Of the other two, one is likely to be Dokimeion, and the

Ident. No	*Description*	*Reg. No*	*BMRL No*	$\delta^{13}C\ ^o/_{oo}$	$\delta^{18}O\ ^o/_{oo}$
1	Capital	1868.10-5.12	32771V	2.43	-1.39
2	Screen post Octagonal	1868.10-5.10	32770X	0.56	-7.16
3	Screen post Square	1868.10-5.13	32772T	3.05	-2.37
4	Fragment showing leaves	1868.10-5.16	32774P	3.56	-10.01
5	Screen post Octagonal	1868.10-5.14	32773R	2.81	-1.53

Table 9.1 Stable isotope analysis of marble fragments from Adulis

other is either from a hitherto uncharacterized (isotopically) source, or from Sardis.

Chapter X
Review, discussion and conclusion

David Peacock, Lucy Blue and Darren Glazier

Introduction

The Eritro-British expedition to Adulis has been an unmitigated success, fully achieving its objectives. Through the combination of a variety of different, complimentary, techniques, from non invasive survey through to sedimentological analysis and the re-examination of classical sources, the project has given crucial insights into the past of the ancient town. This chapter reviews the central findings of the research programme, placing them within the broader framework of Red Sea trade.

Ancient Adulis has always been something of an enigma. The site was first identified by Henry Salt in the early 19th century – the mounds on the plain of Zula matched perfectly the location described by the 1st century AD *Periplus*. Combined with the linguistic evidence offered by Salt (1814, 452), that 'Zulla' [*sic*] derived from 'Azoole' equates to Adulis, there appeared little reason to doubt the identification. However, although subsequent archaeological investigations have revealed substantial Aksumite ruins corresponding to the town described by Cosmas Indicopleustes in the 6th century, no trace of the 'fair sized village' of the 1st century *Periplus* had been recovered (*e.g.* Sundström 1907; Paribeni 1907; Anfray 1974). The 6th century harbour of Adulis, Gabaza, was tentatively identified by Sundström around the hills today known as Galala.

The apparent absence of any 1st century material was problematic. The *Periplus* states that the port was an important staging post in the early Roman Imperial period, articulating commerce between the Roman Mediterranean, East Africa, India and the Orient, with a harbour at Diodorus Island, later removed to Oreinê for increased security. Yet no Roman period imports have been recovered from Adulis. Paribeni's (1907) excavation in the south-west corner of the site appeared to suggest that the Aksumite town was preceded by an archaic settlement and between the two was a gap in occupation which may have encompassed the 1st century AD, through to the fourth.

The work described here has, however, identified the ports of Adulis described by the *Periplus*. Though we cannot yet say whether occupation at the site was continuous, it has been possible to identify occupation at the site ranging from at least the 1st century AD, through to the 7th. The presence of pottery assemblages and sedimentological analysis has allowed us to identify Diodorus Island as an offshore skerry, lying just off the eastern-most tip of the Galala Hills, while the harbour at Orienê lay in an enclosed lagoon on the island of Dese, approached by a channel on the western side of the island. Radiocarbon dates on shell fragments associated with the archaic pottery identified by Paribeni at the main site of Adulis also suggest that the pottery may not be as early as previously thought, and may be local production of the Roman period, unrecognised as such because of the dearth of Mediterranean imports. The wider implications of these discoveries will be explored in this chapter.

Adulis and its harbours

Ancient Adulis was served by two harbours: the ports of Diodorus and Orienê, datable to at least the 1st century AD, and the Aksumite port of Gabaza, the later manifestation of the island of Diodorus. Indeed, given that Adulis was 20 stades from the sea (according to the *Periplus*) it is somewhat surprising that the town should be regarded as a port at all. This is not, though, unusual in the ancient world: Piraeus, the port of Athens, and both Ostia and Portus, the ports of Rome, are some distance away from the cities they serve, whilst the port of Tyre was originally situated on an island opposite the mainland settlement (Keay 2006; Blackman 1982; Frost 1995). Separating port and town in this manner has a number of distinct social, political and economic advantages, including greater protection against sea-borne attack, prevention of contact between the indigenous populace and potentially subversive foreign traders, and ensuring the maintenance of law and order within the environs of the town itself. Market trading can also be an explosive affair: the 'peace of the market' is an important consideration and creating a distinct area for trade ensures greater ease of regulation and control. The market thus effectively becomes a 'neutral ground', an area away from the main settlement where trade can occur under the supervision of a central authority (Blackman 1982; Blue 1995; Karmon 1985), a phenomenon originally documented in the markets of the Berber highlands (see Benet 1957).

The ports of Adulis do therefore seem to be true 'ports of trade', or the places at which trade actually occurred. Interestingly, Adulis is described in the *Periplus* as a 'legally designated emporion', or 'legally limited port', 'ἐμπόριον νόμιμον', a title only ascribed to two other ports in the text, Muza on the Yemen coast and Apologos at the head of the Persian Gulf. There has been considerable debate amongst scholars about what this actually means (see for example Palmer 1951; Huntingford 1980; Casson 1989 and Chapter II, above); clearly it cannot mean that trade conducted at any other Red Sea or Indian Ocean port was illegal. The situation at Adulis seems to suggest that the phrase 'legally designated emporion' is indicative of an area in which trading *had* to occur outside of the town, within an officially designated area, an interpretation which seems more logical than the traditional view forwarded by Palmer (1951) that such ports were 'a law abiding mart' or a place 'where traders are protected by law', a necessity of any market. This is supported by the lack of recognisably Roman imported material within Adulis, suggesting that the local population (or at least the majority of it) did not have access to the luxuries accrued from sea-borne commerce. It was suggested by Aristotle that a city should have two agoras, one for political and administrative purposes, the other a trading area segregated from the city because of basic hostility towards traders. In ancient Greece, foreign traders were not normally allowed into the city and the *emporion* was devised to facilitate overseas trade without admitting aliens into the city (Stanley 1983). It is entirely possible that this arrangement applied at Adulis, separating the cultures of Rome and East Africa.

Significantly, the ancient settlements of both Muza (modern Mocha, or al Mukha) and Apologos (Ubulla, near Basra on the Shatt al Arab) are as enigmatic and uncertain as Adulis once was, perhaps for the same reason: separating town and port deprived the settlements of the Mediterranean imports which would have led to their easy identification. Removal of these trading restrictions would also explain the growth of the settlement from the 'fair sized village' of the *Periplus* to the bustling, cosmopolitan centre described by Cosmas Indicopleustes in the 6th century AD.

It is interesting to note that the two Roman harbours discovered in this study are of a very different genre. It would appear that Diodorus Island was essentially a mooring, with ships sheltering in the lee of the island: sedimentological analysis suggests that the rock was once surrounded by open sea, whilst the *Periplus* describes a causeway linking the island to the mainland, though it is unclear whether this causeway was permanently accessible or reliant upon the tide. In contrast, the harbour on Dese is a lagoon, providing ships with ample shelter from adverse weather. It is uncertain whether there would have been significant harbour structures around Diodorus Island, but they may have existed on Dese; it is possible that linear features visible on the satellite image are indicative of such structures, and it is a matter of regret that we were unable to return to Dese to investigate further. Both harbour types were common along the ancient route to India. The enclosed type is paralleled by Aden, Moscha Limen and Myos Hormos, whilst the open is found at Berenike, Qana' and probably Muza (see appendix for further discussion). There seems to be no consistent nomenclature that links either to typology or topography, with some referred to as 'Hormos' others as 'Limen'. Casson (1989, appendix 1) translates the former as harbour and the latter as port, but it appears the terms were interchangeable (Flemming 1980; Blue 1995).

Analysis of ceramics recovered from the harbours has provided us with chronological indicators for both Diodorus Island and Oreinê. The amphorae suggest a late 1st century BC – early 1st century AD date for Diodorus Island, with fine-ware dating to the 1st century BC through to the Augustan period. Dese, however, would appear to be later: the fine-ware is certainly Augustan, but the presence of the handle of a possible Gauloise 4 amphora could date the site to between perhaps AD 50 through to even the end of the 3rd century AD. The evidence is unfortunately scant, but broadly favours activity in 1st century BC or early 1st century AD for Diodorus Island, overlapping with Dese which could then have continued in use until at least the latter part of the same century or beyond. The *Periplus* suggests that during the mid 1st century Orienê was the favoured harbour, as attacks from local *barbaroi* had made the use of Diodorus Island untenable. Fresh water was apparently available at the latter, but the water of Dese is brackish and scarce. If Orienê was to be used for a prolonged period then an adequate infrastructure would have to be in place to provide the harbour with logistical support from the mainland. The evidence from this survey would thus appear to support the descriptions of the *Periplus*, though both harbours may have been known and in use at least by the Augustan period. The *Periplus* does not, however, provide any indication of how long Dese had been utilised as an alternative anchorage, nor can we know for how long the *Periplus* remained 'current'. It is possible that both harbours were in use frequently, with external circumstances or security issues determining which one was utilised at different times.

The location of the Aksumite harbour of Gabaza is, however, reasonably certain. Sundström (1907) recorded both Aksumite pottery and structures on the Galala Hills, though he wrongly labelled them Gamez. In contrast to the earlier period, there must have been harbour installations: the 6th century *Martyrdom of St Arethas*, describing the military expedition to the Arabian peninsula requested by Emperor Justin in Constantinople in retaliation for the killing of Christians in Najran, indicates that ships were built at Gabaza, and the port also seems to have been a point of embarkation for journeys across the Red Sea. None of these installations were found, but as the coring suggests considerable siltation in this area, they may be very deeply buried; a programme of geophysics, using methods designed to penetrate this overburden, may resolve the issue. The sixty ships gathered by King Kaleb of Aksum for the punitive expedition mentioned in the *Martyrdom* would suggest that the harbour could accommodate a large number of vessels, although these may have lain offshore.

Trade

It is clear that there was a thriving market at Adulis during the Roman period. The *Periplus* describes a market for:

> articles of clothing for the Barbaroi, unused, the kind produced in Egypt; wraps from Arsinoe; coloured abollai [cloaks] of printed fabric; linens; double fringed items; numerous types of glass stones and also of millefiori glass of the kind produced in Diospolis; brass, which they use for ornaments as well as cutting up into coins; copper honey pans (?) for cooking and for cutting up into armlets and anklets for certain of the women; iron which is expended on spears for elephants and other wild animals as well as for war. Likewise there is also a market for: axes, adzes, knives; large round copper drinking vessels; a little Roman money for resident foreigners; wine of Laodicea and Italy, limited quantity; olive oil, limited quantity. For the king, silverware and goldware fashioned in the local manner; in clothing, abollai and kaunakai [heavy cloaks], with no adornment and modest in price. Likewise also, from the interior of Ariake: Indian iron and steel; cotton cloth of the broader make, the so-called monache and sagmatogene; girdles; kaunakai; garments of molochinon; garments of cotton in limited number; lac dye. Exports from this area are: ivory, tortoise shell, rhinoceros horn. Most exporting from Egypt to this port of trade is from January to September, that is from Tybi to Thoth; the best time for departure from Egypt is around the month of September (Casson, 1989, 54–5).

Of this impressive list we have very little archaeological evidence at Adulis or its ports, with the exception of the Italian wine jars recovered from Diodorus Island and Dese. Interestingly the Laodicean amphorae highlighted by the *Periplus* have not yet been recognised in the archaeological record, though they do appear to be something of an archaeological enigma: the presence of Laodicean wine throughout the Roman world (and especially Roman Egypt) is well documented in the classical sources (see Tomber 1998), and it is testimony to the importance of the market at Adulis that this wine reached the peripheries of the empire, in whatever quantities. These amphorae are merely the tip of an iceberg, standing proxy for a huge range of perishable goods or valuable items. The connection with Roman Egypt is also supported by small pieces of obsidian recovered from excavations at Quseir al-Qadim that can be sourced to the Eritrean coastline (see above) and the presence of small fragments of local pottery similar to that found at Adulis and Diodorus Island (Tomber 2005b).

The presence of large quantities of imported amphorae makes the Aksumite trade of Adulis somewhat easier to determine. Though we naturally know little of the perishable goods, the 6th century writings of Cosmas Indicopleustes suggest that incense and spices were important objects of trade:

> The region which produces frankincense is situated at the projecting parts of Ethiopia, and lies inland, but is washed by the ocean on the other side. Hence the inhabitants of Barbaria, being near to hand, go up into the interior and, engaging in traffic with the natives, bring back from them many kinds of spices, frankincense, cassia, calamus, and many other articles of merchandise, which they afterwards send by sea to Adulê, to the country of the Homerites, to further India and Persia (McCrindle 1897; Wolska-Conus 1968, 356).

The 'country of the Homerites' can be equated to modern Yemen, whilst the production region must be the highlands of what is now Somaliland. It is significant that Cosmas mentions this area, but not the main production region of southern Arabia. It is possible that by this period Arabian incense went across the desert once again, following the traditional route to Gaza, and Cosmas knew only of the seaborne trade; equally the trade from Somaliland may have overtaken southern Arabia in importance by the beginning of the 6th century. This latter view is supported to some extent by the archaeological evidence from Qana', which suggests that the port was in decline throughout this period (Sedov 2007).

The import of both Cassia and Calamus to Adulis is also interesting. Cassia (*Cinnamomum cassia*) is sometimes known as False Cinnamon – a bark similar in appearance and taste to true Cinnamon, which originated in China and flourishes in hot, wet climates. It is a spice which is often used as flavouring, but also has medicinal attributes as a tonic, carminative or stimulant and in the treatment of nausea and diarrhoea. Calamus (*Acorus calamus*, or Sweet Flag) is a grass with a root which, when ingested, has hallucinogenic properties. It is a hardy semi-aquatic plant, growing almost anywhere in the northern hemisphere where there is ample water and sunshine. Both Calamus and Cassia were known in Biblical times as key ingredients of 'holy anointing oil' (*Exodus* 30, 22–25); Calamus, along with frankincense, would be utilised in church liturgy which is almost certainly why Cosmas, the biblical zealot, felt it necessary to record them. Adulis was well endowed with churches: three have been excavated, two by Paribeni (1907) and one by the British Museum in 1868 (Munro-Hay 1989a; see also Chapter II).

It is doubtful, however, whether such quantities of incense would have been destined solely for use in the churches of Adulis. Adulis was, above all, a trade centre, and it is probable that much of the incense would have been in transit elsewhere. Indeed, Cosmas himself states that

> On the coast of Ethiopia, two miles off from the shore, is a town called Adulê, which forms the port of the Axômites and is much frequented by traders who come from Alexandria and the Elanitic Gulf [Gulf of Aqaba]. (McCrindle 1897; Wolska-Conus 1968, 364).

We have yet to find traces of Alexandrian traders at Adulis, but the maritime connection with Suez is confirmed by the mention of ships from Clysma (Suez) in the *Martyrdom of St Arethas*. Suez may well have been a transit point on the route to Alexandria – the Trajanic canal connecting the Red Sea and the Nile was operational at this period, and from *c.* AD170 it would have been possible to sail between Alexandria and Clysma (Jackson 2002, 76). In contrast, the traders from Aqaba are well represented in the archaeological material. The surface of the site is littered with pottery, the bulk of which are 6th–7th century amphorae, costrels and coarse-ware from the kilns at Aqaba (Melkawi, 'Amr and Whitcomb 1994; Tomber 2004b). The same type is found at Aksum and Qana', though only one example (in Bodrum Museum) is known from the Mediterranean (Phillipson, 2000, fig 283; Alpözen, Özdaş and Berkaya, 1995, 101). It seems probable therefore that incense traded through Adulis, would have found its way to Aqaba, thence to the region of modern Jordan and Israel.

It is difficult to gauge what might have been carried in these Aqaba amphorae. Aqaba itself is surrounded by desert, so there seem to be but two possibilities: fish products or dates from the oasis, unless they contained produce brought from the hinterland. We discuss the problem above, favouring either wine or date products as the most probable content. Late Roman 1 from southern eastern Turkey or Cyprus, and Late Roman 2 from the Aegean have also been recovered from the site, though in lesser quantities. These are most densely concentrated in the northern and eastern areas of the site which most likely relate to the later stages of occupation at Adulis. The contents of both are a matter of debate but wine seems probable in the case of late Roman 1 (Pieri 2005). Very little Late Roman 3 is present, though what is found at Adulis is likely to have originated in Asia Minor. Perhaps the most exotic amphorae are the Africana, usually represented by body sherds. Again these are mostly concentrated in the northern and eastern areas of the site. It is possible that these amphorae contained oil, but some might also have borne fish sauces (see http://ads.ahds.ac.uk/catalogue/archive/amphora_ahrb_2005 for more details).

Marble also seems to have been imported in considerable quantities, mostly, if not exclusively, for use in church architecture. The predominant type was Proconnesian from the Turkish island of Marmaris or alabaster, probably from Egypt – though as Keith Matthews notes above, it is significant that not all of the marbles recovered from Adulis were Proconnesian in origin. Cosmas Indicopleustes was similarly explicit in his statement that the throne at Adulis was made of 'costly white marble' *not* from the quarries of Proconneseus. More exotic marbles recovered from Adulis include Porfido Verde from southern Greece, Travertine from the banks of the Tiber and the Bianco e Nero from the Pyrenees, along with a white marble perhaps from Dokimeion. The presence of these marbles in churches in Hagia Sophia suggests that they are likely to have come from Constantinople, arriving in Adulis as items of trade or as gifts from church or state.

Local pottery

One of the major outcomes of our work is the discovery of local pottery in association with Mediterranean imports, thus enabling the construction of at least a tentative chronology for the local wares. However as the material was not excavated but found on the surface, the dating must, of necessity, be taken to be indicative rather than secure. The most important site is Diodorus Island, where all the imports are closely datable and include no later, Aksumite material. The local wares can thus with some certainty be dated to the early 1st century AD, or perhaps the latter part of the 1st century BC at the earliest. The fabrics are of types which Tomber (2004b) regards as typical of the Adulis region.

The site of Adulis itself has produced local wares which appear to be of two dates. The earlier material from the south west corner could potentially be Roman in date, though this is not certain. The association with shell fragments radiocarbon dated to the 1st to 3rd centuries AD is, however, suggestive and implies that the hand-made wares need not be so archaic as previously thought. The hand-made wares from the rest of the site appear to be Aksumite in date, loosely associated with later imports. The fabrics of both the early and later ceramics are very similar, suggesting local use of the same or similar raw materials.

Adulis and Aksum

The relationship between Adulis, on the coast of modern Eritrea, and Aksum, in the highlands of modern Ethiopia is a contentious one; more so given the history of hostility and cross-border tensions following Eritrean independence in 1993. It follows therefore that any statement discussing the relationship between the two cities in antiquity has the potential to be utilised for different agendas in the present. It is nevertheless essential that we examine the relationship between Adulis and Aksum if we are to place either site within its contemporary social, political and economic context.

There is ample evidence that, in the Aksumite period, Adulis was the port of Aksum itself. Archaeologically, the presence of Ayla-Aksum and Late Roman 1 imported amphorae on both sites suggests at the very least a close trading relationship (Williams 2000, 494–6), which may also be indicated by the common coarse-ware forms. Without detailed petrographic study of the fabrics on both sites, it is, however, unwise to suggest a movement of coarse pottery. Architecturally, too, the sites demonstrate great similarities, with the presence of 'stepped walls' or 'graduated masonry' and spiral columns at Adulis, Aksum and other Aksumite towns of the period (see Bent 1896; Sundström 1907; Wenig 2002), though this may of course be merely indicative of a regional aesthetic. The result of the geophysics provides us with a potential insight into the relationship between Adulis and Aksum in the fourth, 5th and 6th centuries – the apparent lack of a defensive wall, mirrored in other Aksumite towns in the region (Munro-Hay 1989b, 9), must surely indicate a centralised military power in the region, guaranteeing the protection of such an economically and politically vital port. Inscriptions at Aksum highlight the ruthlessness of the Aksumite kingdom in subjugating neighbouring peoples and in putting down revolts (Munro-Hay 1989b, 8), and it is almost inconceivable that a fully independent state would not feel the need to protect itself with a substantial defensive wall on the doorstep of Aksum, one of the superpowers of antiquity.

The historical sources would also seem to indicate an intimate connection between the two cities. Cosmas relates that the king of the Aksumites showed considerable interest in trade, particularly in gold, salt and iron mining and it is reasonable to assume that this interest resulted in the obvious growth of Adulis from a 'fair-sized village' to the metropolis of the late antique, visible in the geophysical survey. Perhaps most significantly, we are told by Cosmas that he was asked to copy the inscriptions of the *Monumetum Adulitanum* for Elesbaas [Kaleb], king of the Aksumites, doubtless to lend historic justification to his punitive expedition to Arabia, launched from Gabaza. That the inscription outlining the achievements of an Aksumite King was to be found at Adulis, and that Gabaza was chosen as the rallying point for the expedition without apparent reference or deference to local authorities, would suggest that Adulis of the 6th century was at the very least a client kingdom of Aksum, if not part of the Kingdom itself. It is noteworthy that the title *negusa negast*, King of Kings, found upon royal inscriptions at Aksum refers to the King of Aksum himself, suggesting that he had authority over a number of regional, subordinate authorities (Munro-Hay 1989b, 8).

The theory that Adulis was a client kingdom is lent further credence by the mausolea at Samidi, identified by the project 7 kilometres to the north of the Adulis itself. The presence of small quantities of Aqaba and Late Roman amphora suggest a 6th century date and argue against anything but a ceremonial function for the site. The prominent location of the mausolea, overlooking the full expanse of the plain and the Gulf of Zula, and in the case of the southern mound at least dominated by a sophisticated architectural structure, must indicate internment of people of rank, supported by the inclusion of the site within the work of Cosmas Indicopleustes. It is feasible to speculate that the mausolea at Samidi are royal tombs, the last resting place of the Kings of Adulis (*c.f.* the Royal burial chambers and rock-cut tombs of Aksum itself, see Munro-Hay 1989b; Phillipson 2000). Significantly, Procopius still refers to the 'harbour of the Adulitae' in the 6th century (*History of the Wars* I xix) whilst inscriptions recorded by Littmann (1913) and Schneider (1974) at Aksum appear to indicate that separate tribal or ethnic groups retained individual identities long after they were subsumed within the expanding Aksumite empire.

The evidence for the relationship between Adulis and Aksum in the Roman period is, however, a little more ambiguous. Munro-Hay (1996a) argues that Adulis first begun trading with the Arabian peninsula in the first millennium BC, prior to the development of Aksum itself. The classical sources are also intriguing, with both Pliny (*NH* VI, 72) and later Claudius Ptolemy (*Geography* IV, 7, 8) appearing to distinguish between the populations of Adulis and the east African interior and highlands – though this may of course be indicative of the client relationship postulated above. The *Periplus* too refers to the 'city of the Aksumites' and to Zoscales, the ruler of Adulis, though it also states that it is a journey of some eight days from Adulis to the *metropolis itself*, suggesting that Aksum was already more prominent than Adulis. Though others have argued that Zoscales himself was an early King of Aksum (Munro-Hay 1989a, 43; *cf.* Huntingford 1980, 148), the evidence would seem to suggest that Adulis retained a greater degree of autonomy in the 1st century than the 6th, whilst maintaining close economic ties to Aksum. Perhaps the best modern parallel is the relationship between China and Hong Kong, the latter continuing to operate as a separate entity following its transition to Chinese rule in the late 1990s. Such a relationship would enable Aksum to benefit economically, whilst allowing Adulis to gain from the administration of the market at the port and its own affairs. Whoever 'controlled' the region in the 1st century, their influence was not yet great enough to guarantee the protection of ships at Diodorus Island, resulting in the removal of harbour operations to the island of Dese.

It is clear however that neither Adulis nor Aksum would have risen to prominence without the support of the other. Adulis was Aksum's link to the outside world, the focal point of a trade and communication network that stretched from the Mediterranean to the Indian Ocean, whilst the military and political might of 'the metropolis' provided protection for Adulis, in a geographically isolated position on the coast of the Red Sea. The relationship between Adulis and Aksum was thus a symbiotic one, with both drawing upon the other as a source of power and prestige.

The origin and end of Adulis

An understanding of the origins of Adulis must await further excavation. It is plausible that some of the archaic wares discovered by Paribeni will prove to be much earlier than the Roman date postulated here. The inscriptions on the basanite stone erected by Ptolemy III Euegertes of Egypt (247–222 BC) and later copied by Cosmas, implies a Ptolemaic beginning, but at present no trace has been found. Similarly, we have little indication of the date of the marble throne itself, clearly an important historical monument in the town, though it would appear that the inscription relates to the exploits of a King of Aksum. It has been suggested that the stone tablet, already inscribed, was brought to Adulis at a later date, with Ptolemais Theron a possible source (see Kirwan 1972 and above). It is worth noting that there appears to be no mention of Adulis in the inscription itself, simply the region of the Troglodytes and Ethiopia. If a settlement did exist at Adulis prior to the 1st century AD it is perhaps likely to have been a relatively small trading post and thus difficult to document archaeologically.

The end of Adulis is equally difficult to discern. The most remarkable feature of the site is its complete destruction: it is almost unique for an ancient city in southern latitudes as not a single building or ruin can be seen above ground. It is possible that this is the result of a considerable earthquake, though it is unlikely that an earthquake would result in such comprehensive destruction; the characteristic fall patterns have not been noted (Stiros and Jones 1996) and there is no record for substantial seismic activity in this part of the Red Sea in the 7th or 8th centuries (Ambraseys, Melville and Adams 1994). It has been suggested therefore that the destruction of Adulis was a consequence of human agency. We have little record of the site from the 7th century, and none from the 8th, correlating with the conflict between the Muslim Arabs and the Christian Aksumites (Pankhurst 1961). It is clear from the excavations of both Paribeni (1907) and Sundström (1907) that fierce fires raged across the site, destroying substantial buildings and fusing together metal objects, and it has been postulated that the site was destroyed by the Arab naval expedition of 'Umar ibn al-Khattab in 640 (*e.g.* Budge 1928, 274; Pankhurst 1961, 56). Given that Munro-Hay (1982, 117) records coinage from the site up to *c.* 700AD, this hypothesis would appear to be untenable.

It may be that no single factor can be attributed to the demise of Adulis. Political shifts in the 7th century associated with the emergent Islamic empire certainly disrupted the trade routes that were the life-blood of the port, whilst factors internal to the Aksumite Kingdom cannot be overlooked. The evidence from Aksum itself would seem to indicate an increasing number of revolts throughout this period, whilst material from the city suggests that it too fell into decline in the latter stages of the 7th century, when the political capital was moved elsewhere (Butzer 1981). These events correlate well with the decline of Adulis, and its is reasonable to assume therefore that administrative or political upheaval resulted in a shift of emphasis away from the traditional trade routes of the Red Sea and the port of Adulis. The fires that clearly ravaged the site may or may not have been set deliberately; it is unlikely that we shall ever know the answer. It is clear however that, by the beginning of the 8th century, the port was no longer considered important enough to rebuild.

Appendix
The topography of Periplus ports: a comparison

David Peacock and Lucy Blue

Introduction

The discovery of the location of the ports of Diodorus Island and Oreine raises the question the reasons for choice and whether these locations are typical of other ports mentioned in the *Periplus*. In order to limit the problem environmentally, only those in the Red Sea and the Gulf of Aden will be considered, with the exception of Mosyllon, the site of which remains very uncertain. Qana, Aden, Mocha, Quseir and Berenike were visited and thus their location was assessed at first hand. However, the others are less accessible either because they have not been located or because they lie in difficult areas: these have been assessed from satellite images.

Myos Hormos (Quseir al-Qadim)

This is the most northerly of the Egyptian Red Sea Ports. As a result of recent work (Peacock and Blue 2006), we now know that the town was sited on a peninsula, with the sea on one side and a lagoon, now silted on the other. Excavations have revealed substantial, if somewhat crude, harbour installations in the lagoon. The town was in a naturally defensive situation, but it was not possible to establish whether the peninsula was cut by a defensive ditch or wall, or was left undefended. There must have been a military element at Myos Hormos as Strabo (*Geog*. 17.1.45) tells us that there was a naval base here and that Aelius Gallus disembarked here after his campaign in Arabia (*Geog*. 16.4.24). The port seems to have operated from the Ptolemaic period (for which there is minimal evidence) to some time in the 3rd century AD, when it was abandoned.

Berenike (Berenice)

Berenike, which seems to have operated from the Ptolemaic period to the 6th century AD, and has been extensively excavated by a Dutch-American team (Sidebotham and Wendrich, 1995, 1996, 1999, 2000). The site is on a headland with a silted lagoon to the south, which would have been the ancient habour. Today it is cut off by a sand bar, the formation of which probably led to the demise of the port in the 6th century. Again there is no trace of landward defences. Pottery ranges in date from Ptolemaic to 5th century AD and the very last mention of the site is in the *Martyrdom of St Arethas* (above, p.10). It seems to have been the favoured port for voyages to and from India with a much longer lifespan than Myos Hormos, presumably because it would avoid ships battling for a further 300 km against the northerly winds, which are a persistent feature of the Red Sea at this latitude. It is very similar to Myos Hormos in general topography and siting.

Ptolemais Theron (Aqiq)

The site of Ptolemais Theron has yet to be located, but there are some strong indications. The location of the site has been a matter discussion for many years, with proposed locations ranging from Suakin to Marsa Maqdam, Trinkitat and Aqiq, although Aqiq is the favoured locality because of Crowfoot's discovery of Graeco-Roman moulding embedded in a later structure (Casson 1989, 101; Burstein 1989). The area was briefly re-examined in 2004 (Seeger *et al.* 2006).

However, it is possible to make some deductions from the ancient sources, two of which are significant: the *Periplus* and the Geography of Strabo. Both of these proved incredibly accurate when applied to Quseir. The *Periplus* (Casson 1989, 51) tells us that Ptolemais Theron lay 4000 stades from Berenike. Assuming the length of a stade to be 166.67 m, 4000 stades would be 667 km (see below under Avalites). Measuring this distance from Berenike leads to the bay of Aqiq.

Strabo (*Geog.* 16.4.7), tells us that the port was founded as a base to support hunting elephants by Eumedes, who had been sent there by Ptolemy II Philadelphus (286–246 BC). Eumedes,

> secretly enclosed a kind of peninsula with a ditch and a wall, and then, by courteous treatment of those who tried to hinder the work, actually won them over as friends instead of foes.

The Pithom stele suggests that this might have taken place between 270 and 264 BC (Seeger *et al.* 2006, 8). From this it seems clear that the site was on a peninsula. However, by the time of the *Periplus* it was said to have no harbour and had to be approached in small boats. By then it was a source of ivory and tortoise shell rather than elephants. However, it would have been impossible to load elephants onto small boats so the implication is that the harbour had silted up and it might be even more silted today. In other words we should look for a peninsula and adjacent silted harbour.

There are very few places in the Aqiq region that fulfill these criteria and examination of them on satellite images points to one particular spot 18° 11′ 18.38″N, 38° 21′ 58.86″E. Here there is a peninsula with a unique texture giving the appearance of blocks which might well be house foundations. There is nothing like it anywhere in the area and it therefore seems unlikely to be natural. All the other peninsulas are different and evidently entirely geological. The structure of the anomalous peninsula bears a striking resemblance to Islamic 'Aydhab in the Halaib triangle, although less crisp as might be expected for a much older site. Next to it is what might have been a silted harbour.

Recently, fluted column fragments have been found about 15 km away near the village of Aqiq (http://www.barnard.nl/desert/ptolemais.html, Seeger *et al.* 2006). It is possible that Ptolemais Theron was located in this area, but it is 3 km from the sea and there is no sign of a fossil peninsula showing on the satellite image. There will of course have been coastal change, but experience at Adulis leads to the expectation that this might be limited to the coastal 500 m, where the satellite image reveals a colour change to brown sediment. It seems more probable that the column fragments represent an extramural building, perhaps a rural temple, but this can only be ascertained by more survey preferably accompanied by geophysics.

Adulis

The two harbours of Diodorus island and Oreinê were located in the course of the present field work. The location contrasts with the above as there is no peninsula for the settlement, which lay at Adulis some distance away. The Red Sea winds are less ferocious here and it seems that in times of inclement weather the ships would moor in the lee of the Diodorus island or the adjacent Galala Hills. Oreinê has a magnificent lagoonal harbour and an adjacent settlement in the central valley of Dese.

Okêlis and Muza

These two sites have never been satisfactorily located, although Muza is thought to equate with modern Mocha in Yemen. If this is correct there was virtually no natural harbour here. The bay around the old town is protected to some extent by a spit of land which on Heuglin's map of 1852 is marked 'Nord Fort'. It seems to comprise an island connected to the land by a tombolo. In the middle of the bay is a projecting mole marked 'Hafendamm' (http://www.lib.utexas.edu/maps/historical/red_sea_1860.jpg). This still shows on the satellite image as a dark submerged structure. There is a vague suggestion of a further structure running at right angles to it cutting off a corner of the bay. If this is the ancient harbour, which has not been confirmed, it would have been an artificially created one, perhaps similar to that at Acre. Examination of the site on the ground produced no evidence for the harbour and underwater investigations would be needed.

Okêlis is believed to lie on the Yemeni side of the Bab el-Mandeb. The position of Okêlis is given rather precisely in the *Periplus* (25–26). It is said to be on the straits, 1200 stades (200 km) west of Aden. Casson (1989, 158) plausibly suggests that the site is located at Shaykh Sa'îd or Khawr Ghurayah, where there is a lagoon, possibly a silted harbour. It is described as not so much a port, but a watering station for those sailing on. Another possibility might be the village of Dhubab, 30 km further north, which is precisely 200 km from Aden by sea. The village is situated on a headland which has what appears to be a natural promontory jutting southwards cutting off a sheltered south facing bay. There are, in effect, two harbours – a northern and a southern on either side of the headland. It might repay archaeological investigation, but a short visit in May 2007 produced no evidence either way.

Avalites

Assab has been equated with Avalites of the *Periplus* (13–14) and it has an adequate harbour. The main reason for this is the statement that it lay in the narrowest point between Africa and Arabia of the trading with Okêlis and Muza. The problem is that the distance given from Adulis to Avalites is 4800 stades.

The problem of the length of a stade was reviewed by Schoff (1912, 54). It appears that three different measures were in vogue at the time of the *Periplus*. However, now that it has been established that Myos Hormos equates with Quseir al-Qadim (Peacock and Blue 2006) we can calculate the length of a stadium accurately for we are told that it is 1800 stadia from Myos Hormos to Berenike, a distance of exactly 300 km. This gives the length of a stadium as 166.67 m. This in turn means that the distance between Adulis and Avalitês was 800 km. It is possible that the *Periplus* is in error, but testing the above formula on other known points of reference suggests that generally it is incredibly accurate. As Assab is only about 400 km from Adulis, any error would be of the order of 100%, which seems unlikely. An alternative contender is Saylac or Zeila in Somaliland which is exactly 800 km from Adulis. This is supported to some extent by another co-ordinate, because the distance from Avalites to Malaô is given as 800 stades. The latter is almost certainly modern Berbera, which is about 200 km from Zeila, more like 1800 stades. On the other hand the distance from Assab to Berbera is about 400 km or 3,500 stades. The odds are stacked more favourably in favour of Saylac rather than Assab. Placing Avalites in Somaliland resolves many problems, not least why it is referred to as the first of the 'far side' ports. If we assume that the author was referring, not to the narrows of the Bab el Mandeb, but to the narrowest point of crossing the Gulf of Aden to Arabia everything begins to fit into place. However, it is worth noting that Claudius Ptolemy (Book 4, Chapter 7), writing in the 2nd century AD quite unequivocally places Avalitês 'after the strait in the Red Sea' (Stevenson 1932, 107).

No Roman antiquities have been found at Saylac, although there is a bay, now much silted, which might have formed a harbour. However, Curle (1937) records an Islamic settlement on Saad al Din island, about 6 km to the north. It is possible that earlier Roman period remains underlie the Islamic ones. If this is correct, Avalites would have been located on an island.

Eudaimon Arabia (Aden)

Aden is, even today, a major port and is one of the very few to remain viable from the time of the *Periplus*. The *Periplus* (26:8.22–32) describes it as the meeting place for ships coming from India and those coming from Egypt as neither dare make the full journey. The author adds the remark that 'not long before our time, Caesar sacked it' implying that it was no longer used for this purpose or that it now played a much reduced role. This was almost certainly during the campaign of Aelius Gallus in 16–25 BC, the only known Roman attack on South Arabia. Casson (1989, 160) reviews the extensive debate which this statement has generated.

However, analysis of basalt ballast from Myos Hormos / Qusier al-Qadim suggests that 30% originated at Aden (Peacock, Williams and James 2007). This might be Islamic, but there is no evidence for Islamic use of ballast and if Roman it suggests that the fortunes of Aden revived in the 1st and 2nd centuries AD.

The harbour is sheltered and capacious. It is about 10 km wide and 5 km deep between the twin volcanic massifs of Jebel Shamsan and Little Aden. It is thus on a different scale to any of the ports hitherto considered. The precise location of the Roman period settlement has yet to be discovered, but presumably it lies well buried under modern Aden town.

Kane (Qana)

The site of Kane is well known and has been the subject of many years of excavation by a Russian team. Sedov (2007) conveniently summarises the main findings. The site lies on a peninsula guarded by the citadel of Husn al-Ghurab. There are sandy bays to the north and south which would have been admirable for beaching boats although no harbour installations have yet been found. The rock of Husn al-Ghurab might have provided shelter in the lee of which ships could moor. Sedimentological investigation is needed for a more detailed appreciation of the location of the harbour or harbours.

Moscha Limen (Khor Rori)

Moscha Limen was clearly an important port in the frankincense trade – a collection point for resin which was then taken to Qana. It was however used as an over-wintering point for ships that had arrived too late to catch the Monsoon wind to India (Casson 1989, 172–3). The site, which is almost certainly to be located at Khor Rori, lies some 37 km east of Salalah in the Dhofar region of Oman and has been extensively excavated in recent years (Avanzini 2002). The town lies on an elevated knoll, about 1 km from the sea on a deep sheltered inlet, which at this point is about 300 m across. It is today cut off from the sea by a sand bar, but would have been an admirable, south facing and secure harbour.

Malaô

It is generally agreed that Malaô equates with modern Berbera in Somaliland. Here there is a fine harbour protected by an east-west spur of land from the sea. Like Aden it is still a viable and important port. Nothing is known of the archaeology as no-one has looked.

Mundu

Casson (1989, 126) suggests that Mundu is to be located at Heis on the Somaliland coast. The *Periplus* states that at Mundu there was an island very near the shore. This is precisely the case at Heis and on it Chittick (1979, 1981) recorded Roman pottery and glass of the 1st to 5th centuries AD. There is at present no reason to question this attribution.

Conclusion

It appears that there was a preference for ports either on an island or on a peninsula guarding a lagoon. Only Aden, Malao and possibly Kane seem to have been located by bays. This clearly reflects the need for both ease of access and defence. Interestingly, all the supposed Ptolemaic installations are on a peninsula of some sort which suggests some sort of deliberate choice and policy, at least in the earliest phase of exploitation.

Harbour works have been found at Quseir and they might exist at Muza as this is on a relatively exposed piece of coast. It may well be that these are the exception and that normally locations were left in their natural state, with minor modifications, although Aden is such a pivotal point it would be surprising if they did not exist there.

Bibliography

Aharoni, Y., Evenari, M., Shanan, L., and Tadmor, N.H., 1960. The ancient agriculture of the Negev. *Israel Exploration Journal*, 10, 23–36.

Alpözen, T.O., Özdaş, A.H., and Berkaya, B., 1995. *Commercial amphoras of the Bodrum museum of underwater archaeology. Maritime trade of the Mediterranean in ancient times.* Bodrum.

Ambraseys, N.N., Melville, C.P., and Adams, R.D., 1994. *The Seismicity of Egypt, Arabia and the Red Sea. A historical review.* Cambridge.

Anfray, F., 1974. Deux villes Axoumites: Adoulis et Matara. *VI Cong. Int. di Studi Etiopici*, Rome, 745–65.

Avanzini, A., 2002. *Khor Rori Report 1.* Pisa

Bailey, D.M., 1980. *A catalogue of lamps in the British Museum. Vol. 2 Roman lamps made in Italy.* London.

Benet, F. 1957. Explosive markets: Berber Highlands. In K. Polanyi, C.M. Arensberg and H.W. Pearson (eds) *Trade and Market in Early Empires.* Glencoe, Illinois, 188–217.

Bent, J.T., 1896. *The sacred city of the Ethiopians. Being a record of travel and research in Abyssinia in 1893.* London.

Blackman, D.J., 1982. Ancient Harbours in the Mediterranean. Part I & II. *International Journal of Nautical Archaeology,* 11, 79–104, 185–212.

Blue, L.K., 1995. *A topographical analysis of the location of harbours and anchorages of the eastern Mediterranean in the Middle and Late Bronze Ages, and their relation to routes of trade.* Unpublished Oxford DPhil thesis.

Borghini, G., 1997. *Marmi antichi.* Rome.

Brun, J–P. 2004. *Archéologie du vin et de l'huile dans l'Empire Romain.* Paris

Budge, E.A.W., 1928. *History of Ethiopia, Nubia and Abyssinia, volume 1.* London.

Burstein, S.M., 1989. *Agatharchides of Cnidus: on the Erythraean Sea.* London.

Butzer, K.W., 1981. Rise and fall of Axum, Ethiopia. A geo–archaeological interpretation. *American Antiquity,* 40, 471–95.

Caley, E.R. and Richards, J.C. 1956. *Theophrastus on stones.* Columbus.

Cann, J.R. and Renfrew, C., 1964. The characterisation of obsidian and its application to the Mediterranean region. *Proc. Prehist. Soc.*, 8, 111–133.

Casson, L., 1981. The location of Adulis (Periplus Maris Erythraei 4). In L. Casson and M. Price (eds) *Coins, culture and history in the ancient world.* Detroit, 113–22.

Casson, L., 1989. *The Periplus Maris Erythraei.* Princeton.

Chittick N., 1979. Early ports in the Horn of Africa. *International Journal of Nautical Archaeology,* 8, 273– 277.

Chittick, N., 1981. The Periplus and the spice trade. *Azania*, 16, 187– 8.

Coleman, N., and Walker, S., 1979. Stable isotope identification of Greek and Turkish marbles, *Archaeometry*, 21, 107–112.

Connah, G., 1987. *African civilizations: Precolonial cities and states in tropical Africa. An archaeological perspective.* Cambridge.

Craig, H., 1957. Isotopic standards for carbon and oxygen and correction factors for mass spectrometric analysis of $C0_2$, *Geochim. Cosmochim. Acta*, 12, 133–149.

Craig, H., and Craig, V., 1972. Greek marbles: determination of provenance by isotopic analysis, *Science*, 176, 401–403.

Curle, A.T., 1937. The ruined towns of Somaliland. *Antiquity*, 11, 315– 27.

Dodge, H., and Ward–Perkins, B., 1992. *Marble in antiquity. Collected papers of J.B. Ward–Perkins.* British School at Rome, Monograph 6.

Dolinka, B., 2002. *Nabataean Aila from a ceramic perspective*, British Archaeological Reports Supplementary Series 1116. Oxford.

Doresse, J., 1967. *Ethiopia: Ancient cities and temples*. London.

Edwards, D.N., 1996. *The Archaeology of the Meroitic State. New perspectives on its social and political organisation.* Cambridge Monographs in African Archaeology, 38. BAR International Series, 640.

Emery, W.B., 1948. *Nubian treasure. An account of the discoveries at Ballana and Qustul.* London.

Fattovich, R., 1980. Materiali per lo studio della ceramica pre-Aksumita Etiopica. *Annali Istituto Orientale Napoli*, Suppl. 25. Naples.

Flemming, N.C., 1980. Cities under the Mediterranean. In K. Muckelroy (ed.) *Archaeology underwater: an atlas of the world's submerged sites.* New York, 162–7.

Francaviglia, V.M., 1995 Discriminating between Mediterranean obsidians. *Proc. Geosciences and Archaeology Seminar*, 381–398.

Frost, H., 1995. Harbours and Proto–Harbours: Early Levantine Engineering. In V. Karageorghis, and D. Michaelides (eds) *Cyprus and the Sea.* Proceedings of the International Symposium. Nicosia.

Gardiner, A., 1961. *Egypt of the Pharaohs*. Oxford.

Glueck, N., 1959. *Rivers in the desert*. London.

Gnoli, R., 1971. *Marmora romana*. Rome.

Gupta, S., 2007. Frankincense in the 'triangular' Indo–Arabian–Roman aromatics trade. In D. Peacock and D. Williams (eds) *Food for the gods: new light on the ancient incense trade.* Oxford, 109–18.

Heuglin, Th. v. 1860. *Reise in Nordost–Afrika und längs des Rothen Meeres in Jahre 1857. Mittheilungen aus Justen Perthes geographische Anstalt über wichtige neue Erforchungen auf der Gesammtgebiete der Geographie von Dr A Petermann.* Gotha, 325–62.

Hill, J.E., 2003. *The Western Regions According to the* Hou Han shu. http://www.depts.washington.edu/uwch/silkroad/index.html.

Hill, J.E., 2004. *The Peoples of the West from the* Weilue *by Yu Huan*. http://www.depts.washington.edu/uwch/silkroad/index.html

Hobbs, J., 1989. *Bedouin life in the Egyptian wilderness*. Cairo.

Holland, T.J., and Hozier, H.M., 1870. *Record of the expedition to Abyssinia*. London.

Hourani, G., 1995. *Arab Seafaring.* Expanded edition. New Jersey.

Huntingford, G. W. B., 1980. *Periplus of the Erythraean Sea*. London, the Hakluyt Society.

Jackson, R.B., 2002. *At Empire's edge. Exploring Rome's Egyptian Frontier*. Yale.

Karmon, Y., 1985, Geographical components in the study of ancient Mediterranean ports. In A. Raban (ed.) *Harbour Archaeology. Proceedings of the 1st International workshop on Ancient Harbours. Caesarea Maritima.* BAR International Series, 257, 1–6.

Keay, S., 2006. Portus. Rome's other port. *Current world archaeology*, 20, 11–20.

Kirwan L.P. 1972. The Christian Topography and the Kingdom of Axum. *Geographical Journal* 138, 166–177.

Kitchen, K. A., 1971. Punt and how to get there. *Orientalia*, 40, 184–207.

Kitchen, K. A., 1993. The land of Punt. In T. Shaw, P. Sinclair, B. Andah and A. Okpoko (eds) *The Archaeology of Africa, Food, Metals and Towns*. One World Archaeology, 20, London and New York, 587–608.

Kitchen, K.A., 1999. Further thoughts on Punt and its neighbours. In A. Leahy and J. Tait (eds) *Studies on Ancient Egypt in honour of H.S. Smith*. London, 173–78.

Leese, M.N., 1988. Statistical treatment of stable isotope data. In N. Herz and M. Waelkens (eds) *Classical marble: geochemistry, technology, trade*, Dordrecht, 347–354.

Lefebvre, T., 1845. *Voyage en Abyssinie executé pendant les années 1839,40,41,42*. Paris.

Leslie, D.D., and Gardiner, K.H.J., 1996. *The Roman Empire in Chinese sources*. Rome.

Littmann, E., 1913. *Deutsche Aksum Expedition*. Berlin.

Lynn, C.J., 1984. Some fragments of exotic porphyry found in Ireland. *Journal of Irish Archaeology*, 2, 19–32.

Mayerson, P., 1962. *The ancient agricultural regime of Nessana and the central Negev*. London

McCrea, J.N., 1950. The isotopic chemistry of carbonates and a palaeotemperature scale. *J. Chem. Phys*. 18, 849–857.

McCrindle, J.W.,1897. *The Christian Topography of Cosmas an Egyptian Monk*. London.

Miller, J.I., 1969. *The Spice Trade of the Roman Empire*. Oxford

Melkawi, A., ‘Amr, K., and Whitcomb, D.S., 1994. The excavation of two seventh century pottery kilns at Aqaba. *Annals Department of Antiquities Jordan*, 37, 447–68.

Munro–Hay, S.,1982. The foreign trade of the Aksumite port of Adulis. *Azania, 17*, 107–25.

Munro-Hay, S., 1989a. The British Museum Excavations at Adulis, 1868. *Antiquaries Journal*, 69, 43–52.

Munro-Hay, S., 1989b. The history and chronology. In D.W. Phillipson (ed.) *Excavations at Aksum*. London: British Institute in East Africa, 7–26.

Munro-Hay, S., 1991. *Aksum. An African civilization of late antiquity*. Edinburgh.

Munro-Hay, S., 1996. Aksumite overseas interests. In J. Reade (ed.) *The Indian Ocean in Antiquity*. London, 403–416.

Myatt, F., 1970. *The march to Magdala. The Abyssinian war of 1868*. London.

Palmer, J., 1951. Periplus Maris Erythraei: ἐμπόριον νόμιμον and other expressions, *Classical Quarterly*, 45, 156–8.

Pankhurst, R. 1961. *An Introduction to the Economic History of Ethiopia*. London.

Parker, S.T. 1998.The Roman ‘Aqaba project: the 1996 campaign, *Annual of the Department of Antiquities of Jordan* 42, 375–94.

Parker, S.T. 2000.The Roman ‘Aqaba project: the 1997 and 1998 campaigns, *Annual of the Department of Antiquities of Jordan* 44, 373–94.

Paribeni, R., 1907. Richerche nel luogo dell'antica Adulis. *Monumenti Antichi*, 18.

Peacock, D.P.S., 1985. Archaeology of Pantelleria, Italy. *National Geographic Society, Research reports for 1977*, 567–79.

Peacock, D.P.S., 1984. Petrology and origins. In M.G. Fulford and D.P.S Peacock (eds) *Excavations at Carthage: The British Mission, Volume 1.2 The Avenue du President Habib Bourguiba Salammbo. The Pottery and other ceramic objects from the site*. Sheffield, 14–20.

Peacock, D., and Blue, L., 2006. *Myos Hormos – Quseir al–Qadim, Roman and Islamic ports on the Red Sea. Volume 1, Survey and excavations 1999–2003*. Oxford.

Peacock, D., Williams D. and James S. 2007 Basalt as ships' ballast and the Roman incense trade. In D. Peacock and D. Williams (eds) *Food for the gods: new light on the ancient incense trade*. Oxford, 28–71.

Pedersen, R.K., 2003. The Aksumite–Period Shipwreck at Black Assarca Island, Eritrea. http://ina. tamu. edu/assarca.htm.

Pereira, F.M.E., 1899. *Historia dos Martyres de Nagran. Versão Ethiopica*. Lisbon.

Phillipson, D. W., 2000. *Archaeology at Aksum, Ethiopia, 1993–7*. Memoirs of the British Institute in Eastern Africa; no. 17, Report / Research Committee of the Society of Antiquaries of London; 65. London. British Institute in Eastern Africa.

Pieri, D. 2005. *Le commerce du vin orientale à l'époque Byzantine (V^e–VIIe siećle). Le témoinage des amphores en Gaule*. Paris.

Pieri, D. 2007. Les centres de production d'amphores en Mediterranée orientale durant. L'Antiquitié tardive: Quelques remarks. In M. Bonifay and J.C. Treglia (eds) *LRCW 2. Late Roman coarse-ware and amphorae in the Mediterranean: archaeology and archaeometry*. BAR 1662, 611–19.

Rothenberg, B., 1967. *Negev, Archaeology in the Negev and Arabah*. Masada

Reynolds, P., 2005. Levantine amphorae from Cilicia to Gaza: a Typology and Analysis of Regional Production Trends from the 1st to 7th Centuries. In M.A. Gurt i Esparraguera, J. Buxeda i Garigos and M.A. Cau Ontiveros (eds) *LRCW I: Late Roman Coarse Wares, Cooking Wares and Amphorae in the Mediterranean: Archaeology and Archaeometry*. British Archaeological Reports International Series, 1340, 563–612.

Said, R. (ed.) 1990. *The Geology of Egypt*. Rotterdam.

Salt, H., 1814. *A Voyage to Abyssinia and Travels into the Interior of that Country*. London.

Schneider, R., 1974. Trois nouvelles inscriptions royales d'Axoum. *IV Congresso Internazionale di Studi Etiopici, Accad. dei Lincei, Rome* I, 767–86.

Schoff, W., 1912. *The Periplus of the Erythraean Sea*. New Dehli. Reprinted 2001.

Sedov, A., 2007. The port of Qana' and the incense trade. In D. Peacock, and D. Williams (eds) *Food for the gods: new light on the ancient incense trade*. Oxford, 72–108.

Seeger, J.A., Sidebotham, S.E., Harrell, J.A. and Pons, M., 2006. A brief archaeological survey of the Aqiq region (Red Sea Coast) Sudan. *Sahara*, 17, 7– 18.

Sergew, Hable Sallasie, 1972. *Ancient and Medieval Ethiopian History to 1270*. Addis Abbaba.

Siddall, M., Rohling, E.J., Almogi–Labin, A., Hemleben, C., Meischner, D., Schmeizer, I. and Smeed, D.A., 2003. Sea–level fluctuations during the last glacial cycle. *Nature*, 423, 853–8.

Sidebotham, S.E. and Wendrich, W.Z., (eds) 1995. *Berenike '94. Report of the excavations at Berenike (Egyptian Red Sea coast) and the survey of the Egyptian Eastern Desert*. Leiden.

Sidebotham, S.E. and Wendrich, W.Z., (eds) 1996. *Berenike '95. Report of the excavations at Berenike (Egyptian Red Sea coast) and the survey of the Egyptian Eastern Desert*. Leiden.

Sidebotham, S.E. and Wendrich, W.Z., (eds) 1999. Berenike '97. *Report of the excavations at Berenike (Egyptian Red Sea coast) and the survey of the Egyptian Eastern Desert including excavations at Shenshef*. Leiden.

Sidebotham, S.E. and Wendrich, W.Z., (eds) (2000), *Berenike '98. Report of the excavations at Berenike (Egyptian Red Sea coast) and the survey of the Egyptian Eastern Desert, including excavations at Kalalat*. Leiden.

Stanley, P. V., 1983. *Ancient Greek Market Regulations and Controls*. Ph. D. dissertation. Univ. of California, Berkeley.

Stevenson, E.L., 1932. *Claudius Ptolemy. The Geography*. Dover reprint, 1991.

Stiros, S., and Jones, R.E., 1996. *Archaeoseismology*. Athens

Sundström, R., 1907. Report on an exp edition to Adulis. *Zeitschrift für Assyriologie*, 20, 171–82.

Tomber, R.S., 1998. "Laodicean wine containers in Roman Egypt." In O.E. Kaper (ed.) *Life on the*

Fringe. Living in the Egyptian deserts during the Roman and early Byzantine periods. Leiden, 213–20.

Tomber, R., 2004a. Rome and South Arabia: new artefactual evidence from the Red Sea. *Proc. Seminar Arabian Studies*, 34, 351–60.

Tomber, R., 2004b. Amphorae from the Red Sea and their contribution to the interpretation of Late Roman trade beyond the Empire. In J. Eiring and J. Lund (eds) *Transport Amphorae and Trade in the Eastern Mediterranean*. Mon. Danish Institute Athens, 5, 393–402.

Tomber, R., 2005a. Aksumite and other imported ceramics from Kamrej. *Journal of Indian Ocean Archaeology*, 2, 99–102.

Tomber, R., 2005b. Troglodites and Trogodites: Exploring interaction on the Red Sea during the Roman period. In J.C.M. Starkey (ed.) *People of the Red Sea*. Proceedings of the Red Sea Project II. BAR International Series 1395, 41–9.

Török, L., 1997. *Meroe City: An ancient African capital: John Garstan's excavations in the Sudan*. London.

Wenig, S., 2002. Enno Littmanns Deutsche Aksum–Expedition 1906 and die German Archaeological Mission to Eritrea (G.A.M.E.) 90 Jahre später. *Nürnberger Blätter zur Archäologie*, 18, 79–98.

Williams, D., 2000. Petrology of imported amphorae. In D. Phillipson (ed), *Archaeology at Aksum, Ethiopia, 1993–7*. Memoirs of the British Institute in Eastern Africa; no. 17, Report / Research Committee of the Society of Antiquaries of London; 65. London. British Institute in Eastern Africa, 494–6.

Williams, D. and Peacock, D., 2005. The eruption of Vesuvius and Campanian Dressel 2–4 amphorae. In J. Pollini (ed.) *Terra Marique*. Oxford, 140–8..

Williams–Thorpe, O., 1993. Obsidian in the Mediterranean and the Near East: a provenancing success story. *Archaeometry*, 37, 217–248.

Wolska–Conus, W., 1968. *La Topographie chrétienne. Sources chétienne III*. Paris.